Study Guide to Accompany Bob Garrett's

# Brain & Behavior

## 4th Edition

Study Guide to Accompany Bob Garrett's

# Brain & Behavior

## An Introduction to Biological Psychology

### 4th Edition

## Bob Garrett

*Visiting Research Scholar,*
*California Polytechnic State University, San Luis Obispo*

## Prepared by Gerald Hough
*Rowan University*

Los Angeles | London | New Delhi
Singapore | Washington DC

Los Angeles | London | New Delhi
Singapore | Washington DC

FOR INFORMATION:

SAGE Publications, Inc.
2455 Teller Road
Thousand Oaks, California 91320
E-mail: order@sagepub.com

SAGE Publications Ltd.
1 Oliver's Yard
55 City Road
London EC1Y 1SP
United Kingdom

SAGE Publications India Pvt. Ltd.
B 1/I 1 Mohan Cooperative Industrial Area
Mathura Road, New Delhi 110 044
India

SAGE Publications Asia-Pacific Pte. Ltd.
3 Church Street
#10-04 Samsung Hub
Singapore 049483

Printed in the United States of America.

ISBN 978-1-4833-1618-5 (pbk.)

This book is printed on acid-free paper.

Acquisitions Editor:   Vicki Knight
Editorial Assistant:   Yvonne McDuffee
Production Editor:   David C. Felts
Proofreader:   Christine Dahlin
Typesetter:   C&M Digitals (P) Ltd.
Cover Designer:   Candice Harman
Marketing Manager:   Shari Countryman

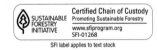

SUSTAINABLE FORESTRY INITIATIVE
Certified Chain of Custody
Promoting Sustainable Forestry
www.sfiprogram.org
SFI-01268
SFI label applies to text stock

14 15 16 17 18 10 9 8 7 6 5 4 3 2 1

# Brief Contents

# Detailed Contents

# Acknowledgments

As with any writing assignment, I would first and foremost like to thank my wife, Kerry, and my two boys, Alex and Ben, who have graciously allowed me the time necessary to revise and update this guide. Revising a study guide takes a tremendous amount of time, and I have been blessed with their support throughout the editing process. Hugs and kisses for everyone now that I'm done! Second, I would like to thank three research mentors over the years who instilled a love of brain and behavior into everything I do: Dr. Erich Klinghammer from Purdue University, where I worked with wolves; Dr. Susan Volman from Ohio State University, who introduced me to the world of neurobiology and the language system of birds; and Dr. Verner Bingman from Bowling Green State University, who introduced me to the hippocampus and its important role in learning and memory. Finally, thanks to my wonderful parents, Gerald and Carole, who in 2014 will celebrate their 50th wedding anniversary—I could not have had a more supportive, loving environment in which to grow up and learn. I love you both very much.

# 1    What Is Biopsychology?

## Learning Objectives

After reading this chapter, you should be able to answer the following questions.

1. How did biological psychology develop from its roots in philosophy and physiology? Be sure to address the contributions of Descartes, Frisch and Hitzig, Helmholtz, Broca, Gall, and Lashley.

2. What is the mind-brain problem? How do most brain scientists currently think about this problem?

3. What are genes, and how do they work?

4. How are heredity and environment interrelated in the development of behavioral characteristics?

5. What is the human genome project, and why is it so crucial to our understanding of physical and mental health issues?

## The Origins of Biopsychology

### Summary and Guided Review

After studying this section in the text, fill in the blanks of the following summary.

_____ (1) is the multidisciplinary study of the nervous system and its role in behavior. During the 1990s, also known as the Decade of the _____ (2), intensive research into the role of biology in behavioral problems led to new treatments for depression, addiction, and age-related memory impairment. Advances were also made in the area of genetics, including a(n) _____ (3) of all human genes and a greater understanding of the genes involved in diseases such as _____ (4).

_____ (5) is the branch of psychology that studies the relationships between behavior and the body, and it attempts to answer questions about the biological basis of diverse phenomena such as mental illness, emotions, perception, cognition, and consciousness. Psychology emerged as a separate discipline in 1879 when _____ (6) established the first psychology laboratory, and biopsychology arose as a distinct subfield of psychology some time after this.

Biopsychology addresses the _____ (7) problem, which concerns the nature of the relationship between the physical brain and the mind. Most modern neuroscientists believe that the _____ (8) is not a real thing but rather is a concept we use to explain our awareness of experience. This position is known as material _____ (9) and assumes that everything is physical. The position that the mind is nonmaterial and separate from the physical brain is called _____ (10). This issue of lack of consensus on the mind-brain problem is not a new one: Among the ancient Greek philosophers, Democritus and _____ (11) were monists, whereas _____ (12) was a dualist.

Scientists often use _____ (13) to help them explain how things work. The hydraulic model of behavior was developed by the 17th-century French philosopher _____ (14) to explain the physical basis of behavior. According to this model, when the mind willed the body to action, the _____ (15) gland pumped animal spirits through the nerves (believed to be hollow tubes) to the muscles, resulting in movement. The pineal gland, therefore, was considered the seat of the _____ (16). This model was ultimately shown to be wrong based on the approach of _____ (17), which involves use of the methods of observation and experimentation.

Important principles of nervous system anatomy and physiology were discovered during the 1700s and 1800s. Work by several physiologists showed that nerves operated via _____ (18), not "animal spirits." However, the German physiologist _____ (19) performed experiments that indicated that nerve conduction was not as fast as electricity conducted through wires, which suggested that something more than just electricity was operating in the nervous system.

In the 1800s, well-documented cases of brain injury suggested that specific parts of the brain have specific functions, a concept known as _____ (20). For example, railroad worker _____ _____ (21) underwent extreme changes in personality following an accident in which an iron rod was driven through his skull and _____ (22) lobes. Another case was reported by the French physician _____ (23); his patient was unable to speak, and after the patient died, it was discovered that he had damage in the _____ (24) hemisphere of his brain. Gall took the localization concept to an extreme in his theory of

_____ (25), which stated that several emotional and intellectual faculties were located in specific areas of the brain based on bumps on the skull. On the other extreme, Lashley's theory of _____ (26) argued that brain functions are evenly distributed across the brain. Currently, brain researchers know that brain functions are both localized and _____ (27), which means that several brain areas interact to produce specific experiences such as learning or emotion.

Evidence that the mind-brain problem is not resolved comes from researchers allied with the Discovery Institute, the headquarters for _____ _____ (28). This group studies nonmaterial neuroscience and points to studies in which _____ (29) altered brain function in obsessive-compulsive patients as evidence for their position. Material neuroscientists interpret these findings as the _____ (30) changing the brain. Nonmaterial neuroscientists are now focusing on _____ (31), which they believe cannot be explained by materialism.

## Short Answer and Essay Questions

Answer the following questions.

1. Give two examples of the types of research questions that biological psychologists might ask. For each, explain how someone from a biological background might approach each research question differently than someone from a psychological background.

2. Regarding the mind-brain question, compare monism and dualism. What are (or were) the problems with each position? How do most modern neuroscientists explain the relationship between the brain and mind? What is the opinion of neuroscientists associated with the Discovery Institute?

3. Why was the case of Phineas Gage important for brain science? What did it reveal about the localization of function issue?

4. Compare the theories of localization and equipotentiality. What is the current position of brain researchers on this issue?

# Nature and Nurture

## Summary and Guided Review

After studying this section in the text, fill in the blanks of the following summary.

The question of _____ versus _____ (32) asks how important genes and environment are in influencing behavior. Evidence is accumulating that many behaviors have a genetic or _____ (33) component. _____ (34), which direct cellular processes and transmit inherited characteristics, are located mostly on _____ (35), which are paired in all cells, with the exception of some in the sex cells. The sex of an individual is determined by the sex chromosomes: Females are _____ (36), and males are _____ (37). Most body cells have _____ (38) chromosomes, but _____ (39) and egg cells have 23. When conception occurs, the fertilized egg, or _____ (40), contains half of each parent's genetic material. For the first 8 weeks following conception, the developing baby is considered a(n) _____ (41), and then it is called a(n) _____ (42) until it is born.

Genes are composed of a double strand of molecules known as _____ (43), or deoxyribonucleic acid. The strands are connected by pairs of nucleotides (adenine, _____ (44), guanine, and _____ (45) that carry instructions for producing _____ (46), which are used in the construction of the body or act as _____ (47). Researchers at the Weizmann Institute are building computers out of _____ (48); in test tubes, these can identify and kill _____ cells (49).

Different versions of a gene are called _____ (50). In some cases the effects of the two alleles blend to produce a result; one example of this would be _____ (51). A(n) _____ (52) allele will produce its effects regardless of which gene it is paired with. In order for a(n) _____ (53) trait to be expressed, there must be a copy of the same allele on each chromosome. Individuals who possess two copies of a dominant allele are _____ (54) for that gene, and will have the same _____ (55), or characteristic, as those who possess one dominant and one recessive allele (who are _____ (56). An X-linked characteristic is produced by a gene on the X chromosome that is not paired with one on the Y chromosome. If a recessive gene is located on the X chromosome, the trait it influences is more likely to be seen in _____ (57); red-green color blindness is an example of a(n) _____ (58) trait. Traits such as height and intelligence are _____ (59), meaning they are influenced by more than one gene.

During the first half of the 20th century, psychologists came to believe that the _____ (60) was more important in contributing to behavior than genes. By the end of the century, a more balanced view was adopted. Psychologists now believe that genes influence many human behavioral traits, and _____ (61) is the behavioral trait whose genetic origins have received the most research attention. However, it is important to remember that genes control only the production of proteins, so they influence behavior indirectly through physiological systems.

Locating genes that influence traits is difficult and time-consuming. However, in 2000, several genetics laboratories published a rough draft of the human _____ (62), which will be useful in locating specific genes. This effort, known as the International Human Genome Project, has revealed that humans have between _____ and _____ (63) individual genes, and that 97% of the genome is made up of "_____" (64) DNA, which are sections of chromosomes whose function is uncertain, though some of it controls _____ (65). Although the map does not tell scientists what each gene does, it will allow them to more easily locate specific genes that contribute to specific traits. For example, although researchers in the 1980s knew that the gene for Huntington's disease was located on chromosome 4 near two _____ (66) genes, it took them ten more years to locate the specific gene. Scientists now predict that they can locate important genes much more quickly because of the map. Such knowledge is expected to lead to genetic-based treatment of many more disorders.

The notion that offspring are like clones of their parents is incorrect. Children inherit _____ (67) of each parent's DNA, and because of the 60 to 70 trillion possible _____ (68) of genes resulting from sexual reproduction, no two individuals are genetically exactly alike (unless they are identical twins!). This variability of traits is the cornerstone of Darwin's theory of _____ _____ (69), which states that organisms possessing traits that are most conducive to survival are more likely to pass their genes on to offspring. Genes are not _____ (70) in their operation. They are not all active at the same time. They may produce more proteins at some times than at others. They may become active during certain _____ (71), such as when an organism is learning. Clearly genes are not the sole dictators of behavior. Instead, they give us predispositions for certain characteristics.

Comparisons between identical and _____ (72) twins allow researchers to estimate the percentage of variation in characteristics due to heredity, or _____ (73). It appears that heritability for intelligence is about _____% (74). Personality characteristics show a heritability of _____ – _____% (75). If half of the variation in behaviors is due to genetics, then the other half must be due to _____ (76). However, it is important to understand that the more similarity there is between people's environments, the _____ (77) the degree of heritability.

Scientists now argue that genes contribute to our predisposition or _____ (78) for certain traits. The genes we inherit may result in a predisposition for a disorder such as schizophrenia, but the disorder will emerge only under certain environmental conditions. Clearly both factors are important.

## Short Answer and Essay Questions

Answer the following questions.

5. What do genes do? Describe the ways in which the actions of genes can be variable.

6. What is the rationale for comparing identical and fraternal twins in order to measure the heritability of traits?

7. Angelina Jolie tested positive for a defective gene (BRCA1) that triggers breast cancer in 87 percent of women with that particular defect. As a result, she removed all of her natural breast tissue through a procedure called a double mastectomy despite not having any symptoms of cancer. Do you agree with her decision? Explain using information gleaned in this section from both points of view.

8. Janet and Charles are expecting their first baby. They are both highly intelligent, and they assume that their child will inherit their intelligence through the genes it shares with them. They feel that the environment has little or no impact on intelligence. After having read the section "Heredity: Destiny or Predisposition?" what would you tell this couple about the scientific evidence for their claim? (Be sure to address the concept of **predisposition** in your answer.)

## Post-test

Use these multiple-choice questions to check your understanding of the chapter.

1. Which of the following did NOT occur during the Decade of the Brain (1990s)?
   a. Genes contributing to the development of Alzheimer's disease were identified.
   b. It was discovered that neurons conduct electricity.
   c. Drugs that block addiction were discovered.
   d. New treatments for depression were developed.

2. Who among the following is credited with establishing the first psychology laboratory in Germany in 1879?
   a. Wilhelm Wundt
   b. Hermann von Helmholtz
   c. Gustav Fritsch
   d. Franz Gall

3. Dr. Locke is a philosopher who believes that there is no distinction between the physical brain and the mind. This position is known as
   a. materialistic monism.
   b. idealistic monism.
   c. dualism.
   d. materialistic dualism.

4. ___ was a dualist.
   a. Aristotle
   b. Plato
   c. Democritus
   d. Descartes

5. According to the hydraulic model of the nervous system,
   a. nerves were like electrical wires that conducted electricity.
   b. nerves were hollow tubes that allowed animal spirits to flow through them.
   c. nerves were not responsible for behavior.
   d. none of the above

6. Descartes believed that the "seat of the soul" was located in
   a. the frontal lobes of the brain.
   b. animal spirits.
   c. the pineal gland.
   d. the left hemisphere.

7. Through their experiments, Fritsch and Hitzig showed that
   a. the muscle in a frog's leg can be made to move by stimulating the nerve connected to it.
   b. the rate of nerve conduction is about 90 feet per second.
   c. the left hemisphere controls speech.
   d. muscle movement is the result of brain stimulation.

8. Who discovered that nerves conduct electricity at a rate significantly slower than the speed of light?
   a. Hermann von Helmholtz
   b. Rene Descartes
   c. Luigi Galvani
   d. Phineas Gage

9. Broca's mute patient had damage to his
   a. pineal gland.
   b. frontal lobes.
   c. left hemisphere.
   d. motor cortex.

10. The 19th-century belief that over 35 different mental faculties were located in specific parts of the brain was known as
    a. equipotentiality.
    b. extreme localization.
    c. phrenology.
    d. biopsychology.

11. With the exception of egg and sperm cells, all human body cells have
    a. 23 chromosomes.
    b. 46 chromosomes.
    c. 23 genes.
    d. 46 genes.

12. If you underwent a procedure to test for a particular disease that is triggered by a defective protein inherited from your parents, what SPECIFIC genetic component will they be looking for?
    a. A particular chromosome in your genome
    b. A particular gene on a chromosome
    c. A particular allele of a gene
    d. A particular base in an allele

13. Female humans have
    a. two X chromosomes.
    b. two Y chromosomes.
    c. one X and one Y chromosome.
    d. one X chromosome.

14. At six weeks after conception, a developing human is known as a(n)
    a. zygote.
    b. ova.
    c. embryo.
    d. fetus.

15. How many different bases make up DNA?
    a. 20
    b. 10
    c. 5
    d. 4

16. Enzymes
    a. are proteins.
    b. are produced as a result of genetic mechanisms.
    c. modify chemical reactions in the body.
    d. all of the above

17. The allele for right-over-left hand clasping preference is recessive. John and Sue both show this hand clasping preference. What preference will their children have?
    a. all left
    b. half left, half right
    c. all right
    d. not enough information is given to answer the question

18. Which of the following is FALSE regarding red-green color blindness?
    a. It is an X-linked trait.
    b. A female cannot be red-green color blind.
    c. Males are more likely to have it.
    d. It is a recessive trait.

19. George is heterozygous for the dominant allele for hand clasping preference (left-over-right), and his son Jason is homozygous for the dominant allele. Which of the following statements is TRUE?
    a. George and Jason have the same phenotype but different genotypes.
    b. George and Jason have the same phenotype and the same genotype.
    c. George and Jason have different phenotypes but the same genotype.
    d. George and Jason have different phenotypes and different genotypes.

20. A trait is polygenic if
    a. it is influenced by a gene on the X chromosome.
    b. it is influenced by a gene on the Y chromosome.
    c. it is influenced by more than one gene.
    d. it is influenced only by a single gene.

21. Which of the following is believed to have a genetic basis?
    a. sexual orientation
    b. drug addiction
    c. personality
    d. all of the above

22. Which of the following is TRUE of the human genome?
    a. Nearly all of the base-pair sequences have been mapped.
    b. Most of our DNA is directly involved in coding for proteins.
    c. The functions of all genes are well documented.
    d. There are about 80,000 genes.

23. The differential survival of organisms with more adaptive traits is known as
    a. sexual reproduction.
    b. predisposition.
    c. natural selection.
    d. heritability.

24. Which of the following is NOT true of gene activity?
    a. Once a gene becomes inactive, it remains inactive.
    b. Genes may fluctuate in the amount of protein they code for at different times.
    c. A gene may become active at only a certain time of the life cycle.
    d. The activity of a gene may be influenced by experience.

25. Which of the following traits has the HIGHEST degree of heritability?
    a. intelligence
    b. personality
    c. height
    d. occupational interests

26. If people from similar environments are sampled, estimates of heritability for traits will be ___ people from different environments are sampled.
    a. lower than if
    b. higher than if
    c. the same as when
    d. either a or b may be correct

27. The BEST way to think about the relationship among genes, environment, and intelligence is that
    a. genes set the potential range, and environment determines the actual capacity.
    b. environment is more important than genetic inheritance.
    c. our genes are more important than the environment.
    d. a person's intelligence is equally influenced by each parent's genes.

## Answers

### Guided Review

1. Neuroscience
2. Brain
3. map
4. Alzheimer's
5. Biopsychology
6. Wilhelm Wundt
7. mind-brain
8. mind
9. monism
10. dualism
11. Aristotle
12. Plato
13. models
14. Descartes
15. pineal
16. soul
17. empiricism
18. electricity
19. Helmholtz
20. localization
21. Phineas Gage
22. frontal
23. Broca
24. left
25. phrenology
26. equipotentiality
27. distributed
28. intelligent design
29. psychotherapy
30. brain
31. consciousness
32. nature versus nurture
33. heredity
34. Genes
35. chromosomes
36. XX
37. XY
38. 46
39. sperm
40. zygote
41. embryo
42. fetus
43. DNA
44. thymine or cytocine
45. cytosine or thymine
46. proteins
47. enzymes
48. DNA
49. cancer
50. alleles
51. type AB blood
52. dominant
53. recessive
54. homozygous
55. phenotype
56. heterozygous
57. males
58. X-linked
59. polygenic
60. environment
61. intelligence
62. genome
63. 20,000 and 25,000
64. junk
65. gene expression
66. marker
67. half
68. combinations
69. natural selection
70. rigid
71. experiences
72. fraternal
73. heritability
74. 50
75. 40–50
76. environment
77. higher
78. vulnerability

## Short Answer and Essay Questions

1. There are several possible answers, but all must mention that biological psychologists look for a connection between the nervous system and a specific behavior or set of behaviors. Though not completely separate in approaches, biologists will tend to approach questions using molecular, genetic, functional, mechanistic, or physiological methods, while psychologists might use interviews, questionnaires, or therapeutic or cognitive methods.

2. Monism assumes that the mind and brain are composed of the same thing or substance. Most monists are materialistic, meaning that they believe everything, including the mind, is physical and therefore has no separate existence. Dualists, however, believe that while the brain is physical, the mind is also real, although not material, and exists separately from the brain. The problem with dualism is that it cannot explain how something nonphysical (the mind) can affect something physical (the body). The problem with materialistic monism is explaining how the brain causes subjective, mental experience. Most modern neuroscientists are materialistic monists. They believe that the mind is not a real entity but rather a concept we use to describe what our brains are doing. Therefore, the mind really is the brain or, more precisely, the activity of the brain. However, nonmaterial neuroscientists funded by the Discovery Institute are keeping the brain-body debate alive by arguing that if psychotherapy can change brain function, then the mind must exist to have an impact on the brain. Material monists would argue that this phenomenon demonstrates that the brain affects the brain.

3. It was important because it showed that damage to a particular part of the brain resulted in disruption of some types of functions but not others. Following his accident, Gage was still able to speak and move normally, and he showed no change in memory or intelligence, but his personality changed, and he became impulsive and hard to deal with. This suggested that the part of the brain damaged by his injury was involved in some types of behaviors but not in others.

4. Localization is the theory that different brain areas are in control of different functions. Equipotentiality assumes that the brain as a whole contributes to all functions. Most brain researchers now believe that while specific functions are located in specific brain regions, several different brain areas work together to produce behaviors and experiences; thus, the brain's functions are both localized and distributed.

5. Genes direct the production of proteins. Genes are variable in their effects, because they may not always be active and because they can vary the amount of a protein that is produced. They may also change functioning as the body ages. Alleles are different forms of genes, which necessarily make different proteins. An allele that encodes for an abnormal or nonfunctional protein (such as sickle cell anemia and its characteristically misshapen hemoglobin molecule) is what we look for when performing a genetic screening test on an individual.

6. Identical twins have the same genes, whereas fraternal twins have about 50% of their genes in common. If we compare identical twins and fraternal twins on some trait such as intelligence, and we find that identical twins are more similar than fraternal twins, then we can assume that genes are responsible for some of the similarity between the identical twins.

7. While individual answers will vary, the following points need to be understood: (a) the presence (or absence) of a particular allele never completely corresponds with the presence (or

absence) of a particular disorder. (b) Environmental factors play a key role in expression of defective genes. (c) Removing potentially cancerous tissue (that is currently healthy) does not completely remove the risk of developing the disease. (d) Surgical procedures carry their own inherent risks—does the benefit gained through surgery outweigh the risks/costs of that procedure?

8. The evidence suggests that genes and environment are both important. The heritability of intelligence is around 50%, so this means that the environment contributes just as much as genes do. Furthermore, what genes contribute is better thought of as a predisposition; the environment will always have a significant impact.

## Post-test

1. b　2. a　3. a　4. d　5. b　6. c　7. d　8. a　9. c　10. c　11. b　12. c　13. a　14. c　15. d　16. d　17. c　18. b　19. a　20. c　21. d　22. a　23. c　24. a　25. c　26. b　27. a

# 2  Communication Within the Nervous System

---

## Chapter Outline

The Cells That Make Us Who We Are
> *Neurons*

**APPLICATION**: Targeting Ion Channels
> *Glial Cells*

CONCEPT CHECK

How Neurons Communicate With Each Other
> *Chemical Transmission at the Synapse*
> *Regulating Synaptic Activity*
> *Neurotransmitters*

**APPLICATION:** Agonists and Antagonists in the Real World
> *Of Neuronal Codes, Neural Networks, and Computers*

**IN THE NEWS:** The Human Brain Project

CONCEPT CHECK

In Perspective

Summary

Study Resources

---

## Learning Objectives

After reading this chapter, you should be able to answer the following questions.

1. Describe the structure and function of neurons.

2. How are neurons specialized to conduct information?

3. How do glial cells support the activity of neurons?

4. How does social deprivation affect glia?

5. How do neurons communicate with each other?

6. What strategies do neurons use to increase their capacity for information processing?

7. What are the functions of some of the major chemical transmitters?

8. What are neural networks and why are they important? How are artificial neural networks useful to neuroscientists?

## The Cells That Make Us Who We Are

### Summary and Guided Review

After studying this section in the text, fill in the blanks of the following summary.

The human brain consists of about 100 billion ___neurons___ (1) cells that carry messages and underlie our thoughts, feelings, and behaviors. It also contains many more ___glial___ (2) cells, which have a variety of functions. Neurons exist in many different forms, but they share similar structures and functions. The ___soma___ (3), or cell body, is where the cell's nucleus containing DNA is located as well as other _____ (4) located in the cytoplasm that carry out the functions of the cell. Branching out from the cell body are ___dendrites___ (5), structures that receive messages from other cells. A single tail-like structure called the ___axon___ (6) extends away from the cell body and carries messages to other neurons. The end bulbs, or ___terminals___ (7) of the axon, contain chemical messengers called ___neurotransmitters___ (8) that enable the neuron to communicate with other cells. Although axons are quite thin (at most 0.1 mm in mammals), they can be up to _____ (9) m long. ___motor___ (10) neurons, which are multipolar, carry information to muscle and gland tissue, whereas ___sensory___ (11) neurons, which are either unipolar or bipolar, are stimulated by internal or environmental events and transmit information about those events to the brain and spinal cord. Neurons with short or no axons that transmit information between adjacent neurons in the same area of the brain are called ___interneurons___ (12), and they are the most abundant type.

The membrane of a neuron is composed of a double layer of lipid molecules and contains _____ (13) molecules. Fluid is found both inside and outside the cell. Some molecules, such as oxygen, can pass through the membrane, while others are prevented from getting in; this property is known as selective ___permeability___ (14). Because ions (charged particles) are distributed in different concentrations on each side of the membrane, the membrane is ___polarized___ (15) (electrically charged). When the cell is at rest, the inside is negatively charged relative to the outside, typically around ___-70___ mV (16). This is known as the ___resting___ (17) potential. ___sodium___ (18) and chloride ions are more concentrated outside the cell, and potassium ions and protein anions are more concentrated inside. Ions are attracted to the side of the membrane where their type is less abundant by the force of ___diffusion___ (19). Because of _____ (20), ions are also attracted to the side of the membrane with the opposite charge (so positively charged ions are attracted to the negative side of the cell). The _____-_____ (21) pump helps to maintain the balance of ions within and outside of the cell.

Sodium ions are attracted inside the cell by both _____ (22) and _____ (23), but they are kept out because they cannot pass through the membrane. However, if the membrane is stimulated by an activating stimulus, then _____ (24) channels in the membrane will open, allowing sodium into the cell. This results in the cell becoming _____ (25), with the inside less negative than before. If enough sodium enters the cell, its polarity will reach a threshold at which the cell will generate a(n) _____ (26) potential; sodium ions enter so rapidly that the cell becomes suddenly positively charged at the site of the depolarization. Shortly after this, the sodium channels close, and _____ (27) channels open. Potassium moves out by diffusion and as a result of the increasingly positive charge inside the axon. All of this occurs in about 1 _____ (28). Once it occurs, an action potential spreads down an axon, because it causes adjacent sodium channels to open and _____ (29) another portion of the membrane. The outflow of potassium ions restores the resting potential; the displaced ions are eventually returned to their resting locations by the sodium-potassium pump. This wave of action potentials sweeps down the length of the axon until it reaches the axon _____ (30) and signals the next neuron.

Depolarizations and action potentials are not identical. Whereas the initial depolarization or local potential is _____ (31), the action potential is not. Action potentials occur according to the _____ or _____ (32) law, which means that a cell's action potentials are all of the same strength. Also, unlike local potentials, action potentials are _____ (33), meaning they maintain their full strength until they reach the axon terminal.

Immediately after an action potential occurs, the sodium channels are unable to open again, and therefore the cell is unable to produce another action potential right away. This is known as the _____ (34) refractory period. The cell is also subject to a relative refractory period, when the _____ (35) channels are still open and the inside is slightly more _____ (36) charged for a short time. In order for an action potential to occur at this time, the stimulus must be _____ (37) than normal. More intense stimuli will produce earlier and, therefore, more frequent action potentials; this is the _____ (38) law.

Puffer fish and snake venoms contain _____ (39) that affect potassium and sodium channels; some animal toxins also affect calcium channels. Sometimes blocking sodium channels can be useful, as is the case with _____ _____ (40), whereas opening potassium channels (causing hyperpolarizations) is one way that _____ _____ (41) work. A new strategy that uses _____ (42) to control ion channels allows more precise targeting of neurons; potential applications range from tracing neural pathways to therapeutic brain stimulation.

Glial cells are an important component of the nervous system. For example, the fatty substance _____ (43) insulates axons and also increases conduction speed, which allows the nervous system to transmit signals faster without having to produce larger axons. In the central nervous system, myelin is made by _____ (44), while _____ (45) cells produce myelin for the rest of the nervous system. Action potentials occur only at the gaps between myelin cells known as nodes of _____ (46), where most of the cell's sodium channels are located. The action potential jumps from one gap to the next rather than traveling down the entire length of the axon; this is known as _____ (47) conduction; it is faster and uses less _____ (48) than conduction in unmyelinated neurons. When myelin is destroyed, as in the disease _____ _____ (49), the neurons cease to function properly.

Glial cells, which are far more numerous than neurons, also perform a number of important functions. By acting as a scaffold, they _____ (50) developing neurons to their destinations. They support and keep mature neurons functioning properly. When deprived of glial cells, neurons lose some of their _____ (51) with other neurons. Brain complexity in different species is correlated with higher ratios of _____ (52) to neurons.

## Short Answer and Essay Questions

Answer the following questions.

1. Identify the key parts of a typical neuron and describe their functions.

2. How are sensory and motor neurons different in terms of their functions and structure?

3. What does it mean that the neural cell membrane is selectively permeable? How do water, oxygen, and carbon dioxide molecules enter the cell? How do ions and other substances necessary for functioning enter the cell?

4. Of all the ions involved in neuronal depolarization, sodium ($Na^+$) ions are most strongly attracted across the membrane. Give two reasons for this.

5. Identify the two "key players" or ions in the action potential. Describe the sequence of events that occur during the action potential.

6. When an axon is depolarized to threshold, it fires an action potential at the site of depolarization. How does that action potential spread to the rest of the axon? Why does that action potential spread in only one direction (toward the axon terminals)?

7. One way in which the intensity of a stimulus is coded or represented in the sensory neuron is by the frequency with which action potentials are generated. For example, a more intense stimulus produces more action potentials per second than a less intense one, although the action potentials themselves are of the same strength. What role does the relative refractory period play in this effect?

8. Explain why action potentials are conducted more quickly, and more efficiently in terms of energy used, in myelinated cells than in unmyelinated cells.

9. What are some functions (other than myelination) of glial cells?

# How Neurons Communicate With Each Other

## Summary and Guided Review

After studying this section in the text, fill in the blanks of the following summary.

The fact that neurons are not physically attached to one another was discovered by Spanish anatomist _____ (53) in the 19th century with the help of the _____ _____ (54) that identifies a small number of particular neurons. In the 20th century, _____ (55) showed that neurons communicate with one another chemically. He did this by first stimulating the vagus nerve of a frog heart, which resulted in the heart rate _____ (56). Then he collected the salt solution he had placed in the heart and administered it to another heart, which also _____ (57) its rate of beating. Later research has shown that neurons can also communicate by electricity and by gas. At chemical synapses the _____ (58) are located in small sacs in the axon terminals called _____ (59). When an action potential reaches the axon terminal,

_____ (60) ions enter the cell and cause the vesicles to fuse with the presynaptic cell membrane, dumping their contents into the synaptic cleft. The neurotransmitter molecules then attach to receptors on the _____ (61) membrane, causing ion channels to open and producing a graded potential. An immediate response in the postsynaptic cell is seen when _____ (62) receptors are opened, while prolonged effects follow the opening of _____ (63) receptors.

Neurotransmitters can affect the postsynaptic cell by causing hyperpolarization (inhibition) or _____ (64) (excitation). Inhibition in the nervous system is important for many reasons, including its role in controlling excitation. Neurotransmitters that cause _____ (65) channels to open lead to EPSPs of the soma and dendrites, whereas those that cause potassium and/or chloride channels to open lead to _____ (66). EPSPs and IPSPs are _____ (67) potentials, and when they reach the axon _____ (68), they either increase or decrease the rate of action potentials. EPSPs may ultimately have inhibitory effects, if they increase output to inhibitory neurons. The stimulant drug _____ (69) is believed to calm hyperactive children by increasing frontal lobe activation, which in turns inhibits behavior.

A single cell is continuously receiving messages from as many as _____ (70) other cells, most of which have only very small effects on the polarity of the cell. The incoming information is integrated by the postsynaptic neuron. When two or more postsynaptic potentials arrive simultaneously but at different parts of the cell, _____ (71) summation occurs. Because the effect of a graded potential takes a while to dissipate, when postsynaptic potentials arrive in close succession, _____ (72) summation can occur. A good way of thinking about the neuron is that it serves as both an information integrator in handling information from a variety of sources and as a(n) _____ (73) maker about whether it will fire and at what rate.

Once it has attached to the postsynaptic receptor and had its effect on the postsynaptic cell, the _____ (74) is inactivated in some way. Often this is accomplished as the presynaptic cell absorbs it, a process called _____ (75). The neurotransmitter may also be broken down by the _____ (76) acetylcholinesterase. Also, glial cells absorb some transmitters. Drugs may affect behavior by interfering with these mechanisms in some way.

Synaptic transmission can be altered by _____ (77) synapses on the terminals, which affect the release of the neurotransmitter from the presynaptic neuron through presynaptic excitation or_____ (78). Additionally, _____ (79) on the presynaptic axon terminals can monitor the amount of neurotransmitters in the synapse and adjust the cell's release of it, and the postsynaptic membrane regulates the number and sensitivity of its _____ (80). _____ (81) cells also regulate synaptic activity in a number of ways, including absorbing neurotransmitters from the synapse and releasing neurotransmitters.

There are many different neurotransmitters, and each may have different effects through different receptor types. For example, acetylcholine has an excitatory effect at _____ (82) receptors, while at _____ (83) receptors, it may have excitatory or inhibitory effects. A single neuron can release more than one type of neurotransmitter at the same synapse. One of these may be _____ _____ (84) and have an immediate effect on the postsynaptic cell, while the others (such as neuropeptides) enhance the effects of the first through more prolonged mechanisms. Some cells appear to release two fast-acting transmitters at the same time, and some release both excitatory and inhibitory transmitters at different _____ (85).

Many drugs affect neural functioning. Nicotine, for example, is a(n) _____ (86) at acetylcholine receptors. Amazonian Indians tip their darts with an acetylcholine antagonist, _____ (87), to paralyze animals.

It is difficult to understand how neural activity controls behavior if we limit ourselves to simple trains of impulses in a chain of individual neurons. However, researchers have been able to record temporal variations in firing during taste stimulation that form a(n) _____ (88) that can then be duplicated as electrical pulses to produce the same behavior in other animals. However, complex processing such as color vision or sound discrimination requires groups of neurons that function together as a(n) _____ _____ (89). Because working with actual groups of neurons is a daunting task, researchers have created _____ _____ _____ (90) on computers. These networks are not programmed to perform a specific task; instead they _____ (91) to carry out their tasks.

## Short Answer and Essay Questions

Answer the following questions.

10. Describe the experiment by Otto Loewi. How did he arrive at the conclusion that neurons communicate via chemical transmission?

11. What happens to a cell's polarity and firing rate when an IPSP occurs? Why does the firing rate change?

12. Why is the model consisting of a single chain of neurons inadequate for explaining how the brain works? Give two reasons. (Hint: In your answer, consider both postsynaptic integration and how synaptic activity may be regulated.)

13. Explain temporal and spatial summation in terms of what happens at the synapse, then phrase each as an example from daily activity such as getting a child to clean up his or her room.

## Post-test

Use these multiple-choice questions to check your understanding of the chapter.

1. Scientists estimate that there are about ___ neurons in the brain.
   a. 1 million
   b. 100 million
   c. 1 billion
   d. 100 billion

2. In the nervous system, which of the following types of cells is MOST numerous?
   a. glia
   b. motor neurons
   c. sensory neurons
   d. interneurons

3. The nucleus of a neural cell is located in the
   a. axon.
   b. dendrites.
   c. soma.
   d. axon hillock.

4. A neuron that transmits information between the central nervous system and a muscle is called a(n)
   a. motor neuron.
   b. sensory neuron.
   c. interneuron.
   d. projection neuron.

5. A ___ neuron has an axon and several dendrites projecting away from the cell body.
   a. bipolar
   b. multipolar
   c. unipolar
   d. monopolar

6. Which of the following statements regarding interneurons is TRUE?
   a. They receive input directly from the external environment.
   b. They send information across long distances.
   c. They may have no axon at all.
   d. They are found only in the brain.

7. The neural membrane is selectively permeable to all of the following substances EXCEPT
   a. sodium.
   b. potassium.
   c. oxygen.
   d. chloride.

8. When a neuron is at rest, ___ ions are more plentiful outside of the cell.
   a. Na$^+$
   b. K$^+$
   c. anions
   d. all of the above

9. The TYPICAL resting potential of a neuron is
   a. −70 V.
   b. −35 mV.
   c. 70 mV.
   d. −70 mV.

10. When the cell is at rest, K$^+$ ions are strongly attracted across the cell membrane
   a. mostly because of electrostatic pressure.
   b. mostly because of the force of diffusion.
   c. equally because of electrostatic pressure and force of diffusion.
   d. by neither electrostatic pressure nor force of diffusion.

11. All of the following are able to pass through the membrane under certain conditions EXCEPT
   a. Na$^+$
   b. Cl$^-$
   c. K$^+$
   d. A$^-$

12. Which of the following statements regarding the sodium-potassium pump is FALSE?
   a. It requires a lot of energy.
   b. It works against diffusion.
   c. It pumps sodium into the cell.
   d. It helps maintain the resting potential.

13. Neurons undergo depolarization when
    a. $K^+$ ions enter the cell.
    b. $Na^+$ ions enter the cell.
    c. either $K^+$ or $Na^+$ ions enter the cell.
    d. $Cl^-$ ions leave the cell.

14. Depolarization is MOST similar to
    a. hypopolarization.
    b. hyperpolarization.
    c. action potential.
    d. electrical gradient.

15. When the neuron is at resting potential, $Na^+$ ions are strongly attracted across the cell membrane because of
    a. electrostatic pressure.
    b. diffusion.
    c. both electrostatic pressure and diffusion.
    d. neither electrostatic pressure or diffusion.

16. A neuron will fire an action potential when it is
    a. depolarized by 10 mV.
    b. hyperpolarized by 10 mV.
    c. depolarized by 15 mV.
    d. depolarized to its threshold.

17. The outflow of $K^+$ ions during an action potential results in
    a. hypopolarization.
    b. hyperpolarization.
    c. depolarization.
    d. another action potential.

18. The action potentials generated by a specific neuron
    a. are the same strength.
    b. occur at the same frequency.
    c. are graded.
    d. are decremental.

19. Which of the following statements regarding the absolute refractory period is FALSE?
    a. The potassium channels are closed and cannot be opened.
    b. The sodium channels are closed and cannot be opened.
    c. An action potential cannot be generated.
    d. It ensures that the action potential will travel only in one direction.

20. During the relative refractory period,
    a. the neuron is hyperpolarized.
    b. a stronger stimulus may result in another action potential.
    c. potassium channels are open.
    d. all of the above

21. The maximum speed at which a neuron can conduct an action potential seems to be about
    a. 10 m/s.
    b. 1,000 m/s.
    c. 120 m/s.
    d. 1.2 m/s.

22. The ___ the axon, the ___ the action potential.
    a. thicker; slower
    b. thicker; faster
    c. longer; slower
    d. thinner; faster

23. In the central nervous system, myelin is formed by
    a. Schwann cells.
    b. protein.
    c. oligodendrocytes.
    d. vesicles.

24. In myelinated axons,
    a. action potentials occur along the entire length of the axon.
    b. action potentials occur only at the nodes of Ranvier.
    c. action potentials occur only where the myelin is in contact with the axon.
    d. action potentials travel more slowly than on unmyelinated axons.

25. Myelination results in all of the following EXCEPT
    a. increased capacitance.
    b. increased speed of conduction.
    c. saltatory conduction.
    d. less work required by the sodium-potassium pump.

26. Which of the following was not mentioned as a function of glial cells?
    a. Storing neurotransmitters.
    b. Guiding developing axons.
    c. Assisting in the development of synapses.
    d. Transmitting action potentials.

27. Who discovered that neurons are separate cells and are NOT in contact with each other?
    a. Ramón y Cajal
    b. Golgi
    c. Loewi
    d. Dale

28. Who demonstrated that synaptic transmission is chemical?
    a. Ramón y Cajal
    b. Golgi
    c. Loewi
    d. Dale

29. When an action potential reaches an axon terminal, ___ ions enter the cell and trigger the release of the neurotransmitter.
    a. $Na^+$
    b. $K^+$
    c. $Cl^-$
    d. $Ca^{2+}$

30. Fast-acting receptors involved in muscle activity and sensory processing are referred to as
    a. metabotropic.
    b. autoreceptors.
    c. ionotropic.
    d. presynaptic.

31. Under normal circumstances, the neurotransmitter molecules released by a *single* neuron can do all of the following EXCEPT
    a. cause ion channels to open.
    b. trigger a graded depolarization.
    c. trigger an action potential.
    d. inhibit the postsynaptic cell.

32. An IPSP will occur if
    a. sodium channels open.
    b. potassium channels open.
    c. chloride channels open.
    d. b or c

33. Action potentials are first produced
    a. at the axon hillock.
    b. in the soma.
    c. in the dendrites.
    d. in the axon terminals.

34. In order for spatial summation to occur,
    a. several EPSPs must arrive at the same time from different inputs.
    b. several EPSPs and/or IPSPs must arrive at the same time from different inputs.
    c. several EPSPs must arrive in quick succession from a single input.
    d. EPSPs and IPSPs must arrive in quick succession from a single input.

35. If a neuron has a resting potential of −70 mV and a threshold of −60 mV, which of the following combinations of simultaneous postsynaptic potentials will result in an action potential?
    a. 15 EPSPs of 1 mV each and 20 IPSPs of 1 mV each
    b. 50 EPSPs of .5 mV each and 20 IPSPs of .5 mV each
    c. 50 EPSPs of .2 mV each and 15 IPSPs of .2 mV each
    d. 25 EPSPs of 1 mV each and 20 IPSPs of 1 mV each

36. Acetylcholine is removed from the synapse by
    a. reuptake by the presynaptic neuron.
    b. absorption by the postsynaptic neuron.
    c. enzymatic deactivation.
    d. absorption by glial cells.

37. Neurotransmitters interact with receptor sites like a ___.
    a. key into a lock.
    b. slip cover over a sofa.
    c. bird sitting next to another bird on a wire.
    d. train passing another train in the night.

38. Which of the following statements regarding nicotinic receptors is FALSE?
    a. They are inhibitory.
    b. They are stimulated by acetylcholine.
    c. They are found in the brain.
    d. They are found in muscles.

39. Regarding the types of neurotransmitters that a neuron can release, which of the following statements is FALSE?
    a. A neuron may release more than one fast-acting neurotransmitter.
    b. There are neurons that are incapable of releasing any neurotransmitters at all.

c. A neuron may release one fast-acting and one slower-acting neurotransmitter.

d. A neuron may release one fast-acting and several slower-acting neurotransmitters.

40. Which of the following is an antagonist at acetylcholine receptors?

a. nicotine

b. muscarine

c. naloxone

d. curare

41. In an artificial neural network, MOST of the processing occurs in which layer of neurons?

a. input

b. hidden

c. output

d. excitatory

42. The ability of neurons to carry information is increased by

a. variations in the size of the neural impulse.

b. its maintenance of the same firing rate regardless of the stimulus.

c. the neuron's consistency in producing excitation or inhibition.

d. varied time intervals of neural bursts.

43. The solution to the problem that chains of single neurons are inadequate to handle the brain's tasks is

a. neural networks.

b. artificial neural networks.

c. labeled lines.

d. temporal coding.

# Answers

## Guided Review

1. neurons
2. glial
3. soma
4. organelles
5. dendrites
6. axon
7. terminals
8. neurotransmitters
9. 1
10. Motor
11. sensory
12. interneurons
13. protein
14. permeability
15. polarized
16. −70
17. resting
18. Na⁺ or Sodium
19. diffusion
20. electrostatic pressure
21. sodium-potassium
22. diffusion
23. electrostatic pressure
24. sodium
25. depolarize or hypopolarize
26. action
27. potassium
28. millisecond
29. depolarize or hypopolarize
30. terminals
31. graded
32. all-or-none
33. nondecremental
34. absolute
35. K⁺ or potassium
36. negatively
37. stronger
38. rate
39. neurotoxins
40. local anesthetics
41. general anesthetics
42. light
43. myelin
44. oligodendrocytes
45. Schwann
46. Ranvier
47. saltatory
48. energy
49. multiple sclerosis
50. guide
51. synapses
52. astrocytes
53. Cajal
54. Golgi stain
55. Loewi
56. decreasing
57. decreased
58. neurotransmitters
59. vesicles
60. calcium
61. postsynaptic
62. ionotropic
63. metabotropic
64. depolarize or hypopolarize
65. Na⁺ or sodium
66. IPSPs

67. graded

68. hillock

69. Ritalin

70. 1,000

71. spatial

72. temporal

73. decision

74. transmitter

75. reuptake

76. enzyme

77. axoaxonic

78. inhibition

79. autoreceptors

80. receptors

81. Glial

82. nicotinic

83. muscarinic

84. fast-acting

85. terminals

86. agonist

87. curare

88. code

89. neural networks

90. artificial neural networks

91. learn

## Short Answer and Essay Questions

1. A typical neuron has a cell body or soma, containing the nucleus (which contains the genetic material) and organelles that keep the cell alive and functioning. Dendrites are the receiving components of the cell, whereas the axon carries information to the terminals. The terminals contain transmitters that communicate with the next cell.

2. Sensory neurons carry information about internal and environmental stimuli to the central nervous system, whereas motor neurons carry messages away from the central nervous system to the muscle and glandular cells of the body. Structurally, sensory neurons are usually bipolar or unipolar. Motor neurons are usually multipolar, with dendritic branches extending in several directions.

3. A membrane that is selectively permeable allows only certain substances to pass through it. Neurons can be readily permeated by water, oxygen, and carbon dioxide but not by other substances that they need for proper functioning. Protein channels embedded within the membrane control the flow of ions and various kinds of molecules. These substances can get in only when the protein channels are open.

4. $Na^+$ ions are more concentrated on the outside of the cell, so they are attracted across the membrane by the force of diffusion. And, because they are positively charged, they are also attracted into the cell because the inside of it is negative relative to the outside (electrostatic pressure).

5. If the excitatory inputs exceed the inhibitory inputs to an adequate degree, the cell will depolarize to a threshold at which sodium channels will open, and sodium will enter, further depolarizing the cell. Potassium channels will also open, and as potassium leaves the axon the cell will return to the resting potential and actually become hyperpolarized for a time.

6. The action potential spreads because it causes the sodium channels near it to open, thereby depolarizing the adjacent part of the membrane to threshold. This propagates the action potential across the length of the axon. The action potential cannot spread backward toward the soma because once the sodium channels at the site of depolarization close, they cannot be opened for a brief period (the absolute refractory period).

7. During the relative refractory period, a neuron is slightly more negative inside than while at rest, and so it requires a stronger stimulus to initiate an action potential. Therefore, stimuli of stronger intensities will have a greater effect than those of weak intensities. A stronger stimulus will cause the neuron to fire again earlier in the recovery period and, therefore, more frequently.

8. The axons of myelinated cells contain gaps between the myelin where the action potential actually occurs. In between those gaps, the cell undergoes a graded depolarization that spreads more quickly than an action potential. This depolarization then triggers the action potential at the next gap. Because the action potential is generated at fewer points along the axon and transmission is faster between nodes, it travels more quickly. Furthermore, fewer ions are exchanged, and therefore, the cell does not have to work as hard (via the sodium-potassium pump) to restore the resting potential.

9. Glial cells provide support and guidance for developing neurons. They also support synapses (neurons lose synapses in the absence of glial cells). They absorb and recycle neurotransmitters from the synapse. They release glutamate into the synapse, which may alter the function of neurons.

10. First, Loewi isolated the hearts of two frogs and kept them beating. Then he stimulated the vagus nerve of one heart, which caused it to slow down. He transferred fluid from this heart to the other heart, which also slowed down. Then he caused the first heart to speed up and repeated the procedure of transferring fluid. The second heart also increased its rate of contractions. He concluded that something in the fluid, some chemical released by the nerve he stimulated, had caused the change in heart rate.

11. The cell becomes slightly hyperpolarized, and this makes it more difficult for the neuron to fire. This is because in order for the cell to be depolarized to threshold, a stronger than normal stimulus (perhaps in the form of several additional EPSPs) is required.

12. First of all, a single postsynaptic neuron usually receives information from more than one presynaptic neuron. Therefore, its activity is a result of the integration of excitatory and inhibitory information it receives from all of these different sources. Second, synaptic activity may be modulated by a number of mechanisms, including glial cells, autoreceptors, and presynaptic excitation or inhibition from a third neuron.

13. Temporal summation occurs when two or more postsynaptic potentials occurring in close temporal (time) proximity have a cumulative effect on a neuron. For example, while a single EPSP will not cause a neuron to fire or increase a cell's firing rate, several EPSPs occurring very close together in time will have a cumulative effect. Spatial summation occurs when simultaneous postsynaptic potentials arriving at nearby locations influence the likelihood of firing or the firing rate of a neuron. For example, while a single IPSP may not have much effect on the postsynaptic cell, several IPSPs occurring together may reduce the frequency of action potentials. An example in real life: A child may clean up his or her room after being asked several times in a row by the same person (temporal) or after several family members asking at the same time (spatial).

## Post-test

1. d  2. a  3. c  4. a  5. b  6. c  7. c  8. a  9. d  10. b  11. d  12. c  13. b  14. a
15. c  16. d  17. b  18. a  19. a  20. d  21. c  22. b  23. c  24. b  25. a  26. d
27. a  28. c  29. d  30. c  31. c  32. d  33. a  34. b  35. b  36. c  37. a  38. a
39. b  40. d  41. b  42. d  43. a

# 3 The Organization and Functions of the Nervous System

## Learning Objectives

After reading this chapter, you should be able to answer the following questions.

1. What are the major functions of each of the cerebral hemispheres?

2. What are the locations and major functions of the thalamus, hypothalamus, midbrain, hindbrain, and cerebellum?

3.  Describe the structure and function of the spinal cord.

4.  What features of the central nervous system protect it?

5.  What structures make up the peripheral nervous system, and what are their functions?

6.  What happens in the nervous system during each of the stages of neural development?

7.  How does the nervous system change in response to experience?

8.  What are the barriers to recovery from damage in the nervous system? What new techniques are being developed to overcome some of these barriers?

## The Central Nervous System

### Summary and Guided Review

After studying this section in the text, fill in the blanks of the following summary.

The central nervous system (CNS) is composed of the _____ (1) and the _____ _____ (2). In the CNS a bundle of axons is called a(n) _____ (3) and a group of cell bodies is known as a(n) _____ (4). In the peripheral nervous system (PNS), an axon bundle is called a(n) _____ (5) and a group of cell bodies is a referred to as a(n) _____ (6). Early in development, the CNS begins as a hollow tube and quickly differentiates into a spinal cord and three brain areas, the _____ (7) (which in humans becomes the largest area), the _____ (8), and the _____ (9).

The forebrain contains two _____ (10) hemispheres, the _____ (11) that receives sensory information, and the underlying _____ (12). The hemispheres are separated by the longitudinal _____ (13). For the most part, each hemisphere receives information from and controls movement in the _____ (14) side of the body. The outer layer of the cerebral hemispheres, the _____ (15), is wrinkled in appearance and contains many _____ (16) (ridges) and _____ (17) (grooves). The surface is composed mostly of cell _____ (18), which accounts for its gray appearance. Its convoluted structure allows for greater _____ (19) area and more efficient connections for axons. The interior of the cortex, composed mostly of axons, appears _____ (20). Furthermore, the cortex is arranged in six _____ (21) in most areas. The layers are organized in _____ (22) that run perpendicular to the cortical surface area; these provide a vertical unity to the layers and are considered the primary _____ (23) processing unit in the cortex.

Among humans, having a larger brain is not usually an indication of superior _____ (24). In comparing different species, the overall size of the brain is in proportion to the body, with larger animals having larger brains. The intelligence of a species appears to be more related to the _____ (25) of the brain rather than its size. Among the most intelligent species, the cortex is _____ (26) in proportion to other brain areas. The nervous system itself is arranged in a(n) _____ (27), with complexity in structure and in the behaviors controlled increasing from the spinal cord up to the cortex.

Each hemisphere is divided into four lobes, and each lobe contributes to somewhat different functions. One function that the _____ (28) lobes are involved in is movement, as well as some of the most complex human capabilities. Different parts of the body are mapped onto areas of the _____ _____ (29), the location of the primary motor cortex, in the form of a(n) _____ (30), such that the parts of the body that are capable of fine motor movements (such as the fingers) are represented by a larger portion of the brain. The primary motor cortex also works with neighboring _____ (31) motor areas and subcortical structures such as the _____ _____ (32) in the control of movement. _____ (33) area, another frontal lobe structure, is involved in _____ (34) production and grammar.

The _____ (35) cortex, which is the anterior portion of the frontal lobe and the largest area of the human brain, contributes to a number of cognitive functions. Damage to this area can lead to many types of problems, including an inability to plan or organize actions, learn from experience, control impulsive behavior, or make decisions. It is also believed to be involved in mental illnesses such as schizophrenia and _____ (36). In the 1940s and 1950s, it was common practice to "disconnect" the prefrontal cortex from the rest of the brain through a procedure known as a(n) _____ (37). Over 40,000 of these were performed in the United States on people with mental illnesses of various types. The success of this procedure was limited, and it eventually fell into disfavor, especially when effective _____ (38) treatments become available in the 1950s. The importance of the frontal lobes was clearly demonstrated in the case of _____ _____ (39) who suffered specific deficits as a result of an accident in which a dynamite tamping iron pierced his skull and brain.

The parietal lobe contains the postcentral gyrus, which includes the _____ (40) cortex, onto which the body senses are projected. This area is structured to represent the body in much the same way as the primary motor cortex. The parietal lobe _____ _____ (41) provide further processing of sensory information, integrating several different types of sensory input. A person with damage to this area may experience _____ (42), a condition in which objects, people, and activity on the side opposite the damage are ignored.

The _____ (43) lobe contains the auditory cortex and (on the left hemisphere) _____ (44) area, which is involved in language comprehension and production. Visual identification of objects is carried out in the _____ (45) temporal cortex; people with damage to this area have difficulty recognizing objects by sight, including familiar people. People have reported experiencing specific events or memories when parts of the temporal cortex have been stimulated during brain surgery. Most of this brain stimulation research was conducted by the neurosurgeon _____ (46).

The entire occipital lobe is devoted to the sense of _____ (47). The primary projection area is organized like a map of the retina (the back part of the eye). The remainder of the occipital cortical areas process different components of images, such as color, form, and movement.

Other major structures of the forebrain include the _____ (48), which serves as a relay station for sensory information, and the _____ (49), which is important in emotions and motivated behavior. The hypothalamus controls the _____ (50) or master gland, which in turn controls all other glands in the body. Bodily cycles such as sleep are controlled in part by the _____ (51) gland.

One way in which the hemispheres communicate with each other is via structures such as the corpus _____ (52), which is found at the bottom of the longitudinal fissure. In cases of severe epilepsy, the corpus callosum may be surgically disconnected. People who have had this procedure can lead normal lives, but they show that to a certain extent that the two hemispheres have different functions, the left hemisphere being more involved in _____ (53) and the right in _____ (54) tasks and recognizing faces. Fluid-filled cavities called _____ (55) are located in the brain. They contain _____ (56) fluid, which transports nutrients to and wastes away from the CNS.

The midbrain contains several important structures. The superior and inferior _____ (57) are involved in eye movements and locating sounds, respectively. The midbrain also contains areas involved in movement; degeneration of cells in the _____ _____ (58) is implicated in Parkinson's disease. The ventral _____ (59) area plays a role in reward. The tube-shaped midbrain and hindbrain make up the brain _____ (60). The hindbrain includes the _____ (61), which is involved in vital functions such as respiration and keeping the heart beating, and the _____ (62), which is involved in sleep and arousal. The _____ (63) formation is a collection of nuclei running through the core of the midbrain and hindbrain. On the back of the brain stem is the _____ (64), which physically resembles the cerebral cortex and is essential in a number of motor and cognitive activities.

The spinal cord communicates between the brain and the body; it contains _____ _____ (65), which are motor programs for repetitive behaviors such as walking, and is responsible for certain reflexive behaviors. The spinal cord contains ascending _____ (66) tracts, which enter the spinal cord through the _____ (67) roots, and descending _____ (68) tracts, which exit the spinal cord through the _____ (69) roots. Some of the sensory neurons form connections directly or indirectly with motor neurons, which allow for spinal _____ (70).

The CNS is protected in a number of ways. It is covered by the _____ (71) (three-layered membrane), and the _____ (72) fluid cushions the brain. Harmful substances are prevented from entering the brain by the _____-_____ (73) barrier. The cells making up the walls of many of the _____ (74) serving the brain are tightly joined, which keeps many substances from passing through them. One area of the brain that is not protected in this way is the area _____ (75); when toxins are detected here, vomiting occurs.

## Short Answer and Essay Questions

Answer the following questions.

1. What is a major advantage of the convoluted structure of the cerebral cortex?

2. Why is brain size alone not a good indication of intelligence of different species of animals (e.g., humans and elephants)? What is a better indication?

3. How are the primary motor and somatosensory cortices organized in relation to the body areas they receive information from or send information to? What determines how much space on the cortex is devoted to a particular area of the body?

4. What is the condition known as *neglect?* What is the likely cause of it?

5. Identify three of the many functions of the temporal lobe.

6. Name three areas in the midbrain and hindbrain that are involved in motor function.

7. Why is the blood-brain barrier important? Explain how the structure of the blood-brain barrier helps keep some harmful substances out of the brain. Why is it advantageous that the area postrema NOT be protected by the barrier?

## The Peripheral Nervous System

### Summary and Guided Review

After studying this section in the text, fill in the blanks of the following summary.

The peripheral nervous system (PNS) is composed of spinal and _____ (76) nerves; it can be divided into the _____ (77) nervous system, which is involved in the control of movement and carries sensory information to the CNS, and the autonomic nervous system (ANS), which is involved in the control of _____ (78) and glands. Two of these are sometimes considered part of the brain: the _____ (79) nerve, which carries information about smell, and the _____ (80) nerve, which carries information about vision.

The ANS has two divisions: the _____ (81), which mobilizes bodily resources, and the _____ (82), which helps to restore energy. The sympathetic nervous system is highly coordinated due to the sympathetic _____ _____ (83). Most of the affected organs are stimulated together when this system is activated. In general, the two branches of the ANS have opposite effects on organs. For example, sympathetic activation _____ (84) heart rate, while parasympathetic activation _____ (85) it. However, both branches are active at the same time, but one may have a stronger effect at one time than the other.

### Short Answer and Essay Questions

Answer the following questions.

8. From the information provided in Figure 3.19, which cranial nerves appear to be involved in eye movement? Which are probably involved in speaking?

9. Why is the sympathetic nervous system able to act in a more coordinated fashion than the parasympathetic? What advantage is there for the coordinated action of the sympathetic nervous system?

## Development and Change in the Nervous System

### Summary and Guided Review

After studying this section in the text, fill in the blanks of the following summary.

Once the neural tube has formed, the nervous system develops in stages. During the first stage, _____ (86), new neurons are formed at a high rate in the _____ (87) zone of the neural tube. In the second stage, the new neurons migrate toward the outer layers of the tube with the support of _____

(88) glial cells. During this time, the neurons have the potential to become many different types of neurons. The next stage is _____ _____ (89) formation, during which axons find their way to target cells and form synapses with them. The chemical environment of the developing nervous system is detected by _____ _____ (90) on the ends of the axons; they are attracted to certain locations and repelled from others by the chemicals. The genes _____ (91) 1 and 3 are involved in getting neurons to their final destination. The nervous system produces many more neurons than it needs, and during the next stage of development, _____ _____ (92), synapses are eliminated and neurons die, leaving only those that are functional and useful. A neuron is more likely to survive this stage if it fires at the same time as its neighbors, in part because postsynaptic neurons release _____ (93) that enhance the development of presynaptic neurons. Circuit pruning may occur before birth, even in the absence of environmental input. In the visual system, for example, waves of activity sweep through the _____ (94), strengthening the connections that have been formed. As synapses are formed, most neurons lose _____ (95), or the ability to undergo modification, while others remain flexible throughout the life span.

During the formation of the nervous system, disruption of development can have serious consequences. For example, periventricular _____ (96), a genetic disorder, produces a smooth cortex, which usually results in severe epilepsy and mental retardation. Prenatal exposure to _____ (97) consumed by the mother may result in neurons migrating to the wrong place or failing to become appropriately organized. Babies with fetal alcohol syndrome often have small and malformed _____ (98) and are mentally impaired. Ionizing _____ (99) is another environmental agent that can interfere with proliferation and migration, particularly if the mother is exposed between the 8th and 15th week of pregnancy. The nervous system is not considered fully mature until _____ (100) is complete, which happens sometime in late _____ (101) or adulthood. This process begins with the lower areas of the brain, and the last areas to mature are the _____ (102) lobes.

Throughout the life span, the nervous system may undergo _____ (103) in response to experience. Through this process, some synapses may be lost while new ones are formed, and areas of the brain devoted to specific functions may actually expand. Reorganization can even violate the doctrine of specific _____ _____ (104), which states that input to a particular sensory area will always result in the same type of sensation. In the blind, for example, some of the visual cortex may be taken over by the _____ (105) system, so the visual cortex actually participates in reading Braille. Sometimes reorganization can have detrimental effects, such as when a limb is amputated and the somatosensory neurons from nearby body parts take over the part of the cortex that was devoted to the missing limb; this is thought to be responsible for _____ (106) pain that amputees sometimes experience. Experiments with cats have revealed that if an animal sees only vertical stripes during early development, it will not be able later to detect objects that are oriented _____ (107).

Recovery from damage in the nervous system is limited. Although in some species, such as _____ (108), damaged neurons easily regenerate, this is not true in all animals. In mammals, regeneration involving the regrowth of a severed _____ (109) occurs in the _____ (110) nervous system with the help of myelin. In the CNS, however, regrowth is unlikely because of the chemical environment, scar tissue, and the presence of glial and _____ (111) cells. Also, in most parts of the nervous system, new cells are not produced once proliferation ends. However, new cell production, or _____ (112), is seen in the hippocampus and the olfactory bulb, as well as at other sites when disease-related damage occurs. It may be possible to enhance regeneration as a treatment for brain damage.

Many people who suffer brain damage do recover some of the functions lost initially from the damage through the process of _____ (113), in which healthy neurons take over the connections that were lost due to the damage. Reorganization may also occur, such as in the case of _____ (114) (language impairment). Occasionally, researchers encounter a person who suffers from profound structural damage but who shows no apparent behavioral impairment. Examples from the text include cases of periventricular heterotopia, which has been discussed previously, and _____ (115), a condition in which blockage of cerebrospinal fluid can lead to severe retardation if untreated. These cases demonstrate that the nervous system is capable of compensating for even extensive damage, although the processes involved are not understood.

There are some other promising forms of therapy that may result in repairing CNS damage, including spinal cord injury and brain damage. One promising molecule, when given to rats with induced stroke, blocks glutamate-induced _____ (116), reducing the area of brain damage by 40%. Embryonic _____ (117) cells are pluripotent and may be used in the mature brain to replace cells damaged by injury or disease.

## Short Answer and Essay Questions

Answer the following questions.

10. During neural development, axons often have to grow over extensive distances, and sometimes across hemispheres, in order to reach their target postsynaptic cells. How is this accomplished? Include in your answer the roles of growth cones and the *Robo1* and *Robo3* genes.

11. It is clear that the nervous system starts out with a lot more neurons than it needs. Why do you think it is advantageous for the nervous system to have so many neurons to start with, if many of them are only going to be lost? Keep in mind that the environment an animal encounters is at least somewhat unpredictable.

12. Maria was exposed to high levels of ionizing radiation during her 32nd week of pregnancy. She is concerned that this will have profound negative effects on her fetus, particularly its nervous system. What would you tell her?

13. What is syndactyly? How does surgical correction of syndactyly and the resulting changes in the brain demonstrate neural reorganization?

14. Describe some ways in which the CNS can compensate at the level of the synapse for the loss of neurons in specific locations.

15. Describe some possible treatments that may be used in the future to correct brain and spinal cord injuries.

## Post-test

Use these multiple-choice questions to check your understanding of the chapter.

1. A ___ is the name for a bundle of neurons in the PNS.
   a. nerve
   b. tract
   c. nucleus
   d. ganglion

2. The spinal cord is part of the ___ nervous system.
   a. central
   b. autonomic
   c. peripheral
   d. sympathetic

3. Which of the following is the largest division of the mature CNS in humans?
   a. forebrain
   b. midbrain
   c. hindbrain
   d. spinal cord

4. The space separating the cerebral hemispheres is called the
   a. lateral fissure.
   b. corpus callosum.
   c. central sulcus.
   d. longitudinal fissure.

5. The surface of the cortex appears gray because it is composed mostly of
   a. unmyelinated axons.
   b. unmyelinated cell bodies.
   c. myelinated axons.
   d. myelinated cell bodies.

6. In the cortex, a ridge is called a
   a. fissure.
   b. gyrus.
   c. tract.
   d. sulcus.

7. What is the name of the 19th-century European anatomist who argued that because women have smaller brains than men, they are less intelligent?
   a. Penfield
   b. Ramón y Cajal
   c. Bischoff
   d. Sperry

8. Animal species that are the MOST intelligent tend to have
   a. bigger brains overall.
   b. more convolutions on the cortex.
   c. a proportionately larger forebrain.
   d. b and c

9. The directional term *anterior* means
   a. in front of.
   b. behind.
   c. above.
   d. below.

10. The brain area controlling fine motor movement is located on the
    a. prefrontal cortex.
    b. precentral gyrus.
    c. postcentral gyrus.
    d. central sulcus.

11. The area of the motor cortex devoted to which of the following body areas is probably the smallest?
    a. lips
    b. tongue
    c. thumb
    d. thigh

12. Damage to the prefrontal cortex is LEAST likely to result in problems with
    a. decision making.
    b. planning.
    c. speech comprehension.
    d. impulse.

13. Who among the following was a proponent of lobotomies as a treatment for mental illness?
    a. Penfield
    b. Gage
    c. Freeman
    d. Bischoff

14. The somatosensory cortex is located in the ___ lobe.
    a. frontal
    b. occipital
    c. temporal
    d. parietal

15. Identifying objects by touch is a function of the
    a. somatosensory cortex.
    b. parietal association cortex.
    c. visual cortex.
    d. inferior temporal cortex.

16. Modern computer studies of the skull of Phineas Gage have revealed the extent of damage to the
    a. frontal lobes.
    b. corpus callosum.
    c. parietal lobes.
    d. brain stem.

17. Which of the following is NOT a function of the temporal lobes?
    a. processing auditory information
    b. language comprehension
    c. fine motor control
    d. visual identification of objects

18. Electrical stimulation of the association areas of the temporal lobe may result in the patient experiencing
    a. intense pain.
    b. buzzing sounds.
    c. bright lights.
    d. vivid memories.

19. The occipital lobe processes ___ information.
    a. visual
    b. auditory

c. somatosensory

d. a and b

20. The thalamus receives information from all of the sensory systems EXCEPT the system for
    a. vision.
    b. hearing.
    c. smell.
    d. taste.

21. The hypothalamus is located ___ the thalamus.
    a. above
    b. below
    c. behind
    d. in front of

22. The ___ is the body's "master" endocrine gland.
    a. pituitary
    b. pineal
    c. hypothalamus
    d. pons

23. The sleep-inducing hormone melatonin is released by the
    a. pituitary gland.
    b. pineal gland.
    c. hypothalamus.
    d. pons.

24. Which statement regarding the corpus callosum is FALSE?
    a. It consists of neuron tracts connecting the two hemispheres.
    b. It is the only place in the brain where information crosses from one side to the other.
    c. It may be severed in order to help control epileptic seizures.
    d. It allows the left side of the brain to share information with the right.

25. Which of the following structures is NOT part of the brain stem?
    a. lateral ventricle
    b. midbrain
    c. pons
    d. medulla

26. All of the following structures are located in the midbrain EXCEPT the
    a. superior colliculi.
    b. ventral tegmental area.
    c. pons.
    d. substantia nigra.

27. Heart rate and breathing are controlled by the
    a. pons.
    b. cerebellum.
    c. superior colliculi.
    d. medulla.

28. A person with damage to the cerebellum may
    a. be blind.
    b. be unable to recognize familiar objects.

c. be insensitive to pain.

d. have problems with movement.

29. The cerebrospinal fluid protects the brain in all of the following ways EXCEPT that it doesn't
    a. provide nourishment to brain cells.
    b. cushion the brain.
    c. remove waste products from the CNS.
    d. prevent toxins from entering the CNS.

30. The skeletal muscles are MOST directly controlled by the ___ nervous system.
    a. autonomic
    b. somatic
    c. sympathetic
    d. central

31. Which of the following cranial nerves is sometimes considered part of the CNS rather than the PNS?
    a. oculomotor
    b. auditory
    c. vagus
    d. optic

32. Which of the following is more a result of parasympathetic than sympathetic activation?
    a. increased digestive activity
    b. increased heart rate
    c. increased blood pressure
    d. increased respiration

33. The stage of neural development in which axons grow toward their target connections is called
    a. proliferation.
    b. migration.
    c. circuit formation.
    d. circuit pruning.

34. Cell proliferation occurs
    a. in the innermost layer of the neural tube.
    b. in the outermost layers of the neural tube.
    c. throughout the neural tube.
    d. in the location of a neuron's final destination.

35. Cells that form a scaffold for neural migration are called
    a. astrocytes.
    b. radial glial cells.
    c. myelin cells.
    d. ladder cells.

36. During the first three weeks after birth, the neurons in a monkey's corpus callosum
    a. triple in number.
    b. increase by about 8 million.
    c. decrease by about 8 million.
    d. undergo very little change.

37. Neural plasticity is retained to the greatest extent in adulthood in which of the following brain areas?
    a. primary visual cortex
    b. somatosensory cortex
    c. primary motor cortex
    d. association cortex

38. Which of the following is NOT a result of fetal exposure to alcohol?
    a. improper migration of cells
    b. failure of cells to form myelin
    c. small brain size
    d. mental retardation

39. Which of the following brain areas is among the last to undergo myelination?
    a. frontal cortex
    b. occipital cortex
    c. spinal nerves
    d. medulla

40. Which of the following is NOT an example of brain reorganization?
    a. larger area of the somatosensory cortex devoted to the index finger in people who read Braille
    b. the occipital cortex of people blind from birth responding to somatosensory information
    c. phantom limb pain following amputation of a leg
    d. regrowth of a severed spinal motor neuron

41. Regeneration is LEAST likely to occur in the
    a. CNS of a frog.
    b. PNS of a frog.
    c. CNS of a mammal.
    d. PNS of a mammal.

42. In the adult mammal, neurogenesis is MOST likely to occur in the
    a. spinal cord.
    b. medulla.
    c. hippocampus.
    d. hypothalamus.

43. Which of the following is NOT true of hydrocephalus?
    a. It results from a blockage of the cerebrospinal fluid.
    b. It can be treated using a drainage shunt.
    c. Even without treatment, individuals usually have normal intelligence.
    d. It affects the development of the CNS.

44. Which of the following is NOT a problem following stroke?
    a. edema
    b. abnormal protein deposits
    c. excitotosis
    d. paralysis

45. Which of the following is FALSE regarding traumatic brain injury? It
    a. can produce Alzheimer-like effects even in young brains.
    b. includes concussion as one of its mild forms.
    c. requires a severe blow, due to the brain's cushioning.
    d. can be minimized by 3 weeks of rest.

# Answers

## Guided Review

1. brain
2. spinal cord
3. tract
4. nucleus
5. nerve
6. ganglion
7. forebrain
8. midbrain
9. hindbrain
10. cerebral
11. thalamus
12. hypothalamus
13. fissure
14. opposite
15. cortex
16. gyri (plural of gyrus)
17. sulci (plural of sulcus) or fissures
18. bodies
19. surface
20. white
21. layers
22. columns
23. information
24. intelligence
25. convolutions
26. larger
27. hierarchy
28. frontal
29. precentral gyrus
30. homunculus
31. secondary
32. basal ganglia
33. Broca's
34. speech
35. prefrontal
36. depression
37. lobotomy
38. drug
39. Phineas Gage
40. somatosensory
41. association areas
42. neglect
43. temporal
44. Wernicke's
45. inferior
46. Penfield
47. vision
48. thalamus
49. hypothalamus
50. pituitary
51. pineal
52. callosum
53. language
54. spatial
55. ventricles
56. cerebrospinal
57. colliculi
58. substantia nigra
59. tegmental
60. stem
61. medulla
62. pons
63. reticular
64. cerebellum

65. pattern generators

66. sensory

67. dorsal

68. motor

69. ventral

70. reflexes

71. meninges

72. cerebrospinal

73. blood-brain

74. capillaries

75. postrema

76. cranial

77. somatic

78. organs

79. olfactory

80. optic

81. sympathetic

82. parasympathetic

83. ganglion chains

84. increases

85. decreases

86. proliferation

87. ventricular

88. radial

89. circuit formation

90. growth cones

91. *Robo*

92. circuit pruning

93. neurotrophins

94. retina

95. plasticity

96. heterotopia

97. alcohol

98. brains

99. radiation

100. myelination

101. adolescence

102. frontal

103. reorganization

104. nerve energies

105. somatosensory

106. phantom pain

107. horizontally

108. amphibians

109. axon

110. peripheral

111. immune

112. neurogenesis

113. compensation

114. aphasia

115. hydrocephalus

116. excitotoxicity

117. stem

## Short Answer and Essay Questions

1. One advantage is that it increases the surface area of the brain without increasing its size a great deal. This means more cortex can be packed into a small area.

2. If we compare between species, brain size is more related to body size than intelligence; the largest animals tend to have the largest brains. A good way of representing the connection between brain and intelligence is its complexity, particularly the degree to which the forebrain is developed. Humans' forebrains are larger and more extensively convoluted than apes' brains, which are larger and more convoluted than monkeys' brains, etc.

3. These areas of the brain are organized like maps of the body. Sensory neurons from adjacent areas of the body project to adjacent areas of the somatosensory cortex, and neurons from adjacent parts of the motor cortex control movement in adjacent areas of the body. Areas of the body that are either especially sensitive (because they contain a lot of sensory receptors) or capable of fine motor movement are represented by a larger area of the cortex than areas that are less sensitive or not involved in fine motor movement. For example, the fingers are represented to a greater extent in both cortices than is the back.

4. This is usually the result of damage to the association cortex in the parietal lobe. It occurs because this part of the brain is involved in various spatial tasks, such as being able to tell where things are in the environment and being able to locate one's own body in space. Persons who suffer damage to this area in the right hemisphere may not pay attention to things on the left side of the body; such an individual may not even recognize that an arm or leg belongs to her or him.

5. The temporal lobes are where auditory information is initially processed and most of language comprehension occurs; the lobes also contain auditory and visual association areas responsible for tasks such as recognition of faces and other visual objects.

6. Three areas with a role in motor function in the midbrain and hindbrain are the substantia nigra, the cerebellum, and the reticular formation.

7. The main route for toxins and other substances to get into organs is through the bloodstream. The brain is especially vulnerable (because most adult CNS neurons do not replicate), so it is especially important to keep toxins out of the brain. In many parts of the brain, the capillaries are structured to do just that. The cells that make up the capillary walls are tightly packed together, so that very few substances can pass through them without going through special channels, and the special channels are selective in what they allow through. However, not all brain areas are protected in this manner. In the area postrema, toxins can get in, and it is actually beneficial that they do in some cases. If a toxin is detected in this area, it triggers the vomiting response, and if the source of the toxin is in the stomach, it will be removed from the body.

8. Cranial nerves III (oculomotor), IV (trochlear), and VI (abducens) control eye movement. Cranial nerves X (vagus) and XII (hypoglossal) are probably involved in speech.

9. The sympathetic nervous system consists of components of several of the spinal nerves serving various internal organs. The activity of its neurons is coordinated because many of them are interconnected within the sympathetic ganglion chain just outside the spinal cord, which allows for a coordinated response. No such structure exists in the parasympathetic division. The advantage of the coordination of the sympathetic division is that it provides a mobilization of most of the body's resources in times of stress.

10. First of all, axons contain a growth cone, which is used to find the correct pathway. The cone is sensitive to the external chemical environment, and it is attracted to certain places and repelled from others. The sensitivity of the growth cone to different chemicals can also change over time as the axon grows into different areas. The *Robo1* gene produces a chemical that repels axons; so when it is active, axons do not grow across the midline of the brain. Activation of the *Robo3* gene leads to axons being attracted across the midline. Once it is deactivated, the axon is no longer attracted to the midline and continues to grow in that side of the brain.

11. By initially overproducing neurons, the nervous system allows for streamlining (elimination of unused and retention of used connections) to eliminate errors in circuit formation. The alternative to overproduction would be more precise circuit formation, which would require complex chemical and genetic codes. In addition, this strategy allows for adaptation to

varied environmental conditions that could not be predicted in advance. An example of such selection occurred in the experiment in which kittens were reared with only horizontal or only vertical stripes.

12. While there may be some detrimental effects, they would probably be worse if she had been exposed earlier, between 8 and 15 weeks of gestation, because that is when proliferation and migration of neurons are occurring at high rates.

13. Syndactyly is a condition in which the fingers are connected by a web of tissue, are of limited usefulness, and are mapped onto overlapping areas of the somatosensory cortex. Within a week following surgical separation, patients' brains showed dramatic changes in that the separated fingers were now represented in distinct locations on the somatosensory cortex.

14. Healthy presynaptic neurons can form new terminals to create replacement connections. Postsynaptic cells can create new receptors to compensate for reduced presynaptic input. And "silent" collaterals, terminals that were inactive, may become active almost immediately following injury.

15. One possibility is introducing new neurons, either from fetal cells or stem cells. The other possibilities involve manipulating the environment of the mature CNS so that it does not inhibit axon regeneration. These mechanisms include providing the nervous system with substances that can promote neural growth, inhibit those substances that inhibit neural growth, serve as scaffolds for developing axons, and/or block the immune response that may be harmful to developing axons. Use of glial and stem cells from the person's own olfactory mucosa may also be helpful in restoration or improvement in function.

## Post-test

1. d    2. a    3. a    4. d    5. b    6. b    7. c    8. d    9. a    10. b    11. d    12. c    13. c
14. d    15. b    16. a    17. c    18. d    19. a    20. c    21. b    22. a    23. b    24. b    25. a
26. c    27. d    28. d    29. d    30. b    31. d    32. a    33. c    34. a    35. b    36. c    37. d
38. b    39. a    40. d    41. c    42. c    43. c    44. b    45. c

# 4 The Methods and Ethics of Research

## Learning Objectives

After reading this chapter, you should be able to answer the following questions.

1.  What roles do theories and hypotheses play in scientific research, and why are scientists often tentative in drawing firm conclusions about the results of their studies?

2.  How do correlational and experimental studies differ?

3.  How are staining, imaging, and microscopic techniques used to study individual cells and their components? What have such techniques revealed?

4.  What are the procedures for measuring and manipulating brain activity?

5.  What are the procedures for imaging brains?

6.  What correlational methods are used for studying heredity in humans?

7.  What are the different types of genetic engineering studies?

8.  What is plagiarism? Fabrication? Why are these problematic for science?

9.  What issues must be considered in research using human participants? Animal subjects?

10. What are the ethical problems associated with gene therapy and stem cell research?

## Science, Research, and Theory

### Summary and Guided Review

After studying this section in the text, fill in the blanks of the following summary.

Science requires that information be derived from observation, a concept known as _____ (1). Scientific observations should be objective, so that two or more people watching the same event will describe it in the same way.

Like many other scientists, biological psychologists are careful about the way they interpret their research results. Knowledge often undergoes _____ (2) over time; what is thought of as a "fact" today may be shown to be incorrect in the future. For example, it was recently discovered that axon regrowth and _____ (3) may occur in the mature primate central nervous system. Many scientists use _____ (4) to explain observations and guide their research. They generate _____ (5), which are testable predictions derived from theories. If a hypothesis is found to be incorrect, then the theory must be revised. The _____ (6) theory of schizophrenia is a very good example of the need to alter theories when new data become available.

An experiment is a study in which the researcher manipulates at least one _____ (7) variable and measures its effects on one or more _____ (8) variables. Experimenters also eliminate _____ (9) variables that might influence behavior, or equate them across subjects. Causal relationships cannot be determined from correlational studies because when two variables are found to be correlated, there may be a(n) _____ (10) variable that accounts for the relationship between the two. Although experimental studies are most useful for determining cause-effect relationships, they are sometimes more artificial than _____ (11) studies. If a researcher measured the extent of frontal lobe impairment in a large group of people and then examined their records for criminal behavior, they might find that criminals are more likely to have frontal lobe deficits than other individuals. This would be an example of a(n) _____ (12) study. This relationship could not be studied as a(n) _____ (13) study for ethical reasons.

## Short Answer and Essay Questions

Answer the following questions.

1. Why do researchers avoid using words like "truth" and "proof" when they discuss the results of their work?

2. If experimental studies are the only ones that allow us to determine cause-effect relationships, why are other studies used at all? What are the limitations of experimental studies?

3. Discuss how the dopamine theory of schizophrenia has evolved. What observations led to the dopamine theory? How was it tested? What were the results of these tests? What is the current status of the theory?

# Research Techniques

## Summary and Guided Review

After studying this section in the text, fill in the blanks of the following summary.

Brain researchers use a variety of techniques to study brain tissue, including staining and imaging neurons. An early method, invented by Camillo _____ (14) and used by Santiago Ramón y Cajal to examine individual neurons, involved staining brain tissue so that about 5% of the neurons would stand out from the rest. Neural pathways (bundles of axons) can be identified by using _____ (15) stains, whereas groups of cell bodies can be identified with _____ (16) stains. Injection of fluorescent substances such as _____ (17), which is transferred between neurons, also allows researchers to trace pathways between neurons. Injecting radioactively labeled glucose allows researchers to see which brain areas are most active during particular activities; this technique is known as _____ (18). Candace Pert used a similar technique to identify _____ (19) receptors in brain tissue. Immunocytochemistry involves attaching a dye, which is usually fluorescent, to _____ (20) to make receptors, neurotransmitters, or other cellular components visible. Using in situ _____ (21), in which radioactive DNA is paired with messenger RNA, researchers have been able to locate specific sites of gene activity.

Light microscopes magnify cells so that their larger components such as cell bodies, some organelles, axons, and _____ (22) are discernible. Electron microscopes can magnify images up to _____ (23) times by passing electrons through objects and onto photographic film. This technique allows researchers to see such things as synaptic _____ (24). A(n) _____ (25) electron microscope produces a three-dimensional image by inducing the object being observed to emit electrons. Two of the newest examples of advances in microscopic technology are the _____ _____ _____ (26) microscope and the _____ _____ (27) microscope.

Brain activity in the form of waves may be measured using electrodes attached to the scalp; the record of this activity is called a(n) _____ (28). This technique has excellent _____ (29) resolution but poor spatial resolution, meaning it is difficult to locate the exact area in which changes are occurring. Researchers can present a specific stimulus several times; the EEGs are recorded and then averaged to cancel out the "noise" from the rest of the brain, producing a(n) _____ (30) potential.

When researchers want to locate a specific brain area for recording or manipulation, a(n) _____ (31) instrument is used to insert an electrode or cannula, in a location determined from a stereotaxic _____ (32). A small electrode may be inserted and left in place to determine what effect stimulation of the brain area containing the electrode will have on the subject's behavior. A(n) _____ (33) is used for single-unit recording while the subject is presented with different stimuli or engages in a certain behavior. A narrow tube called a(n) _____ (34) may be inserted for delivering chemicals to specific brain areas or removing brain fluid, a procedure known as _____ (35).

The study of people with brain damage may give scientists clues about which brain areas are involved in which functions, but more precise methods require experimentally damaging specific areas and observing the effects under controlled conditions. Such studies are done with animals. A procedure called _____ (36) involves removing brain tissue; this may be done with more precision using a vacuum to remove the desired tissue, a technique known as _____ (37). Neural tissue may also be _____ (38), or damaged by the use of electricity, heat, or chemicals. Chilling a brain region or using certain chemicals produces a(n) _____ (39) lesion, allowing the researcher to make comparisons before and during damage and following recovery. In humans, a cannula or electrode may be implanted in order to facilitate surgery or to treat certain conditions (such as epilepsy or Parkinson's disease).

Brain _____ (40) techniques allow for the examination of intact brains; they can reveal areas of damage as well as show which areas are active in response to specific stimulation or during specific behaviors. The first modern imaging technique that was developed was the _____ (41) scan, which takes several X-rays of the brain and combines the different images using a computer; the horizontal "slices" thus form a composite view of the entire brain.. Another technique is _____ _____ (42) imaging, which works by measuring radio-frequency waves from hydrogen (or other elemental) atoms exposed to a magnetic field. A variant of this procedure, _____ _____ (43) imaging, measures the movement of water molecules and is useful for identifying brain pathways. Although these techniques produce pictures of the brain, none shows changes over time. Brain activity may be measured by injecting radioactive chemicals such as 2-DG into the bloodstream and then identifying areas of the brain that take up greater amounts of the chemical. This technique is known as _____ (44), and it allows researchers to determine which brain areas are most involved in specific activities. Another measure of brain activity is the _____ (45) MRI procedure (fMRI), which detects differential oxygen increases. Some researchers are concerned about this technique's lower sensitivity and less-than-perfect test-retest reliability. A relatively new noninvasive technique called _____ (46) uses a magnetic coil to induce changes in electrical activity in the brain. Although this procedure shows some promise as a therapeutic tool, at the moment it is most likely to be useful for _____ (47).

The heredity of behavior in humans may be studied in family, adoption, and _____ (48) studies. By comparing the behaviors of related individuals, researchers can determine the extent to which heredity influences traits among related individuals. For example, family studies have revealed that between parents and their children there is a(n) _____ (49) of about .42 in IQ scores and a rate of about _____ (50) for schizophrenia in the offspring of a schizophrenic parent as compared to the general population rate of 1%. However, _____ (51) studies reveal that when children are adopted out, the correlation of their IQ scores with those of their biological parents drops to .22, indicating that some of the similarity between parents and children stems from the environment. One of the best ways of examining the influence of heredity on behavior in humans is through twin studies. _____ (52) twins, who share the same genetic material, are compared to _____ (53) twins; this comparison controls for environment to some extent, although not entirely. Neither twin nor adoption studies eliminate the influence of the _____ (54) environment or of the time from birth to adoption. Twin studies reveal correlations of IQ scores in dizygotic twins to be around _____ (55) whereas that for monozygotic twins is about _____ (56), suggesting a strong genetic component to intelligence. Sometimes researchers use the term _____ (57) rate to refer to the frequency with which relatives are alike in a characteristic or disorder. Studies show that the concordance rates for schizophrenia in monozygotic twins is about _____ (58) times the concordance rates for dizygotic twins.

At present, the experimental manipulation of genes, or _____ _____ (59), is done mostly with nonhuman animals, particularly mice. One way of changing mice's genetic makeup is by inserting nonfunctioning DNA into mouse embryos and then breeding the offspring, thus creating _____ (60) mice. The _____ _____ (61) procedure is used to alter a gene's activity by blocking the cell's protein-building activity. Gene _____ (62) is a procedure in which a gene from another organism is introduced into a recipient's cells; when the gene is inserted into a developing embryo, the result is referred to as a(n) _____ (63) animal. Gene therapy has been used to treat _____ (64) experienced by individuals like Ashanthi, and doctors have had some success using gene transfer to treat the memory disorder _____ (65).

## Short Answer and Essay Questions

Answer the following questions.

4. What is the advantage of autoradiography over Nissl and myelin staining procedures? Give an example of an important discovery that has resulted from the use of autoradiography.

5. How were immunocytochemistry and in situ hybridization used together to identify the likely protein responsible for night-migration in birds? In your answer, be sure to explain how both of these methods work.

6. What are evoked potentials, and how are they obtained? What do they measure?

7. Describe the uses of a stereotaxic instrument.

8. Why do researchers who want to understand brain damage in humans use ablation and lesioning in animal studies?

9. How do CT and MRI scans work? What does each method reveal about the brain, and what are the limitations of each of these methods?

10. How do PET and fMRI scans work? What does each method reveal about the brain, and what are the limitations of each of these methods?

11. Distinguish between adoption and family studies. Why are adoption studies generally better for studying heredity of traits than family studies?

12. Give some examples of genetic engineering that have been used for research and therapeutic purposes.

## Research Ethics

### Summary and Guided Review

After studying this section in the text, fill in the blanks of the following summary.

Scientists must adhere to guidelines for ethical conduct. These guidelines cover many aspects of scientists' work, including publishing information and using humans and animals in research. One type of ethical violation involves claiming someone else's ideas as one's own; this is known as _____ (66). A more serious violation, in which false or misleading data are published, is _____ (67). These types of violations are potentially damaging for the scientific community.

Scientists are also obligated to treat their human research participants with dignity and respect and to obtain their informed _____ (68) before the individuals participate in the research. This means that participants are fully aware of any potential risks involved in the research. Some behavioral studies, such as the one by Albert Ax described in the book, employ _____ (69), which involves withholding information or giving false information at the outset of a study. Some researchers and subjects' rights advocates say its use is never justified.

Many of the recent advances in medicine would not have been possible without animal research. Animals are used as research subjects for a variety of reasons. Many procedures that are potentially dangerous to humans are performed on animals. Animals' genetic makeup and _____ (70) can be controlled. Consequently, it is easier to interpret results from studies with animals than those from studies with humans. This preference for using animals in potentially harmful studies is considered by some to be a dual ethical standard, which they have labeled _____ (71). Most laboratory animals are _____ (72), and recently NIH stopped all new research grants on _____ (73) (apes most closely related to humans). Animal rights _____ (74), people who work on behalf of the welfare of research animals, may cooperate with animal researchers to improve conditions for research animals, or they may damage or destroy labs and threaten to harm or actually harm the researchers themselves. Scientists who use animals in research are obligated to treat them humanely. Animals must be well cared for, and pain and suffering should be _____ (75). Overall, treatment of research animals seems to be improving, and some researchers are using alternative methods such as tissue _____ (76) and _____ (77) simulations.

Perhaps the most controversial area of medical research using humans is in _____ _____ (78). Such research involves altering the genetic makeup or genetic activity of individuals in order to treat specific problems. As the result of a research participant's death in 1999, stricter _____ (79) for such research are expected. There are other ethical concerns with this type of research as well, including its impact on successive generations of human beings. Evidence of the way in which genetic information might be used, or misused, comes from promises of "_____ (80) babies" created in fertility clinics. Similar efforts are occurring in _____ (81) where children are sent to summer camp to be genetically tested in order to predict abilities and recommend appropriate careers.

The use of human _____ (82) cells has also been a controversial area of research. Stem cells have been used to improve heart functioning, and many researchers expect that stem cells will eventually be used to grow human _____ (83) for transplants, and stem cell research will provide a better understanding of the development of disease. Most human stem cells come from "extra" embryos from fertility treatments. The Bush administration _____ (84) federal funding of research with newly developed stem cell lines, and cells from older lines are of little value for human research. However, _____ (85) reversed this policy in 2009. Because of the complexity of the issue, it is likely that stem cell research will continue to be controversial.

## Short Answer and Essay Questions

Answer the following questions.

13. Describe the study by Albert Ax. Why was this study ethically controversial? Would researchers be able to do this study now? Why or why not?

14. If medical research is done to benefit humans, why are animals used as research subjects?

15. What is speciesism?

16. In what way does the movie *Gattaca* reflect concerns in our society about genetic research and genetic manipulation?

17. What is the major ethical controversy of human stemcell research?

# Post-test

Use these multiple-choice questions to check your understanding of the chapter.

1. A theory is
   a. an established scientific fact.
   b. a prediction that can be tested.
   c. an explanation for our observations.
   d. all of the above

2. Which of the following statements is a biological psychologist LEAST likely to make?
   a. These results suggest that people who drink heavily may suffer from memory loss.
   b. These results show that some people who drink heavily suffer from memory loss.
   c. These results prove that heavy drinking results in memory loss.
   d. From these results, it appears that memory loss may be a result of heavy drinking.

3. A detailed study of a single person showing interesting behavior is called
   a. a case study.
   b. an experiment.
   c. a survey.
   d. none of the above

4. A study that allows researchers to determine if a cause-effect relationship exists between two variables is a(n)
   a. correlational study.
   b. experiment.
   c. naturalistic observational study.
   d. none of the above

5. Dr. Joy observes the behavior of mice in large colonies, taking particular note of social interactions, but does not interfere with the mice in any way. What type of study is this?
   a. an experiment
   b. a case study
   c. naturalistic observation
   d. a survey

6. Dr. Hagen performs a study in which participants are given different amounts of alcohol and then are tested in a driving simulation. In this study, alcohol is the
   a. dependent variable.
   b. correlational variable.
   c. confounded variable.
   d. independent variable.

7. Research volunteers are given either a placebo pill or a drug containing a small amount of amphetamine. Then the volunteers are asked to play a game of chess on a computer. The researchers believe that the amphetamine will interfere with the participants' ability to play well. What is the dependent variable in this study?
   a. the computer game
   b. the placebo
   c. the amphetamine
   d. performance in the chess game

8. Female and male college students are compared on a mathematical test. This is BEST described as a(n)
   a. experiment.
   b. independent variable.
   c. correlational study.
   d. none of the above

9. The dopamine theory of schizophrenia
   a. suggests that the disorder is a result of dopamine hyperactivity in the brain.
   b. was developed after some researchers noticed drug users showing signs of schizophrenia.
   c. does not account for all cases of schizophrenia.
   d. all of the above

10. The staining procedure that allowed 19th-century anatomists to study individual neurons was discovered by
    a. Santiago Ramón y Cajal.
    b. Camillo Golgi.
    c. Candace Pert.
    d. Henrik Mouritsen.

11. If researchers want to find a nucleus (collection of cell bodies) in the hypothalamus, they are MOST likely to use which of the following techniques?
    a. Nissl staining
    b. myelin staining
    c. in situ hybridization
    d. immunocytochemistry

12. ___ is a substance that may be injected into one area of the brain and then transferred to other cells.
    a. Fluorogold
    b. Nissl stain
    c. Golgi stain
    d. Myelin stain

13. Which procedure involves the use of radioactive sugar molecules, which are absorbed by active neurons and then detected on photographic film?
    a. immunocytochemistry
    b. Nissl staining
    c. autoradiography
    d. Fluorogold staining

14. Brain researchers discovered opiate receptors using which technique?
    a. Nissl staining
    b. autoradiography
    c. immunocytochemistry
    d. Golgi staining

15. Immunocytochemistry involves the use of ___, whereas in situ hybridization involves the use of ___.
    a. radioactive DNA; dye-labeled antibodies
    b. dye-labeled antibodies; radioactive DNA
    c. dye-labeled antibodies; radioactive sugar molecules
    d. radioactive sugar molecules; radioactive DNA

16. Cryptochromes are proteins that
    a. bind to opiate receptor sites.
    b. impair the immune system's ability to fight infection.
    c. may be responsible for night-migration in some types of birds.
    d. interfere with messenger RNA.

17. An electron microscope allows us to see images of objects magnified up to ___ times.
    a. 250
    b. 2,500
    c. 25,000
    d. 250,000

18. The EEG has relatively ___ temporal resolution and ___ spatial resolution.
    a. good; good
    b. poor; poor
    c. good; poor
    d. poor; good

19. Researchers who use evoked potentials to study brain activity are MOST likely interested in
    a. studying patients who are asleep.
    b. identifying how the brain responds to brief changes in stimuli.
    c. recording from single neurons.
    d. injecting chemicals in the brain.

20. A stereotaxic instrument may be used to
    a. place a recording electrode in a specific location in the brain.
    b. place a stimulating electrode in a specific location in the brain.
    c. locate a specific area of the brain in which to inject chemicals.
    d. all of the above

21. Microdialysis is a procedure for
    a. removing brain fluid for analysis.
    b. injecting chemicals into the brain to destroy neurons.
    c. injecting radioactive substances into the brain to measure activity.
    d. removing neurons from the brain for analysis.

22. Jerry is undergoing a procedure in which several electrodes are attached to his scalp, and the activity of neurons under the electrodes is recorded. What is this procedure called?
    a. EEG
    b. PET
    c. MRI
    d. CT

23. Aspiration is BEST thought of as a form of
    a. lesioning.
    b. recording brain activity.
    c. ablation.
    d. reversible lesioning.

24. Which of the following brain imaging techniques involves the use of X-rays?
    a. MRI
    b. fMRI
    c. PET
    d. CT

25. If a brain researcher is interested in studying which brain areas are MOST active during a spatial skills task, the procedure of choice would be
    a. MRI.
    b. PET.
    c. CT.
    d. TMS.

26. The effects of heredity and environment on behavior are MOST confounded in
    a. family studies.
    b. adoption studies.
    c. twin studies.
    d. genetic engineering studies.

27. A correlation of −.75 indicates
    a. a weak relationship between two variables.
    b. a strong relationship between two variables.
    c. no relationship between two variables.
    d. a mistake; correlations cannot be negative.

28. When researchers look at the IQ scores of children raised by adoptive parents, there is a correlation of about ___ with the IQ scores of their biological parents.
    a. 0.42
    b. 0.47

c. 0.60

d. 0.22

29. Compared to identical twins, fraternal twins show ___ concordance for schizophrenia.

a. a higher

b. a lower

c. the same

d. no

30. The ___ technique of genetic engineering involves preventing or reducing the expression of a particular gene by occupying the cell's ribonucleic acid with a synthetic strand of DNA.

a. antisense DNA

b. transgenic

c. antisense RNA

d. knockout

31. People with SCID

a. may die if exposed to a normal environment.

b. suffer from severe mental disorders.

c. may be aided by genetic engineering.

d. a and c

32. Jennifer is a graduate student studying the effects of electrical stimulation on the cingulate gyrus in rats' brains. Her initial results are not what she expected, and because she is worried about finishing her dissertation on time, she changes some of her data so that it fits her hypothesis. Jennifer has engaged in

a. plagiarism.

b. deception.

c. fabrication.

d. breaking the law.

33. Researchers who use humans as participants

a. are barred from intentionally deceiving them.

b. may withhold information from them but may not lie to them.

c. must fully inform them about all details of a procedure beforehand.

d. may not withhold information about risks or discomfort that might occur.

34. What percentage of laboratory animals are primates?

a. more than 90%

b. about 50%

c. between 10% and 15%

d. fewer than 5%

35. Regarding animal research guidelines, which of the following is FALSE?

a. Procedures involving pain may not be performed on primates.

b. Stress should be minimized.

c. Procedures must be approved by an Institutional Animal Care and Use Committee.

d. Researchers must provide humane housing and medical care.

36. The researcher Edward Taub, whose laboratory at Silver Springs, Maryland, made national headlines in the 1980s,

a. is currently serving a prison sentence for animal abuse.

b. received an award from the American Psychological Society.

    c. was able to complete his research after his grant was reinstated by the National Institutes of Health.

    d. none of the above

37. Which of the following statements regarding gene therapy research is TRUE?
    a. No human has died from gene therapy research.
    b. Some humans have been treated for diseases using gene therapy research.
    c. Gene therapy research with humans is illegal in the United States.
    d. The idea that "designer babies" can be created is science fiction, not reality.

# Answers

## Guided Review

1. empiricism
2. changes
3. neurogenesis
4. theories
5. hypotheses
6. dopamine
7. independent
8. dependent
9. extraneous
10. confounding
11. correlational
12. correlational
13. experimental
14. Golgi
15. myelin
16. Nissl
17. fluorogold
18. autoradiography
19. opiate
20. antibodies
21. hybridization
22. dendrites
23. 250,000
24. vesicles
25. scanning
26. confocal laser scanning
27. two-photon
28. electroencephalogram (EEG)
29. temporal
30. evoked
31. stereotaxic

32. atlas
33. microelectrode
34. cannula
35. microdialysis
36. ablation
37. aspiration
38. lesioned
39. reversible
40. imaging
41. CT or CAT
42. magnetic resonance
43. diffusion tensor
44. PET (positron emission tomography)
45. functional
46. TMS (transcranial magnetic stimulation)
47. research
48. twin
49. correlation
50. 13%
51. adoption
52. Monozygotic/Identical
53. dizygotic/fraternal
54. prenatal
55. 0.60
56. 0.86
57. concordance
58. three
59. genetic engineering
60. knockout
61. antisense RNA
62. transfer

63. transgenic

64. SCID

65. Alzheimer's

66. plagiarism

67. fabrication

68. consent

69. deception

70. environment

71. speciesism

72. rodents

73. chimpanzees

74. activists

75. minimized

76. cultures

77. computer

78. gene therapy

79. guidelines

80. designer

81. China

82. stem

83. organs

84. banned

85. Obama

## Short Answer and Essay Questions

1. Knowledge, or what we think we know to be true, changes. Many ideas that are currently accepted as fact may someday be shown to be incorrect. Therefore, scientists are usually careful about drawing such conclusions from their research. They prefer to be tentative about their conclusions.

2. There are many types of questions that cannot be answered using experimental procedures. Researchers are bound by ethical and legal rules that forbid the use of humans for many types of potentially interesting studies. Also, there are many variables that researchers are unable to manipulate, such as age, sex, and other factors that are inherent to individuals.

3. The theory was first developed when some researchers noticed that people using certain drugs that increase dopamine activity in the brain showed symptoms of schizophrenia (but these symptoms disappeared when the drugs wore off). It was suggested that schizophrenia is caused by excess dopamine. One hypothesis used to test this theory was that schizophrenics should improve when given drugs that decrease dopamine activity. However, not all schizophrenics show this expected result, and therefore the dopamine theory is recognized as being an incomplete explanation of schizophrenia.

4. Autoradiography allows researchers to see which cells are active, whereas other staining methods only show neurons and their parts against the background. One discovery that stemmed from this method was that the visual cortex contains a map of the retina and the visual field. Another discovery was the identification of opiate receptors in the brain.

5. Immunocytochemistry (in which fluorescent antibodies are used to locate specific cell components, including proteins) revealed that cryptochromes were present in both night-migrating and nonmigrating birds during the day, but that these proteins were present at night only in the night-migrating birds. This suggested that cryptochromes were responsible for migration guided by magnetic fields. Before they did this study, the researchers used in situ hybridization (in which radioactively labeled DNA is paired with the cells' own mRNA) to determine which of two cryptochromes to focus on, CRY1 or CRY2. Results showed that CRY2 was constructed in the nuclei,

while CRY1 was constructed outside the nucleus; because a magnetoreceptor would likely function outside the nucleus, the researchers focused on CRY1.

6. Evoked potentials are EEG recordings that are taken over a number of trials, during which target stimuli are present or absent. They represent an average response of the brain to specific stimuli, because by looking at several different trials, the change in brain activity in response to the stimulus (which is only weakly detected by the EEG) can be filtered out of the rest of the brain's normal activity (background noise).

7. Stereotaxic instruments are used to hold an animal's head in place and to locate a target in the brain where stimulation or measurement is to take place. The instrument is used to implant electrodes to stimulate the brain or measure activity in neurons, or to insert a cannula to deliver chemicals or collect brain fluids.

8. Researchers often want to know the function of a very specific brain area, and studying humans with brain damage is problematic, because brain damage is rarely limited to the areas of interest. Using animals allows researchers to introduce damage to very specific areas of the brain and to learn about the effects of damage under more controlled conditions.

9. A person receiving a CT scan is injected with a dye, and then X-rays of the intact brain are taken from several different angles; finally, the images are compiled by a computer to show a three-dimensional image. In the past, this procedure has been slow to produce the image, but newer technology allows for faster computing. The image, of course, is a still shot of the brain, and it cannot show activity or change as the brain functions. MRI scans measure the radio waves given off by hydrogen atoms in the brain when exposed to a magnetic field. Images are formed because of the different concentrations of this element in different structures. No substances such as dyes or radioactive materials need to be given. This procedure is reasonably fast, and it is becoming less expensive (due to advances in technology), but it also produces a static image.

10. PET scans require the administration of radioactively labeled glucose, which is then taken up to differing degrees by different brain areas according to how active they are. Imaging the radioactivity provides a measure of each brain area's activity during stimulation or task performance. This is an expensive procedure, and it only detects brain changes of at least 45 seconds in duration. Also, the image of the different amounts of radiation must be superimposed on a scan of the brain, usually from an MRI. Functional MRIs measure differences in brain cells' oxygen consumption. They are relatively safe; the biggest disadvantage of this method is its price.

11. The difference between adoption and family studies is that adoption studies look at children raised in homes by adoptive parents, whereas family studies look at children in intact families. Family studies are inherently confounded, because not only do individuals share genes, they also share an environment. Therefore, any similarities between them may be due to either factor or to both factors.

12. Some examples of genetic engineering are the knockout technique, the antisense RNA procedure, gene transfer, gene therapy, and creation of transgenic animals.

13. One part of Ax's experiment involved convincing his participants that they were in physical danger (which they were not) in order to induce fear. Many of the participants indeed seemed very afraid during the procedure. There are two major reasons why this was ethically questionable. First, human research participants should be able to give their informed consent before participating in a research project. This means that they are informed ahead of time of any risks inherent in the procedure and that with this knowledge they voluntarily agree to participate. The second, related, problem is that the participants were deceived. Deception is

allowed in research, but only when the potential benefits of the study outweigh the costs of using it. At the time of the study, standards had not been established for deception and informed consent. It is not likely that such a study would be conducted now, because it involved such an extreme manipulation of fear and because the information divulged while obtaining informed consent would likely make the "threat" unconvincing.

14. There are many procedures that would be unethical to perform on humans. For this reason, procedures that may eventually be used on humans are tested first on animals. Also, the laboratory animal's environment may be controlled, so it is easier to interpret the results (because many potentially confounding variables can be eliminated).

15. It is the assumption that animals have fewer rights than humans and that procedures that would be unacceptable with humans are acceptable with animals.

16. The movie *Gattaca* concerns a future society in which genetically "superior" individuals are more privileged than others. Although the movie is science fiction, some in our society are concerned that genetic engineering of humans could lead to something similar to this, particularly if people are able to select the most desirable traits for their offspring or to engineer those traits in their children.

17. The primary reason the use of human stem cells in research is controversial is because it destroys the embryo.

## Post-test

1. c   2. c   3. a   4. b   5. c   6. d   7. d   8. c   9. d   10. b   11. a   12. a   13. c   14. b
15. b   16. c   17. d   18. c   19. b   20. d   21. a   22. a   23. c   24. d   25. b   26. a
27. b   28. d   29. b   30. c   31. d   32. c   33. d   34. d   35. a   36. b   37. b

# 5 Drugs, Addiction, and Reward

## Learning Objectives

After reading this chapter, you should be able to answer the following questions.

1.  What are the physiological and psychological effects of different forms of opiates? How do opiates produce pain relief?

2.  What are the different types of depressant drugs, and what are their effects?

3.  What are the different types of stimulant drugs, and what are their effects? What do they have in common regarding their effects at dopamine synapses?

4.  What are the effects of psychedelic drugs and marijuana?

5.  Why are addiction and withdrawal considered independent mechanisms?

6.  What brain areas and neurotransmitters are involved in reward? What role is reward believed to play in addiction?

7.  What functions besides reward does dopamine have?

8.  How are drugs used to treat addiction? What are some examples of each type?

9.  How do Type 1 and Type 2 alcoholics differ?

10.  How are genes thought to be involved in alcoholism?

11.  What are the implications of alcoholism research?

## Psychoactive Drugs

### Summary and Guided Review

After studying this section in the text, fill in the blanks of the following summary.

Drugs can affect the brain by acting as ＿＿＿＿＿＿＿＿＿＿ (1) (mimicking the effects of neurotransmitters), or ＿＿＿＿＿＿＿＿＿＿ (2) (blocking or reducing the effects of neurotransmitters). Individuals who become obsessed with obtaining a drug or who use it compulsively are showing signs of ＿＿＿＿＿＿＿＿＿＿ (3). When a person stops taking a drug, she or he may experience symptoms of ＿＿＿＿＿＿＿＿＿＿ (4), which are usually opposite to the effects of the drug. With repeated use, the brain may develop ＿＿＿＿＿＿＿＿＿＿ (5) to a drug, a result of a reduction in quantity or sensitivity of receptors.

Opiates are drugs that come from opium poppies; these drugs have powerful psychoactive effects, including euphoria, ＿＿＿＿＿＿＿＿＿＿ (6), and ＿＿＿＿＿＿＿＿＿＿ (7). Morphine has been used clinically for treating the pain of surgery, battle wounds, and ＿＿＿＿＿＿＿＿＿＿ (8). Another opiate drug, commonly used as a cough suppressant, is ＿＿＿＿＿＿＿＿＿＿ (9). The most commonly abused opiate is ＿＿＿＿＿＿＿＿＿＿ (10), because of its intense effects on the nervous system. In a long-term study of heroin addicts, the most common cause of death was ＿＿＿＿＿＿＿＿＿＿ (11), yet about half of those surviving were still using heroin at the end of the study. Opiate drugs affect the nervous system because the body produces its own natural opioids called ＿＿＿＿＿＿＿＿＿＿ (12), which are internal substances that affect the same receptors as opiates.

Drugs that have inhibitory effects on the central nervous system are called ＿＿＿＿＿＿＿＿＿＿ (13). Alcohol, the most commonly abused drug, impairs motor and _____ (14) functions, as well as causing sedation, euphoria, and _____ (15)-reducing effects. Someone with a blood-alcohol level of _____% (16) is considered too intoxicated to drive. At concentrations of 0.5%, a person may go into a coma or _____ (17). Severe withdrawal symptoms such as hallucinations, delusions, and seizures, also known as _____ _____ (18), may occur following prolonged alcohol abuse. Health problems associated with long-term use of alcohol include cirrhosis of the _____ (19) and a form of brain damage called _____ (20) syndrome. _____ (21) drinkers are more likely to be impulsive and have learning and memory deficits. Alcohol affects the central nervous system by inhibiting the release of _____ (22) and by increasing the release of the inhibitory neurotransmitter _____ (23), which acts on receptors to open _____ (24) channels. Exposure to alcohol during prenatal development may result in a cluster of symptoms (including mental retardation, irritability, and facial anomalies) called _____ _____ (25) syndrome.

_____ (26) are depressant drugs that have been used to treat insomnia, epileptic seizures, and _____ (27). They typically produce _____ (28), resulting in increasing dosages and addiction. Because there is a fine line between therapeutic and toxic levels of these drugs, they have mostly been replaced with much safer _____ (29).

_____ (30) are drugs that produce arousal and elevate mood. Cocaine, which is derived from the coca plant, produces euphoria and relieves fatigue. Pure cocaine, or _____ (31), produces especially rapid, intense effects. A less pure and faster-acting version of cocaine is called _____ (32). Cocaine blocks the reuptake of _____ (33) and serotonin, which results in removal of cortical _____ (34) of lower structures. Although in the past cocaine was not considered dangerous, it is now recognized as being quite addictive, especially when injected or _____ (35). Cocaine users have impairments in memory and _____ (36) functions, and have a high rate of _____ (37) disorders, which makes rehabilitation difficult. In one study where rats could press a lever to self-administer cocaine or heroin, _____% (38) of the cocaine group had died as a result of overdose, compared to only 36% in the heroin group. In addition, a controlled adoption study revealed that _____ (39) exposure to cocaine is linked to lower IQs and problems with language and attention in children.

Due to their tendency to enhance alertness reduce fatigue, _____ (40) such as Dexedrine and the much more powerful drug featured on the television show *Breaking Bad,* _____ (41), are often used by people who want to stay awake for long periods of time. These drugs cause an increase in the release of dopamine and _____ (42). Psychotic symptoms from prolonged use include _____ (43) and delusions similar to those seen in paranoid schizophrenics.

Nicotine, the addictive psychoactive ingredient in tobacco, has _____ (44) effects when taken in short puffs, but depressant effects when deeply inhaled. Most people find that when they quit smoking, the _____ (45) symptoms such as anxiety and headaches are unpleasant, and they return to smoking. The health risks of smoking are high, but they are due to compounds in _____ (46), not nicotine. Children exposed to nicotine prenatally are more likely to be underweight as infants; however, their tendency to display _____ (47) disorder and criminal behavior later in life appears to be linked to genes and not nicotine. In the central nervous system, _____ (48)-releasing neurons are activated by nicotine, leading to cortical arousal. In the periphery, nicotine stimulates _____ (49) receptors.

Caffeine, a milder stimulant than cocaine and amphetamine, affects the nervous system by blocking _____ (50) receptors, which results in an increase in the release of dopamine and _____ (51). Withdrawal symptoms are mild, but common; the most problematic symptom seems to be _____ (52).

Psychedelic drugs cause _____ (53) distortions, such as intensification or changes of visual stimuli and cross-modality perceptions. LSD and drugs derived from the *Psilocybe mexicana* mushroom resemble and stimulate the same receptors as the neurotransmitter _____ (54). _____ (55) comes from the peyote cactus and may be used legally for religious practices by some Native Americans. MDMA, also known as _____ (56), stimulates the release of serotonin and dopamine; this drug has _____ (57) stimulant effects at lower doses and hallucinatory effects at higher doses. Some studies show a decrease in _____ (58) functioning, with persistent but small effects on _____ (59). Phencyclidine (PCP), also known as angel dust or crystal, was initially developed as a(n) _____ (60). However, this drug often triggers symptoms similar to _____ (61) and shows indications of being addictive.

The psychoactive ingredient in marijuana and hashish is _____ (62), a substance that binds to cannabinoid receptors, which are found on axon terminals. Endogenous cannabinoids such as anandamide are _____ (63) messengers. Marijuana's effects on cognition and time perception may be due to its effects on the _____ (64) cortex. Long-term heavy use of marijuana has been associated with reduced volume and impaired white matter connectivity in the _____ (65) as well as damage to the amygdala. Longitudinal studies in individuals who smoked five joints a day had a progressive decline in _____ (66) as well. Prenatal exposure to marijuana is correlational at best, but there does seem to be an increase in _____ (67) problems, such as impulsivity, hyperactivity, and performance in visual-spatial tasks. Marijuana does have beneficial uses, such as relieving _____ (68) associated with chemotherapy. While federal laws prohibit any use of marijuana, numerous states have legalized its use and the Department of _____ _____ (69) announced that it would allow patients treated at its hospitals and clinics to use medical marijuana.

Because withdrawal from marijuana produces very mild symptoms, its compulsive use has often been attributed to _____ _____ (70). However, monkeys will _____-_____ (71) THC when given the opportunity to do so, suggesting that it is indeed an addictive substance.

## Short Answer and Essay Questions

Answer the following questions.

1. What is conditioned tolerance? What evidence is there that heroin use may lead to conditioned tolerance?

2. Describe the structure of the GABA$_A$ receptor complex, and compare the mechanisms by which alcohol, barbiturates, and benzodiazepines affect GABA activity.

3. Compare the effects of withdrawal from opiates, alcohol, cocaine, and nicotine. Which drug produces the most serious withdrawal symptoms?

4. Compare the effects of prenatal exposure to the following drugs: alcohol, cocaine, nicotine, and marijuana.

5. Is marijuana addictive? Support your answer with facts from the text and the web.

# Addiction

## Summary and Guided Review

After studying this section in the text, fill in the blanks of the following summary.

In the past, addiction researchers assumed that addiction to drugs is maintained by the addict's desire to avoid _____ (72) effects. However, this does not explain what motivates drug taking until addiction develops. Initial drug taking apparently depends on the drug's _____ (73) effect, which appears to be a physiologically independent process. Drug researchers have identified the _____ (74) dopamine system as the major drug reward system. Virtually all abused drugs increase dopamine levels in an area of the system called the _____ _____ (75) and drugs that block dopamine in this area tend to reduce self-administration of amphetamine and _____ (76). Eating, drinking, and _____(77) behavior also increase dopamine levels in this area. Chronic drug users release less dopamine and have fewer dopamine _____ (78), but this condition may precede drug use, producing a(n) _____ _____ (79) syndrome. Other neurotransmitters are involved in reward as well; for example, the rewarding effect of alcohol is due in part to _____ (80) receptors, and PCP produces reward by blocking _____ (81) receptors on neurons that mediate the dopamine reward system.

Most people agree that while reward is involved in early drug taking, later stages characterized by craving and withdrawal involve lifelong changes in _____ (82) functioning. Research on learning has been important in trying to understand drug addiction. Recent studies suggest that dopamine activity signals not only reward but errors in _____ (83). This research suggests that some dopamine neurons encode motivational value of a stimulus, while others encode the _____ (84) of a stimulus based on its attention-getting properties. Drugs that increase dopamine release also produce anatomical changes in the nucleus accumbens and _____ (85) cortex in rats. In cocaine addicts, the sight of drug paraphernalia evokes _____ (86), which coincides with changes of activity in brain areas involved in _____ (87) and emotion. Researchers believe that these learning processes lead to long-term changes in the brain that underlie addiction. For example, compulsive use of cocaine may be due to pathological changes in the pathway between the _____ _____ (88) and the _____ _____ (89). The return to drug taking results from _____ (90) release in the prefrontal cortex and glutamate release in the nucleus accumbens.

Quitting an addictive substance can be very difficult. The first step is for the body to rid itself of the drug, a process called _____ (91). Withdrawal symptoms during this period can be intense, and in the case of alcohol withdrawal it may be necessary to administer _____ (92) to prevent life-threatening results. Once the withdrawal symptoms have subsided, abstaining from a drug may involve the therapeutic use of other drugs. For example, _____ (93) is an opiate agonist given to heroin users that has milder effects and can be obtained legally. Antagonist treatments like _____ (94) are used to block the effects of opiates on receptors. The muscle relaxant _____ (95) dampens the reward system by stimulating GABA receptors. _____ (96) is an aversive treatment for alcohol addiction; it works by making the person violently ill if alcohol is consumed. A promising area

of research involves the use of antidrug _____ (97), which stimulate the
immune system to produce antibodies for a drug.

Addiction has been correlated with reduced _____ (98) activity,
and drugs that increase the level of this neurotransmitter are useful in treating both
smoking and _____ (99) addiction. The combination of addiction
and other psychological disorders, or _____ (100), makes addiction
treatment even more challenging. One of the most common psychological disorders
exhibited by drug users is a(n) _____ (101) disorder (such as
antisocial disorder). However, some believe that the use of some pharmacological
treatments, such as methadone for opiate abuse, are not okay because they continue the
_____ (102) of drug taking.

## Short Answer and Essay Questions

Answer the following questions.

6. What are the problems with explaining addiction as the avoidance of withdrawal symptoms?

7. What is reward deficiency syndrome? Why might individuals with this condition be more likely to become drug addicts?

8. How might cocaine-induced brain changes contribute to addiction to the drug?

9. Give an example of each of the following types of treatment for addiction: agonist, antagonist, and aversive. Explain how each works.

10. How might the immune system be manipulated to treat drug addiction? What are the advantages of this approach?

11. Why are pharmacological treatments for drugs controversial? Do you think they should be used? Why or why not?

# The Roles of Genes in Addiction

## Summary and Guided Review

After studying this section in the text, fill in the blanks of the following summary.

Based on results from twin and adoption studies, there appears to be a strong
_____ (103) component to alcoholism. The results of Cloninger and
colleagues' comprehensive study of Swedish adoptees suggested that there are early and late
onset alcoholics. In Type 1 or _____-_____ (104)
alcoholics, problem drinking usually emerges after age _____ (105),
and these people may alternate between abstinence and _____ (106)
drinking. Type 2, or early-onset alcoholics, may begin drinking in adolescence and display
a host of personality traits characteristic of _____ (107) personality
disorder. _____ (108)-onset alcoholics are more likely to be hospitalized.
The environment seems to have a great impact on the development of alcoholism only in the
offspring of _____ (109)-onset alcoholics.

The exact role of genetics in alcoholism is beginning to be understood. For
example, mice lacking either *Homer* or *Clock* genes are more strongly affected by the
rewarding effects of _____ (110). Moderate alcoholics with the
_____ (111), which influences $GABA_A$ receptor functioning, have

more symptoms of alcohol dependence and impulsiveness. Furthermore, addicts who are anticipating a reward or loss have higher activity in the _____ _____ (112). In addition, a lowered amplitude in the _____ (113) wave, which is a dip in the EEG evoked potential after an unexpected stimulus, predicts development of drug abuse disorders by the age of 20. This dip in activity has been seen in a variety of disorders characterized by _____ _____ (114), which is characterized by impulsivity, risk taking, novelty seeking, and poor stress responsiveness.

## Short Answer and Essay Questions

Answer the following questions.

12. Distinguish between early- and late-onset alcoholics in terms of (1) the developmental pattern of the addiction and (2) the personality characteristics of each type.

13. Many alcoholics report that when they started drinking, alcohol seemed to affect them less than others. What genetic and neurological differences may account for this?

14. Describe three ways in which the EEG patterns of alcoholics and those at risk for becoming alcoholics differ from the EEG patterns of nonalcoholics. Why might the EEG be a useful tool for determining who is most at risk for becoming an alcoholic?

15. Imagine you are a scientist who studies the biological basis of alcoholism. You are in the process of seeking a multimillion-dollar grant to fund additional research in this area. The granting agency wants to know why alcoholism should be studied so intensely when there are many other forms of addiction and "more dangerous" drugs. How would you justify your continued study of alcoholism?

## Post-test

Use these multiple-choice questions to check your understanding of the chapter.

1. Which of the following is NOT true of heroin use?
   a. It may lead to an addiction that is difficult to overcome.
   b. It may lead to withdrawal symptoms that are life-threatening.
   c. Users experience intense euphoria followed by relaxation.
   d. It may lead to conditioned tolerance.

2. Arlene has been smoking marijuana three to four times a week for 2 years. She often worries about running out and occasionally steals small amounts from her friends who smoke. She recently tried to quit, but she started again after 1 month of being off the drug. Arlene is experiencing
   a. withdrawal.
   b. tolerance.
   c. addiction.
   d. depression.

3. Alcohol is BEST classified as a(n) ___ drug.
   a. depressant
   b. stimulant
   c. opiate
   d. psychedelic

4. Jerry, a 55-year-old chronic alcoholic, has recently begun experiencing memory loss and motor problems. His doctor informs him that he may be suffering from ___ as a result of his long-term alcohol abuse.
   a. delirium tremens
   b. conditioned tolerance
   c. Korsakoff's syndrome
   d. binge drinking

5. Which of the following drugs influence the activity of GABA?
   a. alcohol
   b. barbiturates
   c. benzodiazepines
   d. all of the above

6. Which of the following is NOT true regarding the early historical use of cocaine?
   a. The freebase form was used by South American Indians for centuries.
   b. It was an ingredient in Coca-Cola until 1906.
   c. In the 1800s, it was used as a local anesthetic.
   d. Sigmund Freud recommended it to his family and friends.

7. Prenatal exposure to cocaine has been linked to which of the following problem(s)?
   a. seizure disorders in children
   b. poor cognitive development
   c. facial abnormalities
   d. all of the above

8. The MOST potent form of amphetamine is
   a. Benzedrine.
   b. Dexedrine.
   c. methamphetamine.
   d. dextroamphetamine.

9. What percentage of people who quit smoking is able to abstain for at LEAST 2 years?
   a. 10%
   b. 20%
   c. 50%
   d. 80%

10. Which of the following is NOT a health problem associated with cigarette smoking or tobacco use?
    a. Buerger's disease
    b. cancer of the mouth
    c. emphysema
    d. Korsakoff's syndrome

11. Which stimulant affects dopamine and acetylcholine levels indirectly through its effects on adenosine?
    a. caffeine
    b. cocaine
    c. nicotine
    d. amphetamine

12. Which of the following psychedelic drugs is found in a cactus?
    a. ecstasy
    b. angel dust

    c. mescaline

    d. psilocybin

13. Which of the following psychedelic drugs is MOST closely related to amphetamines?

    a. ecstasy

    b. angel dust

    c. LSD

    d. mescaline

14. The psychoactive ingredient in marijuana affects the same receptor sites as which of the following ligands?

    a. endorphin

    b. anandamide

    c. dopamine

    d. glutamate

15. The cognitive deficits seen in children exposed to marijuana prenatally seem MOST likely due to impairment of which part of the brain?

    a. hippocampus

    b. basal ganglia

    c. cerebellum

    d. prefrontal cortex

16. The MOST compelling reason to believe that marijuana is an addictive substance is that

    a. some people experience withdrawal symptoms when they stop using it.

    b. many people use it for years.

    c. animals will self-administer it.

    d. it has negative effects on the fetus.

17. Rats will learn to press a lever in order to inject drugs into which of the following brain structures?

    a. medial forebrain bundle

    b. ventral tegmental area

    c. nucleus accumbens

    d. all of the above

18. Addictive drugs may produce euphoric effects by

    a. stimulating the release of dopamine.

    b. blocking postsynaptic dopamine receptors.

    c. eliminating dopamine from the synapse.

    d. inhibiting the release of dopamine.

19. ESB has its greatest effect

    a. on animals missing a specific subtype of dopamine receptor.

    b. when an animal is also given cocaine or amphetamine.

    c. in brain areas where dopaminergic neurons are highly concentrated.

    d. in brain areas where serotonergic neurons are highly concentrated.

20. There is evidence that people with fewer $D_2$ receptors

    a. are highly unlikely to become addicted to drugs.

    b. are more responsive to rewards than other people.

    c. experience greater release of dopamine when using drugs than other people.

    d. like the stimulant drug Ritalin more than other people.

21. Opiates are implicated in the rewarding effects of which drug?
    a. alcohol
    b. cocaine
    c. amphetamine
    d. nicotine

22. PCP inhibits the effects of
    a. dopamine.
    b. glutamate.
    c. serotonin.
    d. endorphins.

23. Recent evidence regarding the role of dopamine in learning suggests that
    a. serotonin is actually more important in learning than is dopamine.
    b. serotonin is primarily a signal that an event is rewarding.
    c. dopamine is more likely to be released when a reinforcer is unpredictable.
    d. dopamine is not involved in reward or reinforcement.

24. Cocaine addicts' compulsive drug-using behavior may be a result of
    a. damage to the hippocampus.
    b. damage to the prefrontal cortex.
    c. damage to the ventral tegmental area.
    d. all of the above

25. When a rat that has learned to press a lever in order to receive a drug reward no lon-ger receives the reward, it will stop pressing the lever. However, electrical stimulation of the ___ reinstates the lever pressing.
    a. nucleus accumbens
    b. ventral tegmental area
    c. hippocampus
    d. lateral hypothalamus

26. Freud suffered from lifelong addiction to
    a. cocaine.
    b. alcohol.
    c. heroin.
    d. nicotine.

27. Sharon was recently admitted to the hospital because she was suffering severe withdrawal symptoms, including seizures. She was given a benzodiazepine to reduce the severity of her symptoms. Which of the following drugs is Sharon MOST likely addicted to?
    a. alcohol
    b. heroin
    c. nicotine
    d. cocaine

28. Nicotine gum is an example of an ___ treatment for drug addiction.
    a. antagonist
    b. aversive
    c. agonist
    d. antidrug

29. Naltrexone may be used to block opiate receptors in people who abuse
    a. nicotine.
    b. cocaine.

     c. amphetamines.

     d. alcohol.

30. Methadone was developed as an analgesic during World War II when ___ was in short supply.

     a. morphine

     b. heroin

     c. codeine

     d. endorphin

31. Which of the following statements is NOT true of antidrug vaccines?

     a. They lead to the destruction of drug molecules before they can reach the brain.

     b. They are more effective than other pharmacological treatments in humans.

     c. They result in fewer side effects than other pharmacological treatments.

     d. Their effects may be longer lasting than other pharmacological treatments.

32. For heroin addicts,

     a. methadone treatment alone is the most effective treatment option.

     b. counseling alone has a high rate of success.

     c. no treatment method has more than a 50% success rate.

     d. methadone plus counseling is quite effective.

33. The heritability for alcoholism is

     a. 5–10%.

     b. 20–30%.

     c. 50–60%.

     d. 80–90%.

34. Which of the following characteristics typifies early-onset alcoholics?

     a. They tend to feel guilty about drinking.

     b. They tend to be novelty seekers.

     c. They may abstain from alcohol for long periods of time.

     d. They are often emotionally dependent.

35. Which of the following is a characteristic of Type 1 alcoholics?

     a. They begin having problems with alcohol in adolescence.

     b. They tend to behave aggressively when drinking.

     c. They are quite cautious.

     d. all of the above

36. Cloninger's study of early- and late-onset alcoholics indicates that

     a. exposure to alcoholism in the home has more of an impact on the children of late-onset alcoholics than the children of early-onset alcoholics.

     b. exposure to alcoholism in the home has more of an impact on the children of early-onset alcoholics than the children of late-onset alcoholics.

     c. exposure to alcoholism in the home has about the same effect on the children of early- and late-onset alcoholics.

     d. late-onset alcoholics are most likely to have children who are early-onset alcoholics.

37. Genes for which of the following transmitters have been implicated in drug abuse?

     a. GABA

     b. endogenous opioids

     c. anandamide

     d. all of the above

38. Which of the following does NOT indicate a high risk for alcoholism?
    a. being the child of an alcoholic
    b. feeling fewer effects of alcohol when drinking
    c. having ALDH deficiency
    d. showing an abnormal P300 wave

39. ALDH is an enzyme that ___. A heritable deficiency in this enzyme is frequently seen in nonalcoholic ____ individuals.
    a. breaks down dopamine; Caucasian
    b. blocks serotonin receptors; German
    c. has an agonistic effect on alcohol; Somali
    d. breaks down alcohol; Japanese

40. The P300 wave
    a. shows promise for diagnosing those at risk for alcoholism.
    b. occurs in response to a novel or unexpected stimulus.
    c. occurs in similar ways among genetically related individuals.
    d. all of the above

# Answers

## Guided Review

1. agonists
2. antagonists
3. addiction
4. withdrawal
5. tolerance
6. analgesic
7. hypnotic
8. cancer
9. codeine
10. Heroin
11. overdose
12. endorphins
13. depressants
14. cognitive
15. anxiety
16. 0.08
17. die
18. delirium tremens
19. liver
20. Korsakoff's
21. Binge
22. glutamate
23. GABA
24. chloride
25. fetal alcohol
26. Barbiturates
27. anxiety
28. tolerance
29. benzodiazepines
30. Stimulants
31. freebase
32. crack
33. dopamine
34. inhibition
35. smoked or inhaled
36. executive
37. psychological
38. 90
39. prenatal
40. amphetamines
41. methamphetamine
42. norepinephrine
43. hallucinations
44. stimulating
45. withdrawal
46. tobacco smoke
47. conduct
48. dopamine
49. acetylcholine
50. adenosine
51. acetylcholine
52. headache(s)
53. perceptual
54. serotonin
55. Mescaline
56. ecstasy
57. psychomotor
58. serotonin
59. memory
60. anesthetic
61. schizophrenia
62. tetrahydrocanabbinol (THC)
63. retrograde
64. frontal
65. hippocampus
66. IQ

67. behavioral

68. nausea

69. Veteran's Affairs

70. psychological dependence

71. self-administer

72. withdrawal

73. reward

74. mesolimbocortical

75. nucleus accumbens

76. cocaine

77. sexual

78. receptors

79. reward deficiency syndrome

80. opiate

81. glutamate

82. brain

83. prediction

84. salience

85. prefrontal

86. craving

87. learning

88. prefrontal cortex

89. nucleus accumbens

90. dopamine

91. detoxification

92. benzodiazepines

93. Methadone

94. naltrexone

95. Baclofen

96. Antabuse

97. vaccines

98. serotonin

99. alcohol

100. comorbidity

101. personality

102. pleasures

103. genetic

104. late-onset

105. 25

106. binge

107. antisocial

108. Early

109. late

110. cocaine

111. GABRA$_2$

112. insular cortex

113. P300

114. behavioral disinhibition

## Short Answer and Essay Questions

1. Conditioned tolerance is a learned tolerance that is specific to the setting where it developed; as a result, the individual shows tolerance to a drug in one context but not in another. Rats are more likely to die of overdose when given a large dose in a novel environment (64% versus 32% of rats in each group died). Likewise, human heroin addicts may be more likely to overdose when they take the same amount of drug in a novel setting. When in a different environment, those cues that trigger the tolerance response are no longer present, and the same dose may have a more powerful effect.

2. The GABA$_A$ receptor complex has at least five different receptor sites, only one of which responds to the neurotransmitter GABA. When GABA binds to its receptor, chloride channels open and the neuron is inhibited. The other receptor types are affected by various drugs. Alcohol fits a different receptor in the complex, and it enhances GABA binding, which produces a stronger inhibitory response. Barbiturates fit yet another receptor in the GABA$_A$ complex, also enhancing the effectiveness of GABA, but at high doses they can actually open

chloride channels without GABA. Benzodiazepines also act at the $GABA_A$ receptor complex in the limbic system, brain stem, hippocampus, and cortex.

3. Opiate withdrawal is like having the flu. Alcohol produces the most serious withdrawal symptoms, including delirium tremens, convulsions, and even death. Less severe withdrawal symptoms of alcohol include anxiety and mood changes. Cocaine produces mild withdrawal symptoms, including anxiety and loss of motivation and pleasure. Nicotine withdrawal includes anxiety, sleepiness, and headaches.

4. Prenatal exposure to alcohol may result in fetal alcohol syndrome, a cluster of symptoms including facial abnormalities, mental retardation, and irritability. Exposure to cocaine prenatally has been linked to impaired IQ and language development as well as attention problems. Prenatal exposure to nicotine is linked to low birth weight. Marijuana exposure before birth may contribute to behavioral and cognitive deficiencies, but these may not be apparent until after 4 years of age.

5. There is evidence that marijuana is addictive, although it produces only mild withdrawal symptoms. Compulsive use in humans has been documented, and monkeys will self-administer THC, which is usually taken as evidence of addiction.

6. One problem is that withdrawal symptoms occur later, so avoidance of withdrawal cannot be the mechanism that maintains early drug use. Second, addicts intentionally go through withdrawal to adjust their tolerance level. Third, many addicts start using a drug again after having quit for a long period of time and are presumably no longer experiencing withdrawal. Finally, the power of addiction of a drug is not related to the severity of withdrawal. For example, alcohol can cause severe withdrawal symptoms, but heroin or stimulants may not.

7. Some people apparently have fewer $D_2$ receptors than other people, probably due to genetic differences. Fewer dopamine receptors and reduced dopamine activity are linked to a reduced experience of reward, even among those who are not addicts. These individuals may find drugs that increase dopamine activity, such as cocaine, particularly reinforcing, and they may be more likely to continue using a drug if they start.

8. Learning is associated with synaptic increases in the prefrontal cortex and nucleus accumbens. In addition, the prefrontal cortex also undergoes pathological alterations in dendrites, reduction in dopamine activity, prefrontal deactivation, and reduced behavioral inhibition. As a result of learning, hippocampal stimulation produces a high level of dopamine release and a return to drug-seeking behavior; brain changes from learning are considered to be the reason drugs have a lifelong effect.

9. Agonist treatments, such as methadone for heroin addiction, involve the replacement of a more harmful substance with a less harmful one that basically has the same effect on the nervous system. Antagonistic treatment involves administration of a drug that blocks the effects of the undesirable drug. For example, Baclofen seems to block dopamine activity normally stimulated by several addictive substances. Aversive treatments produce an undesirable reaction when the harmful drug is taken. Antabuse, for example, produces nausea and vomiting when alcohol is consumed, because it inhibits the metabolism of acetaldehyde.

10. Anti-drug vaccines induce the body to produce antibodies to destroy the drug. They appear to be quite effective and may soon be available for use with humans. The advantages of these drugs are that they do not result in the side effects common to drugs that interfere with neurotransmitters, and their effects may be quite long lasting.

11. Pharmacological treatments are controversial because they involve treating drug addiction by giving a person another drug. In the case of methadone, this means substituting a less problematic addiction for a more problematic one. Other drug treatments (such as treatment with Antabuse and possibly with Baclofen) interfere with drug use without leading to addiction. (The argument for these treatments is that they are generally effective, but some people believe that addiction should be overcome by sheer willpower, and that relying on other drugs to do it is taking the easy way out.)

12. Early-onset alcoholics usually begin drinking prior to the age of 25, many of them in their teens. They are more likely to be male, and they often display impulsive, aggressive, and reckless behavior while being socially and emotionally detached from others. This pattern of characteristics is associated with antisocial personality disorder. Late-onset drinkers usually begin having problems with alcohol after the age of 25, following a period of social drinking. They tend to binge drink, which results in guilt feelings; they may abstain from alcohol for long periods. They tend to be cautious and emotionally dependent.

13. Alcoholics who have the $A_1$ allele for $D_2$ (dopamine) receptors may actually have fewer of these receptors. Because alcohol stimulates dopamine activity, which is experienced as pleasant or rewarding, such individuals would have to consume more alcohol to feel the same level of effect as someone with more $D_2$ receptors. Greater consumption puts them more at risk for becoming addicted.

14. First, when not under the influence of alcohol, male alcoholics and their children show more high-frequency waves than nonalcoholics. Also, alcoholics and their children, who are probably at risk for alcoholism, show a reduced "dip" in the P300 waves in response to novel stimuli, and the P300 wave is also delayed. The EEG may be useful for determining who is most at risk for alcoholism, because children of alcoholics who are not alcoholics themselves often show the same pattern of responses as their parents.

15. Alcoholism is a good model for studying drug addiction. Many of the addictive drugs have very similar effects in the brain, mostly through their effects on the dopamine reward system. Therefore, any discoveries made about the genetic and neurological bases of alcohol addiction may be applicable to other forms of addiction. Furthermore, alcoholism is the most problematic addiction in our society. Its use is linked to violence, traffic accidents, and other serious behavioral problems. Because it is a legal drug, there are more alcoholics than people addicted to other drugs. Consequently, it makes sense to attempt to understand and perhaps control or even eradicate it. In doing so, it may be possible to treat other forms of addiction as well.

## Post-test

| | | | | | | | | | | | | |
|---|---|---|---|---|---|---|---|---|---|---|---|---|
| 1. b | 2. c | 3. a | 4. c | 5. d | 6. a | 7. b | 8. c | 9. b | 10. d | 11. a | 12. c | 13. a |
| 14. b | 15. d | 16. c | 17. d | 18. a | 19. c | 20. d | 21. a | 22. b | 23. c | 24. b |
| 25. c | 26. d | 27. a | 28. c | 29. d | 30. a | 31. b | 32. d | 33. c | 34. b | 35. c |
| 36. a | 37. d | 38. c | 39. d | 40. d |

# 6 Motivation and the Regulation of Internal States

## Chapter Outline

## Learning Objectives

After reading this chapter, you should be able to answer the following questions.

1. What are the differences among instinct, drive, incentive, and arousal theories of motivation?

2. What is homeostasis? How does temperature regulation exemplify this concept?

3. What are the two types of thirst, and what mechanism is responsible for each?

4. What are the five primary tastes, and what is the function of each? How is taste information conveyed in the nervous system?

5. What taste mechanisms help to ensure that we eat a healthy, balanced diet?

6. How does digestion occur? Include in your answer the events of the absorptive and fasting phases.

7. What mechanisms are involved in the stimulation and termination of eating? In controlling body weight?

8. What health problems are associated with obesity? What myths surround obesity?

9. To what extent is heredity believed to be involved in obesity? How about environmental factors? What specific genetic mechanisms might be involved?

10. What role does metabolism play in obesity? How is obesity treated?

11. What are the contributions of environment and genetics for the various eating disorders?

12. What are the characteristics of anorexia, bulimia, and binge eating disorder?

13. What social and biological factors contribute to anorexia, bulimia, and binge eating disorders?

14. How are serotonin, dopamine, and cannabinoids involved in eating disorders?

## Motivation and Homeostasis

### Summary and Guided Review

After studying this section in the text, fill in the blanks of the following summary.

_____ (1) refers to factors that initiate, sustain, and direct behaviors; there are several theories of motivation. Ancient Greeks, as well as some early 20th-century psychologists, proposed that many human behaviors are _____ (2) motivated; a more precisely defined concept continues to be used with animal behavior, but most contemporary psychologists believe instincts have little influence on human behavior. Another explanation for motivation is _____ (3) theory, which proposes that the body attempts to maintain _____ (4), or balance. While this theory helps explain some behaviors, it does not explain behaviors that do not satisfy bodily needs, such as seeking fame or academic excellence. _____ (5) theory accounts for the fact that people are often motivated by external stimuli, such as money. Another theory, _____ (6) theory, suggests that people are also motivated to maintain a preferred level of stimulation, although this level varies from person to person. Perhaps the best way to think about drives is to assume that they represent _____ (7) rather than conditions of the body. This is supported by the fact that many stimuli can motivate a behavior, even in the absence of _____ (8) needs, such as suddenly feeling hungry when smelling food, even after a meal.

A useful way of representing homeostasis and the preferred state of a control system is the _____ (9) point; when conditions deviate too far from this point, the nervous system becomes operative to restore it. For example, all animals must maintain their body _____ _____ (10) within a particular range, or they will die. _____ (11) animals like reptiles rely on the temperature of the external environment, whereas _____ (12) animals like mammals and birds have internal mechanisms that regulate body temperature, although they can also manipulate their environment to maintain a comfortable state. In mammals, body temperature is controlled by the _____ (13) area of the hypothalamus. Here, warmth- and _____-_____ (14) cells respond to the temperature of the blood and to temperature receptors in other parts of the body by initiating physiological activities, such as sweating if the organism is too hot, or _____ (15) if the organism is too cold.

Another drive that nicely fits the homeostatic model is _____ (16). Because water makes up about _____ % (17) of the body, it is essential for the proper function of the bodily systems. Because water is continually lost through urination, defecation, and _____ (18), it is especially important to maintain sufficient liquids in the body. There are two types of thirst: _____ (19) thirst is a result of low intracellular fluid, whereas _____ (20) thirst occurs when blood volume drops. Osmotic thirst is regulated by cells in the _____ (21), along the third ventricle, that detect low levels of intracellular fluid and communicate the deficit to the _____ _____ _____ (22) of the hypothalamus, which initiates drinking. Hypovolemic thirst is detected by pressure receptors in the atrium of the _____ (23) that signal the brain via the _____ (24) nerve to the _____ (25) in the medulla. The _____ (26) also respond to low blood volume by releasing renin; this increases the level of _____ (27) II, which is detected by the _____ (28) organ and induces drinking via the median preoptic nucleus. Homeostasis is not achieved immediately after ingesting water, so there must be some kind of _____ (29) mechanism that recognizes when enough water has been taken and terminates thirst; receptors in the _____ (30) and liver may serve this purpose.

## Short Answer and Essay Questions

Answer the following questions.

1. What is the cause, and what are the consequences, of Prader-Willi syndrome?

2. Why is drive theory alone insufficient to account for motivation?

3. What mechanisms for temperature regulation do ectothermic and endothermic animals have in common?

4. Compare the mechanisms responsible for managing osmotic and hypovolemic thirst. How do researchers know they operate independently?

# Hunger: A Complex Drive

## Summary and Guided Review

After studying this section in the text, fill in the blanks of the following summary.

As a drive, hunger is more complicated than temperature and thirst, because the _____ (31) point can undergo dramatic changes and because there are so many different types of _____ (32) that the body needs.

Humans eat a variety of plant and animal foods, meaning that we are _____ (33); in order to remain healthy, we need to eat a varied diet and at the same time carefully select foods that are not toxic or spoiled. The sense of _____ (34) helps us select nutritious, safe foods and avoid non-nutritious, dangerous ones. We have _____ (35) primary taste sensations, each of which seems to indicate different qualities of food. Foods that taste _____ (36), such as fruits, and those that taste salty are highly preferred. These types of food typically provide nutrients necessary for survival. A recently discovered taste, _____ (37), has been described as "meaty" or "savory"; some researchers believe it could be important in our selection of _____ (38). The other qualities, _____ (39) and _____ (40), often indicate that food is spoiled or toxic, respectively, and should therefore be avoided. Sensory information about taste is transmitted from the taste buds located on the surface of the _____ (41) of the tongue, through the nucleus of the solitary tract in the _____ (42), and via the thalamus to the _____ (43), which is the primary gustatory cortex. Information from different taste receptors travels to the cortex via separate pathways to distinct areas; this is referred to as _____ (44) coding of stimuli.

A food particularly becomes less appealing as we eat more of it, a phenomenon known as _____-_____ (45) satiety, which is an important mechanism for ensuring that we eat a variety of foods. This form of satiety seems to be controlled by the _____ (46). Taste is an important cue for learning which foods may be harmful; experiments with rats have shown that if a certain taste becomes associated with illness, they will _____ (47) items with that taste in the future. Humans also demonstrate these _____ _____ (48) aversions, although the bouts of sickness are often not caused by the foods they become associated with, as in the case of children undergoing _____ (49) who learned to avoid a particular flavor of ice cream. There is even some evidence that rats will form an aversion to food _____ (50) in thiamine. Taste is also an important cue for learning which foods to eat when the nutrients themselves may not be detected; for example, rats deprived of a specific _____ (51) learned to eat a food enriched with it and flavored with anise. When the anise was switched to a nutrient-deficient food, the animals preferred it instead, and the rats switched to that food. This phenomenon is called a(n) _____ (52) taste preference.

_____ (53) begins in the mouth, where _____ (54) is added to food. In the stomach, pepsin and _____ (55) acid are added to food to break it down. If food contains toxins that irritate the stomach too much, or if toxins reach the area postrema via the blood, _____ (56) occurs. The first segment of the small intestine, the _____ (57), is where most food is digested. Here, carbohydrates are converted into _____ (58) such as glucose, and proteins are converted into _____ _____

(59). Fats are converted to fatty acids and _____ (60) in the intestines and _____ (61). These basic nutrients are then _____ (62) into the bloodstream and taken to the liver by the _____ _____ (63) vein. Excess water is reabsorbed in the large _____ (64). Digestion is controlled by the _____ (65) nervous system and can be disrupted by arousal, which may lead to nausea, constipation, or _____ (66).

For the first few hours after a meal, during the _____ (67) phase of the feeding cycle, recently ingested nutrients provide fuel for the body. This is managed by the parasympathetic nervous system, which is activated by _____ (68) levels of glucose. Insulin is secreted by the _____ (69), allowing glucose to be used by the cells. _____ (70) is a result of not producing enough insulin or being less responsive to it. Glucose is also converted to _____ (71) for short-term storage. Excess glucose and proteins are converted to _____ (72) and stored in _____ (73) tissue. When glucose levels in the blood decline, the body enters the _____ (74) phase of the feeding cycle. Parasympathetic activity is replaced by _____ (75) activity, resulting in the secretion of _____ (76) from the pancreas. This substance is instrumental in the conversion of glycogen to _____ (77) and of fat into fatty acids and _____(78), the latter of which is converted into glucose for the brain by the _____ (79). Eating and metabolism are governed by the lateral _____ (80) and the _____ (81).

There are three major signals of hunger; _____ (82) hunger tells the brain that there is a low level of glucose, _____ (83) hunger indicates a deficit in fatty acids, and the third signals low levels of nutrients in the _____ (84). Blood levels of glucose and fatty acids are monitored by the liver; when these levels are low, a message is carried to the medulla via the _____ (85) nerve. Glucose levels in the brain are monitored directly by the _____ (86) in the medulla. Next the message is carried to the _____ (87) nucleus, which in turn sends signals to the PVN and _____ (88) hypothalamus. As the stomach empties during fasting the peptide _____ (89) is released and stimulates the arcuate nucleus to cause eating. Excess ghrelin may be involved in the uncontrollable appetite of people with _____-_____ (90) syndrome. All three of the hunger signals exert their influence through NPY/AgRP neurons in the arcuate nucleus, which releases _____ (91) and _____- _____ (92) protein. Both substances excite the PVN and lateral hypothalamus to increase eating and reduce _____ (93).

There are a number of satiety signals, including those from _____ (94) receptors in the stomach that become active when it is full. The stomach and intestines also release a number of _____ (95) that trigger enzyme release for digestion and also signal the brain. For example, the duodenal hormone _____ (96) detects fats and triggers the release of bile from the _____ _____ (97) and initiates a signal in the vagus nerve to the NST and hypothalamus to stop eating. _____ (98) is another peptide hormone released from the intestines that inhibits NPY release in the _____ (99) nucleus, which decreases caloric intake over several hours. Rats with lesions in the _____ (100) hypothalamus overeat in part because insulin production is increased, which results in nutrients being stored rather than utilized. In _____ (101) rats, in which one was lesioned and one was not, the normal rat reduced its eating in response to a satiety signal that the lesioned rat was insensitive to. The satiety signal turned out to be the hormone _____ (102); obese individuals have _____ (103) blood levels of this hormone. Leptin and insulin decrease eating by inhibiting the NPY/AgRP neurons, but also activating _____ / _____ (104) cells. In turn, these cells reduce feeding by inhibiting the _____ (105) and the lateral hypothalamus.

## Short Answer and Essay Questions

Answer the following questions.

5. As a drive, why is hunger more complex than the drives of thirst and temperature regulation?

6. Why is it advantageous for us to prefer sweet and salty foods and to dislike sour and bitter foods?

7. How does sensory-specific satiety help explain the tendency for some people to over-eat at potluck meals or buffets where many different types of foods are available?

8. As a child, Shirley became ill and threw up several times in one night. Her family had eaten chili for dinner that day. Shirley was the only one who became sick, so there must have been some other cause for her illness. However, for the next 10 years, Shirley refused to eat chili, and even the sight of it made her nauseous. Explain why Shirley stopped eating chili.

9. Why do diabetics feel hungry, even when their blood sugar is high? What is the role of insulin in this?

10. Why may a diet high in sugar and/or protein lead to weight gain?

11. Identify and describe the three major signals for hunger.

12. What happens when rats are given injections of neuropeptide Y? What effects does it have on appetite? On energy consumption?

13. What signals the end of a meal?

# Obesity

## Summary and Guided Review

After studying this section in the text, fill in the blanks of the following summary.

Two thirds of adults in the United States are overweight and a third qualify as _____ (106). Worldwide, obesity has doubled since 1980, in part because of the availability of junk food that is high in calories but not in _____ (107). The degree of obesity is calculated by dividing weight in kilograms by squared height in meters, which yields the _____ (108); the person is considered obese if this value is _____ (109) or higher. Overweight and obese individuals are more at risk for many health problems; for example, in a Swedish study, the more overweight a woman was, the more likely she was to have shrinkage in her _____ (110) lobes. If the trend toward obesity is not reversed, by 2050 the life expectancy gains of the last _____ (111) could disappear. On the other hand, dietary restrictions may prolong life. In elderly subjects who reduced their total number of calories by 30%, they saw improvements in blood pressure, heart health, and even _____ (112) memory.

Obesity seems to be most directly linked to eating high-calorie foods and not getting enough _____ (113). However, research has not supported the popular opinion that obesity is completely under _____ (114) control, is the result of a maladaptive eating style, or is the inability to delay _____ (115).

If obesity runs in families, it is more likely due to _____ (116) than environment, as evidenced by the fact that the correlation of BMI scores in identical twins raised apart is _____ (117), only slightly lower than the 0.74 correlation for those raised together. However, the role of inheritance is complicated, as there are several genes involved, such as the _____ (118) gene on chromosome 6 and the _____ (119) gene on chromosome 4. Coleman used the parabiotic technique described earlier to experimentally study the effects of recessive genes on food intake and weight in mice. The *db/db* mice produced a signal to stop eating but were insensitive to it, while the _____ (120) mice were sensitive to the signal but did not produce it. It was not until later that researchers discovered that the signaling substance was _____ (121). The *ob* and *db* genes are rare and account for few cases of obesity. On the other hand, individuals with a particular allele (A) of the _____ (122) gene have a 30% greater risk of obesity, 70% if homozygous (AA). And mutations of the _____ (123) gene may account for 6% of cases of severe childhood obesity. _____ (124) characteristics are inheritable traits that result from modifications of gene expression rather than changes in the individual's DNA sequence. One form of this occurs if mothers have low levels of carbohydrates while pregnant; this causes _____ (125) of the RXRA gene, which accounts for more than 25% of weight variation in childhood.

A person's basal _____ (126) rate (BMR) largely determines how much food is needed to maintain weight, and someone with a higher BMR needs to take in _____ (127) calories than someone with a lower BMR. When a person loses weight, the BMR usually _____ (128), making additional weight loss difficult. The increase in metabolism is variable among people, partly due to nonexercise forms of spontaneous _____ (129), such as fidgeting; these individuals expend more energy and gain less weight than others. Another factor that may make weight loss difficult is that after a person gains weight, she or he may develop a new _____ _____ (130).

Exercise seems to be an important part of losing weight, more because of its effects on one's _____ _____ (131) than because of the calories expended during the exercise itself. Some medications have been used to treat obesity, but frequently they have side effects that can sometimes be serious. One recently withdrawn drug, _____ (132) or the marketing name Meridia, inhibited reuptake of the neurotransmitter _____ (133), which reduced carbohydrate craving but also increased risk of heart attack and stroke. The drug _____ (134), also called Alli or Xenical, blocks fat absorption but requires a label warning because of rare reports of liver damage. Treatment with the hormone _____ (135) has been shown to be effective in increasing metabolism and reducing fat while sparing lean mass, but it works only in the 5−10% of obese individuals who lack it.

A new approach to understanding and treating obesity is to view overeating as an addictive behavior. One neurotransmitter that plays a key role in both compulsive overeating and addiction is _____ (136). The drug _____

(137) that reduces dopamine has been used experimentally to treat addiction; it also causes weight loss in genetically obese rats. Because drugs and lifestyle changes are not effective with the morbidly obese, surgical procedures such as _____ _____ (138) and lap band may be required to save lives. The former procedure works by limiting meal size and nutrient absorption in the digestive tract, while the latter places a restrictive band around the stomach without surgically altering it. However, because these surgeries have many risks and are expensive, they are often a last resort for weight management.

## Short Answer and Essay Questions

Answer the following questions.

14. Why is obesity considered to be a major problem today?

15. Why is it easier to gain than lose weight?

16. Kelly, who does not exercise, recently moved in with a roommate who likes to cook. Before this, Kelly lived by herself and ate small meals at dinner. Now, because of her roommate's influence, she eats lavish dinners and consumes about 500 more calories per day than she used to. However, she is not gaining weight. How might her energy expenditure have increased to prevent weight gain?

17. Discuss the following anti-obesity drugs: Sibutramine, Orlistat, leptin, and Vigabatrin. Include in your discussion the mechanism of action, side effects (if mentioned), and limitations of their use.

# Anorexia, Bulimia, and Binge Eating Disorder

## Summary and Guided Review

After studying this section in the text, fill in the blanks of the following summary.

Though men are overrepresented among obese Americans, women are three times as likely to be diagnosed with anorexia nervosa or _____ (139) and are _____ (140) times as likely to suffer from binge eating disorder. _____ (141) nervosa is characterized by maintaining weight at an unhealthy low level, which can lead to serious health problems and even death. Anorexics who binge eat and control their weight by vomiting or using _____ (142) are called _____-_____ (143), while _____ (144) are those who simply eat very little food. Health risks associated with anorexia include heart damage, loss of bone density, and deficits in _____ (145) volume. This is not due to a lack of hunger. Anorexics have elevated _____ (146) and _____ (147), and leptin levels are diminished, suggesting that they are experiencing hunger. Weight in individuals with _____ _____ (148) is usually normal. Their _____ (149) levels are a third higher than those of controls and decrease less following a meal. People with _____ _____ (150) disorder eat large amounts of food in a short time and cannot control how much they eat. They usually are obese and feel shame about their eating. This has recently been added to the _____ (151) V, the newest revision of the mental disorders handbook released by the American Psychological Association.

The social environment plays a role in eating disorders, including exposure to thin models in the media. After satellite TV became available in _____ (152) in 1995, almost 75% of the teenage girls reported feeling fat, and the number of those who admitted to vomiting to control their weight rose from 3% to _____ (153). Genetic inheritance also appears to play a role; the concordance rate of anorexia among identical twins is _____ (154) times greater than in fraternal twins. Surprisingly, environment exerts a strong effect on eating disorders in adolescent girls; hormonal changes, stress, and dieting produce _____ (155) changes in the genes that play a role in anorexia and bulimia. In addition, eating disorders typically are accompanied by _____ (156) psychological disorders such as depression, anxiety, and obsessive-compulsive disorders.

Antidepressants that increase the levels of the neurotransmitter _____ (157) reduce bingeing and purging in bulimics and also decrease relapses in anorexics. Anorexics have lower levels, but only when they are underweight, apparently due to malnutrition. Evidence also points to a dysfunctional _____ (158) system in anorexia. Administering amphetamine to control subjects produced euphoria, but it increased _____ (159) in those who were recovering from anorexia. In addition, patients with anorexia and bulimia have more _____ (160) receptors in the insula, which contribute to the rewarding effects of food.

## Short Answer and Essay Questions

Answer the following questions.

18. What evidence points to an environmental influence on anorexia and bulimia?

19. Compare purging and restrictive anorexics to bulimics. Include in your answer the role of serotonin.

# Post-test

Use these multiple-choice questions to check your understanding of the chapter.

1. Christopher, the person described in the introduction to the chapter, exhibited all of the following EXCEPT
   a. poor impulse control.
   b. short stature.
   c. mental disability.
   d. violent outbursts.

2. Which of the following statements regarding motivation is TRUE?
   a. Motivation is controlled by the thalamus.
   b. Motivations are best thought of as instinctive drives.
   c. Motivation refers to bodily states of need.
   d. Motivation is sometimes confused with emotion.

3. The fact that some people need higher levels of excitement than others is BEST explained by ___ theory.
   a. incentive
   b. arousal
   c. drive
   d. instinct

4. Which of the following animals is ectothermic?
   a. elephant
   b. chicken
   c. cow
   d. snake

5. Endothermic animals can reduce their body temperature by
   a. burrowing into the ground.
   b. finding shade.
   c. sweating.
   d. all of the above

6. Warmth-sensitive and cold-sensitive cells that help mammals regulate their body temperature are found in the ___ of the hypothalamus.
   a. preoptic area
   b. area postrema
   c. ventromedial nucleus
   d. nucleus of the solitary tract

7. Jason has just eaten an entire bag of potato chips and suddenly feels thirsty. What type of thirst is he experiencing?
   a. hypovolemic
   b. osmotic
   c. hypervolemic
   d. endothermic

8. Which of the following does NOT result in loss of extracellular water?
   a. exercise
   b. blood loss
   c. ingesting a lot of salt
   d. vomiting

9. Osmotic thirst
   a. results from activation of baroreceptors in the heart.
   b. results from the release of renin by the kidneys.
   c. is controlled by the subfornical organ.
   d. is disrupted when the OVLT is lesioned.

10. Which of the following statements is TRUE?
    a. The set point for temperature is less variable than the set point for hunger.
    b. The set point for thirst is more variable than the set point for hunger.
    c. The set point for temperature is more variable than the set point for hunger.
    d. Once we reach adulthood, the set point for hunger becomes stable.

11. A species of animal that eats only berries and leaves is a(n)
    a. carnivore.
    b. omnivore.
    c. herbivore.
    d. endovore.

12. Of all of the primary taste qualities, ___ is the MOST recently discovered.
    a. umami
    b. sour
    c. bitter
    d. salty

13. Foods that provide the ions necessary for neural transmission are MOST likely to taste
    a. sweet.
    b. salty.
    c. bitter.
    d. sour.

14. Foods that contain toxins tend to taste
    a. sweet.
    b. sour.
    c. salty.
    d. bitter.

15. The taste buds send signals to the ___ area of the cortex.
    a. olfactory
    b. auditory
    c. gustatory
    d. somatosensory

16. Learned taste aversion accounts for all of the following EXCEPT
    a. bait shyness in rats.
    b. coyotes' refusal to eat lamb after consuming a tainted carcass.
    c. rats' decreased responsiveness to glucose placed on the tongue after receiving a glucose injection.
    d. children avoiding certain flavors of ice cream eaten while undergoing chemotherapy.

17. Which of the following statements regarding taste preferences is TRUE?
    a. Rats are better at "listening to what their bodies need" than humans.
    b. Rats deprived of a vitamin can develop a preference for a food high in that vitamin.
    c. Rats' behavior does not change when their diet is missing critical nutrients.
    d. Rats find the taste of cinnamon aversive.

18. Which of the following is released by the stomach as an aid to digestion?
    a. pepsin
    b. leptin
    c. insulin
    d. cholecystokinin

19. Most of digestion occurs in the
    a. large intestine.
    b. small intestine.
    c. liver.
    d. stomach.

20. Glycerol is a product of the transformation of
    a. fats.
    b. proteins.
    c. carbohydrates.
    d. all of the above

21. After nutrients are absorbed into the bloodstream, they are transported to the ___ by the hepatic portal vein.
    a. kidneys
    b. liver
    c. brain
    d. large intestine

22. During the absorptive phase of the feeding cycle,
    a. recently eaten food may be stored.
    b. recently eaten food is used for energy.
    c. the parasympathetic nervous system is activated.
    d. all of the above

23. Which of the following statements regarding insulin is TRUE?
    a. Brain cells can import glucose without it.
    b. All body cells can import glucose without it.
    c. Diabetics produce too much of it.
    d. Its production is activated by the sympathetic nervous system.

24. Which of the following contributes to adipose tissue?
    a. excess protein
    b. excess glucose
    c. fat
    d. all of the above

25. Which of the following statements regarding glucagon is FALSE?
    a. It is secreted by the pancreas.
    b. It transforms proteins to fatty acids.
    c. It transforms glycogen to glucose.
    d. It converts stored fat to glycerol.

26. A rabbit injected with 2-deoxyglucose into its hepatic portal vein will
    a. start eating but will eat only a small amount.
    b. not eat for several hours.
    c. start eating and eat more than usual.
    d. enter a diabetic coma.

27. Which of the following statements regarding neuropeptide Y is FALSE?
    a. It is released by the preoptic area of the hypothalamus.
    b. It stimulates eating.
    c. It is released in response to low glucose.
    d. It may help an animal conserve energy.

28. Satiety may be signaled by
    a. stretch receptors in the stomach.
    b. the release of cholecystokinin.
    c. the presence of nutrients in the liver.
    d. all of the above

29. Rats injected with CCK over several days will
    a. gain a lot of weight.
    b. lose a lot of weight.
    c. stay at the same weight.
    d. lose a little bit of weight but then gain it back when the injections are withheld.

30. In Hervey's parabiotic rats, the rat without a lesion lost weight because
    a. the lesioned rat was digesting all of the food that both rats consumed.
    b. the lesioned rat continually produced a satiety signal that inhibited eating only in the nonlesioned rat.
    c. the nonlesioned rat became insensitive to hunger cues.
    d. the lesioned rat refused to eat.

31. As leptin ___, neuropeptide Y ___.
    a. increases; increases
    b. increases; decreases
    c. decreases; decreases
    d. increases; remains the same

32. Which of the following is NOT a health risk associated with obesity?
    a. loss of bone density
    b. colon cancer
    c. Alzheimer's disease
    d. heart disease

33. A body mass index (BMI) of ___ is considered moderately risky.
    a. 20–25
    b. 30–35
    c. 25–29
    d. 36–40

34. Correlations for BMI are HIGHEST for
    a. identical twins raised together.
    b. identical twins raised apart.
    c. fraternal twins raised together.
    d. fraternal twins raised apart.

35. A rat of normal weight is MOST likely to starve to death when biotically paired with a(n) ___ rat.
    a. *db/db*
    b. *ob/ob*
    c. *db/db* or *ob/ob*
    d. normal

36. Basal metabolism accounts for energy used to fuel the brain and other organs and for
    a. exercise.
    b. digestion.
    c. maintaining body temperature.
    d. physical activity.

37. Mavis, who does not exercise, has reduced her calorie intake by 25% and expects to lose a lot of weight. What is likely to happen?
    a. She will lose as much weight as she wants.
    b. Her metabolism will increase.
    c. Her metabolism will decrease.
    d. It is impossible to predict.

38. Someone who responds to increased caloric consumption by fidgeting a lot
    a. will probably gain a lot of weight.
    b. may gain little or no weight.
    c. will probably lose weight.
    d. may develop other nervous habits.

39. In some obese people, carbohydrate consumption
    a. elevates mood.
    b. leads to depression.
    c. reduces serotonin levels.
    d. a and c

40. Which of the following drugs blocks the absorption of fat?
    a. leptin
    b. sibutramine
    c. PYY
    d. orlistat

41. Serotonin-enhancing drugs are LEAST likely to be useful for treating
    a. obesity.
    b. bulimia.
    c. purging anorexia.
    d. restrictive anorexia.

42. Leptin seems to
    a. increase appetite.
    b. increase metabolism.
    c. decrease appetite.
    d. b and c

43. Based on recent research, the neurotransmitters most involved in anorexia and bulimia are
    a. dopamine and norepinephrine.
    b. serotonin and norepinephrine.
    c. serotonin and dopamine.
    d. dopamine, norepinephrine, and serotonin.

44. The difference between bulimics and purging anorexics is that
    a. bulimics are usually of normal weight.
    b. purging anorexics purge by using laxatives, whereas bulimics rely on vomiting.
    c. purging anorexics are usually male.
    d. bulimics, but not purging anorexics, tend to be impulsive.

# Answers

## Guided Review

1. Motivation
2. instinctively
3. drive
4. homeostasis
5. Incentive
6. arousal
7. brain states
8. tissue
9. set
10. temperature
11. Ectothermic
12. endothermic
13. preoptic
14. cold-sensitive
15. shivering
16. thirst
17. 70
18. sweating
19. osmotic
20. hypovolemic
21. OVLT
22. median preoptic nucleus
23. heart
24. vagus
25. NST (nucleus of the solitary tract)
26. kidneys
27. angiotensin
28. SFO (subfornical organ)
29. satiety
30. stomach
31. set
32. nutrients
33. omnivores
34. taste
35. five
36. sweet
37. umami
38. proteins
39. sour
40. bitter
41. papillae
42. medulla
43. insula
44. labeled line
45. sensory-specific
46. NST
47. avoid
48. learned taste
49. chemotherapy
50. deficient or low
51. nutrient or vitamin
52. learned
53. Digestion
54. saliva
55. hydrochloric (HCl)
56. vomiting or regurgitation
57. duodenum
58. (simple) sugars
59. amino acids
60. glycerol
61. liver
62. absorbed

63. hepatic portal
64. intestine
65. autonomic or parasympathetic
66. diarrhea
67. absorptive
68. high
69. pancreas
70. Diabetes
71. glycogen
72. fats
73. adipose
74. fasting
75. sympathetic
76. glucagon
77. glucose
78. glycerol
79. liver
80. hypothalamus
81. PVN (paraventricular nucleus)
82. glucoprivic
83. lipoprivic
84. stomach
85. vagus
86. NST
87. arcuate
88. lateral
89. ghrelin
90. Prader-Willi
91. NPY (neuropeptide Y)
92. agouti-related
93. metabolism
94. volume or stretch
95. peptides
96. CCK (cholecystokinin)
97. gall bladder

98. PYY (peptide YY3-36)
99. arcuate
100. ventromedial
101. parabiotic
102. leptin
103. higher
104. POMC/CART
105. PVN
106. obese
107. nutrients
108. BMI (body mass index)
109. 30%
110. temporal
111. century
112. verbal
113. exercise
114. impulse or voluntary
115. gratification
116. genetics
117. 0.62
118. obesity (ob)
119. diabetes (db)
120. ob/ob
121. leptin
122. FTO
123. MC4R
124. Epigenetic
125. methylation
126. metabolic
127. more
128. decreases
129. activity
130. set point
131. basal metabolism
132. sibutramine

133. serotonin

134. orlistat

135. leptin

136. dopamine

137. Vigabatrin

138. gastric bypass

139. bulimia

140. three

141. Anorexia

142. laxatives

143. binge-purgers

144. restrictors

145. brain

146. NPY

147. ghrelin

148. bulimia nervosa

149. ghrelin

150. binge eating

151. DSM

152. Fiji

153. 11

154. three

155. epigenetic

156. comorbid

157. serotonin

158. dopamine

159. anxiety

160. cannabinoid

## Short Answer and Essay Questions

1.  This disorder is caused by the failure of a section of the father's chromosome 15 to be incorporated into the fertilized egg. The results of the absence of this genetic material include a number of impulsive behaviors (such as extreme overeating), short stature, and learning disabilities.

2.  Drive theory explains behaviors resulting from tissue deficits, such as eating and drinking, but not other forms of behavior such as sex, striving for achievement, thrill seeking, and even eating when we are not hungry. Most researchers conceptualize motivation in terms of brain states, which can account for all of these forms of motivation.

3. Ectotherms and endotherms can sun themselves, find shade, burrow in the ground, build nests or shelters, and take other external actions to control their body temperature. Only endotherms can regulate their body heat by internal means such as sweating or changing their metabolism.

4. Osmotic thirst is regulated by cells in the OVLT that detect low levels of intracellular fluid. When an animal whose OVLT is lesioned is given an injection of salt water, it will increase its water intake to a lesser degree than one without the OVLT lesion. Hypovolemic thirst is regulated by receptors in the heart, which signals the hypothalamus via the vagus nerve, and the kidneys, which initiate increases in renin and then angiotensin II, which in turn stimulates the SFO. An animal whose SFO is lesioned will not drink in response to the presence of angiotensin II but will drink if its intracellular fluid levels fall too low.

5. First of all, the set point for hunger fluctuates to a greater extent than that for the others. The second difference has to do with the fact that thirst is satiated by water, while satiation of hunger requires a variety of nutrients.

6. Naturally sweet foods are generally nutritious, and those that are salty contain salt, which is converted to ions that we need. Sour foods are often rotten or spoiled, and bitter foods may contain toxins. In both cases, we could become sick from eating them.

7. When we eat a lot of the same food, it becomes less appealing. However, having a variety of foods (and tastes) available seems to maintain one's appetite, and therefore interest in eating. For example, the study by Rolls et al. suggested that more food will be consumed if a greater variety of food is offered.

8. Shirley developed a learned taste aversion to chili. Her illness, although not caused by the chili, was associated with it because she happened to get sick within a few hours of eating it. Through learning, chili became repulsive to her.

9. People with diabetes either have low levels of insulin or are less sensitive to it than others. Because insulin is needed to allow cells to utilize glucose, diabetics cannot use glucose as efficiently as other people. Therefore, they essentially "starve" their cells of glucose, even though it is available in the blood.

10. Excess amounts of either of these types of nutrients is stored as fat.

11. The three major signals for hunger are low levels of glucose (glucoprivic hunger), low levels of fats (lipoprivic hunger), and the release of ghrelin synthesized in the stomach (low level of stomach nutrients).

12. This stimulates the appetite, and they will eat more than normal. There is also evidence that it may reduce energy consumption, because these rats gain weight disproportionately to the amount of food they eat. Under severe deprivation conditions, NPY can reduce body temperature and inhibit sexual behavior, thereby conserving energy.

13. All of the following play a role in satiety: stretch or volume receptors in the stomach, release of CCK in response to food in the duodenum, PYY released in the intestine, leptin secreted by fat cells, and insulin released by the pancreas.

14. Rates of obesity have dramatically increased in both the United States and the rest of the world, causing the World Health Organization to view it as a global epidemic. The number of people who are malnourished is now double those who are undernourished, because they are getting their calories from junk food that is low in nutritional value. There are significant health problems related to obesity such as diabetes, heart disease, stroke, cancer, and even brain degeneration. Certainly obesity has negative effects on life expectancy.

15. The body seems to be programmed to hold on to weight. Under survival conditions this is adaptive, because in times of deprivation the body conserves fat. Although the body for the most part maintains weight around a set point, it is less likely to inhibit weight gain than weight loss.

16. According to information presented in the text, spontaneous activity such as casual walking, fidgeting, and posture maintenance may contribute to an increase in energy expenditure. It is possible that her level of spontaneous activity has increased, and her BMR also could have increased in response to the additional calorie intake.

17. Sibutramine inhibits serotonin reuptake. This works in some people because it inhibits carbohydrate craving (because the drug enhances serotonin, which reduces NPY activity). Orlistat blocks the absorption of fat by about 30%. It also blocks the absorption of water and leads to cramping and diarrhea. Leptin may work for obese people who are sensitive to but deficient in leptin. Increasing leptin levels reduces the sensitive individual's hunger. Vigabatrin is an experimental drug being used to treat drug addiction. It decreases dopamine and it produced weight loss in animal studies.

18. These disorders are more common in cultures where the media tend to portray thin people as beautiful. In Fiji, when television was introduced in the 1990s, the rates of anorexia

and bulimia rose very quickly among adolescent girls, supposedly in response to seeing thin Western actresses.

19. Both purging anorexics and bulimics are more likely to display impulsive behavior, and they also show low levels of serotonin. Purging anorexics are typically much thinner than bulimics, however. Restrictive anorexics, on the other hand, are in some ways more like people with OCD. Following weight gain, they have higher levels of serotonin than purgers or bulimics; starvation may be a means of reducing serotonin and reducing obsessive concerns.

## Post-test

1. c   2. d   3. b   4. d   5. d   6. a   7. b   8. c   9. d   10. a   11. c   12. a   13. b   14. d
15. c   16. c   17. b   18. a   19. b   20. a   21. b   22. d   23. a   24. d   25. b   26. c
27. a   28. d   29. c   30. b   31. b   32. a   33. c   34. a   35. a   36. c   37. c   38. b
39. a   40. d   41. d   42. d   43. c   44. a

# 7 The Biology of Sex and Gender

## Chapter Outline

*Parental Influences on Brain Structure and Function*

*Social Implications of the Biological Model*

CONCEPT CHECK

In Perspective

Summary

Study Resources

## Learning Objectives

After reading this chapter, you should be able to answer the following questions.

1. What occurs during the four phases of the cycle of sexual arousal and satiation? Describe the differences between men and women with respect to what happens after the fourth phase.

2. What role does testosterone play in sexual behavior?

3. What brain structures and neurotransmitters are involved in sexual behavior?

4. What sensory signals appear to influence sexual behavior?

5. How is olfactory information transmitted in the nervous system?

6. How does an individual become male or female?

7. What effects does prenatal exposure to hormones have on the brains of males and females?

8. What biological factors might account for the gender differences in verbal skills, spatial abilities, and aggression?

9. What are the characteristics and causes of 46 XX and 46 XY differences of sexual development (DSD).

10. What do studies of behavior in DSD individuals suggest about the roles of hormones in brain development?

11. What does the case study involving *ablatio penis* suggest about the formation of gender identity? What are the limitations of this study?

12. What genetic and hormonal factors may contribute to homosexuality in males? What brain structures may be involved in male homosexuality?

13. What evidence is there for a biological basis for homosexuality in females?

14. What are the social implications of the biological model of homosexuality?

## Sex as a Form of Motivation

### Summary and Guided Review

After studying this section in the text, fill in the blanks of the following summary.

Sex shares some similarities with other forms of motivation, such as cycles of arousal and _____ (1), and regulation by hormones and specific brain areas. But unlike hunger and thirst, there is no homeostatic _____ (2) need for sex.

The cycle of sexual arousal and satiation in humans was studied extensively by the researchers _____ and _____ (3) in the 1960s. They described four phases: _____ (4), during which physiological arousal increases sharply; _____ (5), during which arousal levels off; _____ (6), marked by intense pleasure, vaginal contractions in females, and _____ (7) in males; and _____ (8), during which the body returns to its resting state. Whereas _____ (9) can re-enter the excitement phase immediately after orgasm, men have a(n) _____ (10) phase during which time they cannot be aroused or have another orgasm. Among some animals, a male will return to arousal more quickly if he is exposed to a novel female rather than the one with which he has most recently mated; this phenomenon is known as the _____ (11) effect.

The role of hormones in sexual behavior is often studied in nonhuman animals, in part because hormones control their behavior to a(n) _____ (12) extent than in humans. The method of _____ (13) involves removing the gonads, the source major of sex hormones; this is done to determine what effects exposure to hormones has on behavior. Occasionally humans undergo castration, and those who do often experience a(n) _____ (14) in sexual interest and behavior, although there is a great deal of variability. Some male criminals have volunteered to undergo physical or chemical castration, which reduces _____ (15), a class of hormones responsible for a number of male characteristics and functions, in order to curb their violent or sexual behavior. The primary compound in that class, which serves as the major sex hormone in male humans, is _____ (16). Apparently, in human males just a small amount of testosterone is needed to maintain sexual interest and behavior.

In many animal species, females will mate only while they are in _____ (17), when they are ovulating and estrogen levels are high. Human females will engage in sex throughout the reproductive cycle, although they are more likely to initiate sex around the time of _____ (18), which corresponds with peaks in _____ (19) and, possibly more important, testosterone. Postmenopausal women's sexual behavior seems to be most closely tied to _____ (20) levels.

Research with animals has revealed several brain areas involved in sexual behavior that probably work in conjunction with one another. The _____ (21) of the hypothalamus is active during copulation in both male and female rats, and studies with monkeys indicate that it is more involved in sexual _____ (22) than motivation. Lesioned monkeys would masturbate but not _____ (23). The _____ (24) amygdala is responsive to sexual stimuli and is also active during copulation. In male rats, when the _____ (25) of the MPOA is lesioned, the result is reduced sexual activity. In female rats, when the _____ (26) hypothalamus is lesioned, they are less likely to copulate. Many neurotransmitters are involved in sexual functioning. _____ (27) activity in the MPOA contributes to sexual motivation in both males and females. In males, as dopamine levels rise, they initially stimulate $D_1$ receptors, activating the parasympathetic response increasing motivation and a(n) _____ (28) in males; later, _____ (29) receptors are activated, leading to ejaculation under _____ (30) control. Dopamine levels in the nucleus

_____ (31) may also be responsible for the Coolidge effect, which is when a recently mated male presented with a new female will show an increase in dopamine levels in that area. The refractory period in males appears to be influenced by the neurotransmitter _____ (32); individuals taking reuptake inhibitors (increasing levels) frequently report an inability to have orgasms.

External factors are also involved in sexual motivation and behavior and are particularly sensitive to _____ (33)—so much so that the nose can be considered a sex organ in many species! Humans may use scent to recognize relatives or people with similar genes, in particular genes in the major _____ (34) complex (involved in immune function and may be related to fertility), and avoid selecting those people as mates. Other effective stimuli might be _____ (35), airborne chemicals released by an animal that have physiological or behavioral effects on another animal of the same species. Airborne odorous materials are detected by receptors in the _____ (36) cavity. Axons from the olfactory receptors pass through openings in the base of the skull and enter the _____ _____ (37), which lie over the nasal cavity. The information then travels to the olfactory cortex in the temporal lobes. Our ability to distinguish between _____ (38) different odors seems to be a result of the combination of a few hundred neurons that are active. The nasal cavity also contains the _____ (39) organ, which is used to detect pheromones. Some researchers believe that this organ has evolved to a diminished size in humans and that the _____ (40) that are responsible for its receptors are no longer functional. This organ sends messages to the _____ (41) and the ventromedial hypothalamus, as well as to the emotion center _____ (42). Studies indicate that pheromones may be involved in _____ (43) synchrony in women living together in dorms, but these findings have been difficult to replicate. Men preferred the scent of T-shirts worn by women who were in the middle of their menstrual cycle at the point of maximal fertility, when they would be expected to be _____ (44). PET scans suggest that pheromones from the T-shirts might activate the _____ _____ (45) area, where structures important for sexual behavior are located.

Mating in prairie voles begins with the release of the neurotransmitter _____ (46) and the neuropeptide _____ (47). Prairie voles, which have the AVPR1A gene that codes for a particular _____ (48) receptor, are monogamous and mate for life due to their increased preference for females they have mated with. In humans, the neuropeptide facilitates bonding and plays a role in muscle contractions in lactation and _____ (49). Oxytocin also contributes to social _____ (50), which is necessary for developing mate preferences.

## Short Answer and Essay Questions

Answer the following questions.

1. Compare hunger and sex as forms of motivation. Point out their similarities and differences.

2. Name the four phases of sexual response as described by Masters and Johnson.

3. What role does testosterone play in sexual motivation in men and women? Discuss the research that indicates this hormone's importance for sexual arousal and for behavior in men and in women.

4. Identify the brain areas most important for sexual behavior in males and females, based on animal studies.

5. What are pheromones? Give an example of how they might affect reproductive function, sexual behavior, or attraction.

# The Biological Determination of Sex

## Summary and Guided Review

After studying this section in the text, fill in the blanks of the following summary.

The term "sex," which refers to the biological characteristics that distinguish males and females, should not be confused with _____ (51), which refers to the behavioral characteristics associated with being male or female, or gender _____ (52), which is the sex an individual identifies herself or himself as being. Sometimes a person's sex does not match the gender or gender identity.

The first step in the determination of sex occurs during _____ (53), when the egg and sperm cells combine. Each sex cell contains only 1 chromosome from each of the 23 pairs of chromosomes. The sex of the fetus is determined by the combination of sex chromosomes. The mother always contributes a(n) _____ (54) chromosome. If the sperm cell contains an X chromosome, the fetus will be _____ (55), and if it contains a Y chromosome, the fetus will be _____ (56). Fetuses of both sexes initially possess identical sexual tissue that will later differentiate into male or female sex organs. In XX fetuses, the primitive (indifferent) gonads become _____ (57), the uterus develops from the _____ (58) ducts, the _____ (59) ducts are absorbed, and the external structures form the _____ (60), part of the vagina, and the _____ (61). In XY fetuses, the _____ (62) gene on the Y chromosome transforms the gonads to become _____ (63). These produce _____ _____ (64) hormone, which causes these ducts to degenerate, and _____ (65), which transforms the Wolffian ducts into the _____ (66) vesicles and vas deferens. The hormone _____ (67) causes the external structures to form into a penis and the testes-containing _____ (68). The permanent effects of male hormones are called _____ (69) effects, because they occur early in development and produce changes that will last throughout the life span. Hormones also have temporary _____ (70) effects, which cause reversible changes if the hormone is no longer present. In humans, sexual maturation is completed during _____ (71), when gonadal hormones are again released in large amounts. Puberty is accompanied by organizing effects, such as maturation of the _____ (72). It also has activating effects, such as breast and muscle development, the release of _____ (73) in females, and production of sperm cells in males.

In many species, sex hormones are largely responsible for sexual behavior. There are _____ (74) periods during development when exposure to a particular hormone alters the brain and thus influences future behavior. In rats, for example, a newborn male that is castrated will be more likely to engage in _____ (75) (presenting its hindquarters for mounting) as an adult. A young female rat exposed to _____ (76) will perform male-typical mounting more often as an adult than females with normal hormone levels. The hormone _____ (77) is critical both for feminizing female brains and masculinizing male brains (through aromatization of testosterone).

Behavioral sex differences in humans are less clear than they are in other animals, in part because of the limitations of research in this area. However, _____ and _____ (78) in a 1974 review of the research literature found consistent differences between males and females. In cognitive performance, girls tended to be better at _____ (79) tasks, whereas boys tended to be better at visual-spatial tasks and _____ (80). Boys were also found to be more _____ (81) than girls. These findings have been controversial because there is considerable _____ (82) between males and females in these characteristics.

The source of these differences has been debated. There is evidence that experience contributes to them, in that the differences have been decreasing over the last few decades, particularly in the area of _____ (83). The dramatic differences in aggression rates in countries suggest that there is a strong _____ (84) component to aggression. However, there is evidence that biological factors contribute to some of the differences. Most researchers attribute the gender differences to hormonal exposure during _____ (85). Males who produce low levels of testosterone during the developmental years have lower _____ (86) ability later in life. Male transsexuals who take estrogen gain in _____ performance (87) but decrease in _____ (88) performance. The opposite is true for female transsexuals taking _____ (89). Elevated testosterone is associated with aggression, but it is unclear whether the hormone is the cause or result of the behavior. For example, winning at sports _____ (90) testosterone, and losing decreases it.

Some researchers explain gender differences in traits by referring to brain anatomy and organization. One explanation for women's superiority on verbal tasks is that they use both _____ (91) of the brain during the tasks, not just the language-based one (usually the left). In terms of spatial rotation tasks, women rely more on _____ (92) areas, whereas men use _____ (93) areas. Males are also more likely to experience disorders like _____ (94), Tourette's syndrome, and attention-deficit/hyperactivity disorder. Women are more likely to suffer from _____ (95).

## Short Answer and Essay Questions

Answer the following questions.

6. Which of the sex organs and structures in females and males develop from the same primitive tissue? What factors are responsible for transforming these primitive structures into the male-typical structures? Be sure to include both internal and external structures.

7. Distinguish between organizing and activating effects of hormones, and give an example of each.

8. Compare the sexual behavior of normal female rats to those that have been "masculinized."

9. What evidence is there that differences in estrogen levels may be partly responsible for the gender differences seen in verbal abilities?

10. Why does the author refer to males and females as "other" rather than "opposite" sexes?

# Biological Origins of Gender Identity

## Summary and Guided Review

After studying this section in the text, fill in the blanks of the following summary.

For decades, gender identity has been assumed to be a combination of genital appearance and parenting. For example, many of the physical differences between males and females are clearly the result of the effects of hormones and genes on development. However, some individuals believe they have been born into the wrong sex, despite being otherwise physically normal. These people are called _____ (96). Males in this category have been studied more extensively than females, and there are striking parallels in the brains of these two groups. The brain areas _____ (97) and _____ (98), both in the hypothalamus, are sized more like females than nontranssexual males, and they have similar responses to the presumed male pheromone AND and the female pheromone EST. These differences were independent of sexual preference.

If there is a physical difference between the sex chromosomes and genitalia, these individuals have a DSD, meaning a _____ of _____ (99). Many of these individuals are born with ambiguous genitalia, although these individuals usually have _____ (100) that match their chromosomal sex. One cause of 46 XY DSD is the lack of the enzyme 17α-_____ (101) that converts testosterone into _____ (102); males with this condition appear female at birth but undergo some masculinization at puberty due to a surge of _____ (103) from the internal, undescended testicles. A similar condition, caused by the lack of 5α-reductase, has a genetic basis; many individuals with this genetic defect live in the country of the _____ (104). In most cases, the individual is reared as a girl, but she begins questioning her gender during childhood. When masculine characteristics develop in puberty, most of these individuals will adopt a male gender role. Although this suggests that hormones are largely responsible for our sense of gender, the fact that males are more valued in this society indicates that _____ (105) may play a role as well. A third condition that produces 46 XY DSD individuals is _____ _____ (106) Syndrome (AIS); due to a genetic mutation, these individuals lack male hormone receptors and have outward physical characteristics of females, although they have undescended and usually normal functioning _____ (107). They undergo further feminization at puberty due to estrogen from the gonads as well as the adrenal glands, developing strong female secondary sex characteristics that include well-developed _____ (108), flawless complexion, and long slender legs. For these reasons, individuals with AIS can frequently outcompete women for modeling jobs.

46 XX DSD typically results from exposure to high levels of _____ (109) such as testosterone during fetal development. These individuals have internal female gonads, but externally they resemble males. The clitoris is enlarged and resembles a(n) _____ (110), and the _____ (111) may be partially or completely fused. One cause of 46 XX DSD is _____ _____ _____ (112), or CAH, which involves excessive androgen production by the adrenal glands. Parents may decide to raise the baby as a boy or a girl; _____ (113) surgery may be performed to alter the appearance of the genitals to match the baby's assigned sex. Some researchers believe that we need to recognize more than two categories for sex, including _____ (114) for individuals who are in the gray areas between maleness and femaleness. This ambiguity was recently highlighted in the case of athlete Caster Semenya in the Application. Following suspicions over her strong

performance and masculine physique, Semenya underwent extensive _____
(115) testing. Despite rumors that Semenya had two testicles and triple the normal amount of
_____ (116) for a woman, she was cleared to compete again. One major result
of this case is the realization that the International Olympic Committee does not have a good
definition of what are _____ (117) levels of male hormone, and it is skirting the
gender issue by banning all individuals with high levels of androgens from female competitions.

There are cognitive and behavioral effects of sex hormones as well. These hormones
strongly influence brain development both within the womb and in early life. For
example, androgen-insensitive males are more like females in terms of their higher
_____ (118) ability and lower _____ (119) ability, and
they are also decidedly _____ (120) in sexual orientation. Although 95%
of XY males with CAH who are reared as girls accept a(n) _____ (121)
gender identity, they are somewhat more likely to display masculine characteristics and define
their sexual orientation as _____ (122) or _____
(123). Furthermore, women who were exposed to the anti-miscarriage drug DES
(diethylstilbesterol) before they were born reported an increased _____
(124) behavior and fantasies.

But what about gender identity in individuals without hormonal anomalies? The debate
between "neutral-at-birth" and "_____ (125)-at-birth" theorists is played
out in the case of an 8-month-old boy whose penis was accidentally destroyed during
_____ (126). The researcher Money (who followed his case) believed
the theory that sexuality is not established until a "critical period" ends after the first several
years of life. His evidence was that the child underwent sexual reassignment surgery and
was reared as a girl after this period and that "Brenda" became a well-adjusted, feminine
child. However, when "Brenda" discovered the truth at the age of 14 after several years of
feeling like a male, she reverted to her original biological sex, took the name David, married,
and adopted a typically masculine role. Two other cases of _____
_____ (127) had similar outcomes: In one, the individual reverted to a
male identity. In the second, the individual remained female but was very masculine, exhibited
a(n) _____ (128) orientation, and had sexual fantasies predominantly
involving women. Therefore, sexuality may be established at birth (or earlier), regardless of
later hormonal or social influences. It is important to keep in mind that these are case studies,
and we must be careful about any conclusions we draw from them.

## Short Answer and Essay Questions

Answer the following questions.

11. If androgen-insensitive males are raised as females, look female even after puberty,
    and typically adopt a female gender identity without question, how may their condi-
    tion be discovered?

12. Will a female with CAH have a uterus? Why or why not?

13. What accounts for the fact that androgen-insensitive males perform more poorly on
    tests of spatial skills than their sisters and other females?

14. Describe the case of Semenya that demonstrates the difficulties with gender determi-
    nation and how this seriously affected her career.

15. Does CAH cause women to engage in homosexual activity? Support your answer.

16. Why are the conclusions that can be drawn about the influence of biology and expe-
    rience on gender from the ablatio penis studies so limited?

# Sexual Orientation

## Summary and Guided Review

After studying this section in the text, fill in the blanks of the following summary.

Identifying the basis of sexual orientation is difficult. However, if we can understand why some people are not attracted exclusively to members of the opposite sex, this may inform us to what aspects of each sex trigger sexual attraction. It is important to understand that many more people have homosexual experiences than are considered homosexuals. The rate of homosexuality in the population is difficult to determine, but in a recent literature review, the average rate in the United States was approximately _____ (129). Although equally prevalent in men and women, there was a much stronger tendency for males to be exclusively _____ (130) than females. Furthermore, an estimated 1% expresses no interest in sex at all and is referred to as _____ (131).

There is evidence that homosexuality develops early in life, but it is unclear if early exposure to homosexual behaviors or individuals has any effect on future sexual orientation. _____ (132) learning and experience have both been implicated in the formation of _____ (133) behaviors. Adult homosexuals are more likely to have displayed gender _____ (134) earlier in life, preferring companions, mannerisms, dress, and activities typical of the opposite sex.

There is strong evidence for a genetic component in homosexuality. For example, early research on identical twins reported a(n) _____ (135) rate of 50%, but the actual figures may be lower due to the "volunteer effect." One researcher, Hamer, claims to have found an area of DNA on the _____ (136) chromosome that contributes to homosexuality in males. Hamer's study group included pairs of gay brothers with gay relatives on the _____ (137) side of the family, and _____% (138) of the brother pairs had identical genotypes in the region in question.

The idea that homosexuality is a heritable trait runs counter to _____ (139) theory, which argues that traits that promote survival and reproduction are the ones more likely to be passed on. However, researchers have found a correlation between genes on the X and 7th chromosomes to both higher birth rates, as well as increased attraction to _____ (140) in both men and women. Additionally, recent evidence indicates that male homosexuality may be related to an epigenetic process known as _____ (141) that involves selective inhibition of one of the mother's X chromosomes rather than inheritance of "gay genes." This could result in a significant change in _____ (142) to sex hormones, and if that change is heritable it could have significant effects on the sexual and gender development of the children.

In animal studies, experimental manipulation of hormone levels can produce homosexual preferences and behaviors. Critics argue that these animals display homosexuality only when isolated from members of the other sex, not as a permanent state of sexuality. But numerous studies have demonstrated homosexual behaviors in mixed-sex groups occurring spontaneously in many different animal species, such as in 10% of _____ (143), and a small number of female gulls remain in stable homosexual pairs for multiple years. The evidence for hormonal influences in humans is weak, but there is compelling evidence that hormonal factors may alter the brain _____ (144) during gestation, which in turn may contribute to differences in sexual orientation.

Additional research revealed differences in brain structure between homosexual and heterosexual men. Swedish researchers discovered that both male homosexuals

and male-to-female transsexuals responded atypically high to the male sex pheromone
_____ (145) in a way similar to females, and the opposite effect for
nonheterosexual females with respect to the female sex pheromone EST. Simon LeVay
reported that the INAH-3 (third interstitial nucleus of the _____
_____) (146) is smaller in gay men and heterosexual women than in
heterosexual men. In another study, the _____ (147) nucleus was larger
in gay men than in heterosexual men and contained twice as many cells that secrete the
neuropeptide _____ (148). Whether the above differences contribute
directly to sexual behavior in humans is unclear.

Understanding _____ (149) homosexuality also represents
a challenge. But two ways in which lesbians resemble men of all sexual orientations
are as follows: their _____ to _____-
_____ (150) ratios, and the strength of evoked _____
(151) emissions when the inner ear is stimulated. Because both of these traits are influenced
by prenatal exposure to _____ (152), it may be that the timing of
exposure results in masculinization of mechanisms for sexual orientation. One intriguing idea,
called the _____ _____ (153) hypothesis, suggests that
a mother builds up antibodies to male-specific proteins after each male child is born, which
affects the development of subsequent male children. A gene on the Y chromosome has been
shown to do just that in mothers of multiple sons.

The social implications of the biological model are important. If sexual preference is
a voluntary _____ (154), then those who display homosexuality are
not eligible for civil rights protection since a minority group is defined as one with clearly
defined, inborn, and unalterable characteristics. However, if sexual preference has a clear
_____ (155) basis, as many homosexuals claim, then their status should be
protected. Although the majority of homosexuals believe that they are "born that way," some
are opposed to the model because of its association with a disease explanation, and fear of
efforts to eliminate the "problem" through _____ (156) manipulation or
abortion. Other homosexuals embrace the biological model, because they think it will make
homosexuality more _____ (157) in society. The increases in legal same-
sex marriage and benefits seen across the nation and across the world lend this argument
strong empirical support.

## Short Answer and Essay Questions

Answer the following questions.

17. What can studying homosexuality tell us about heterosexuality?

18. What evidence is presented for the social learning hypothesis of homosexuality? What
    are the problems with interpreting this evidence?

19. Why is homosexuality difficult to explain from an evolutionary standpoint? What
    evidence is there that homosexuality may be the result of epigenetic processes?

20. One criticism of the studies of brain differences in homosexuals is that they rely too
    much on older individuals and those who have died from AIDS. Why is this a prob-
    lem? What limitations do these samples place on the conclusions that can be drawn
    from the results?

21. Why are some members of the homosexual community opposed to the biological
    model of homosexuality? What benefits could be gained if this model is accepted?

# Post-test

Use these multiple-choice questions to check your understanding of the chapter.

1. As forms of motivation, how are hunger and sex different?
    a. Sex, but not hunger, involves arousal and satiation.
    b. Hunger, but not sex, is under the influence of hormones.
    c. Hunger, but not sex, represents a homeostatic tissue need.
    d. Sex, but not hunger, is entirely under the control of external stimuli.

2. Penile and clitoral erection first occur in the ___ phase of the sexual response.
    a. excitement
    b. plateau
    c. orgasm
    d. resolution

3. Which of the following statements regarding the refractory phase of the sexual response is TRUE?
    a. Females have a shorter refractory phase than males.
    b. During the refractory phase, orgasm cannot occur.
    c. Males typically have a refractory phase of 3–5 hours.
    d. all of the above

4. Anti-androgen drugs
    a. may block the production of testosterone.
    b. may reduce deviant sexual behaviors.
    c. may reduce sexual fantasies.
    d. all of the above

5. Which of the following statements regarding sexual activity in females is TRUE?
    a. Only female humans will engage in sexual activity when they are not ovulating.
    b. Women on birth control pills are less likely to initiate sex mid-cycle than at other times.
    c. In women, the increased likelihood of initiating sex corresponds with an increase in sex hormone levels.
    d. Women are less likely to engage in sexual intercourse during ovulation than at other times of the cycle.

6. Which of the following brain areas is active during copulation in female, but not male, rats?
    a. medial preoptic area
    b. medial amygdala
    c. sexually dimorphic nucleus
    d. ventromedial nucleus

7. Which of the following neurotransmitters increases in the nucleus accumbens during sexual activity?
    a. dopamine
    b. serotonin
    c. norepinephrine
    d. endorphin

8. Which of the following statements regarding the major histocompatibility complex is FALSE?
    a. Couples with similar MHCs may have more fertility problems.
    b. People who are unrelated are more likely to have similar MHCs.

  c. The MHC includes genes involved in the immune system.
  d. all of the above

9. Which of the following statements regarding olfactory receptors is TRUE?
  a. Humans can distinguish approximately 1,000 odors.
  b. Humans have more genes for them than mice.
  c. Humans have 500–750 genes for odor receptors.
  d. There are as many different odor receptors as odors that can be detected.

10. Receptors in the VNO project to which TWO of the four areas of the hypothalamus listed below?
  a. lateral geniculate nucleus (LGN)
  b. sexually dimorphic nucleus (SDN)
  c. medial preoptic area (MPOA)
  d. ventromedial nucleus of the hypothalamus (VMH)

11. Which of the following statements regarding pheromones in humans is FALSE?
  a. Women's menstrual cycles may be synchronized by pheromones.
  b. Men wearing pheromones are more likely to engage in intercourse than controls.
  c. Pheromones have been linked to sexual behavior, but not nonsexual behaviors like aggression.
  d. Women wearing pheromones are more likely to engage in intercourse than controls.

12. Oxytocin
  a. plays a role in bonding.
  b. is important in social recognition.
  c. causes muscle contractions involved in lactation and orgasm.
  d. all of the above

13. Which of the following statements regarding egg cells is TRUE?
  a. They contain both X and Y chromosomes.
  b. They contain only Y chromosomes.
  c. They contain only X chromosomes.
  d. They contain either an X or a Y chromosome.

14. Which of the following internal structures must be actively inhibited in order for the normal pattern of male genitalia to form?
  a. Müllerian ducts
  b. Wolffian ducts
  c. ovaries
  d. testes

15. The penis in males and the ___ in females develop from the same embryonic tissue.
  a. vagina
  b. labia
  c. uterus
  d. clitoris

16. What hormone(s) is (are) responsible for masculinization of the external genitalia in males?
  a. testosterone
  b. dihydrotestosterone
  c. Müllerian-inhibiting hormone
  d. a and b

17. Which of the following represents an activating effect of a hormone?
    a. maturation of the genitals at puberty
    b. the enlargement of the SDN in male rats
    c. production of a mature egg cell during ovulation
    d. masculinization of the genitals during prenatal development

18. Which of the following statements regarding sexual behavior in rats is TRUE?
    a. Among male rats, castration does not affect sexual behavior because it occurs after birth.
    b. Androgenized females will mount other rats but do not display lordosis.
    c. Castrated males do not display lordosis.
    d. Normal females occasionally mount other females.

19. Which is NOT true of the hormone estradiol?
    a. It is critical for masculinization of the male brain.
    b. It is critical for feminization of the female brain.
    c. It can be converted by the aromatization of testosterone.
    d. It is only found in females.

20. Which of the following gender differences has NOT been found in the research literature?
    a. Females are more emotional than males.
    b. Females tend to score better on verbal tasks than males.
    c. Males tend to score better on spatial tasks than females.
    d. Males tend to be more aggressive than females.

21. Which of the following is NOT a sex difference reported in the literature?
    a. Males are more susceptible to autism.
    b. Women are more affected by stress than males.
    c. Females are genetically more resistant to pain than males.
    d. Attention-deficit disorder is more common in males.

22. Which hormone may be linked to enhanced verbal fluency?
    a. testosterone
    b. estrogen
    c. progesterone
    d. dihydrotestosterone

23. Which hormone may be linked to enhanced spatial skills?
    a. testosterone
    b. estrogen
    c. progesterone
    d. dihydrotestosterone

24. Which of the following statements regarding sex differences in aggression is FALSE?
    a. The cultural influence on aggression is weak compared to other factors.
    b. Studies indicate that males are much more likely than females to kill another person.
    c. Studies indicate that aggression is moderately heritable.
    d. Studies indicate that testosterone is related to aggression.

25. Steve believes he should have been born into a woman's body, and he wishes to get gender reassignment surgery to fix the apparent "mistake." However, he is still sexually attracted to women. If Steve's doctor were to examine his brain, what area would be sized smaller than his homosexual and heterosexual male friends?
    a. central bed nucleus of the stria terminalis (BSTc)
    b. third interstitial nucleus of the hypothalamus (INAH3)

   c. ventromedial hypothalamus (vmH)
   d. medial preoptic area (MPOA)

26. Which of the following will NOT result in 46 XY DSD?
   a. 17 α-hydroxysteroid deficiency
   b. androgen insensitivity syndrome
   c. 5 α-reductase deficiency
   d. congenital adrenal hyperplasia

27. Which of the following statements regarding 46 XX DSD individuals is TRUE?
   a. They are always raised as girls.
   b. They have ovaries.
   c. The external genitalia are clearly male in appearance.
   d. They lack testosterone receptors.

28. Which of the following groups tends to score the LOWEST on spatial tasks?
   a. CAH females
   b. 46 XX DSD individuals
   c. normal females
   d. normal males

29. Regarding the case of "Bruce-Brenda-David," which of the following is TRUE?
   a. Brenda wanted to become a boy before she knew her true sex.
   b. Brenda was comfortable with her feminine role until adolescence.
   c. Brenda's identical twin brother also exhibited many feminine characteristics.
   d. This case clearly demonstrated that the "neutral-at-birth" position is incorrect.

30. The study of 46 XY DSD in the Dominican Republic found that
   a. the source of the condition was androgen insensitivity.
   b. most individuals developed a sexual preference for male partners.
   c. although raised as girls, most of the individuals adopted male gender identities.
   d. all of the above

31. An early study indicated that, compared to other females, CAH females
   a. were more oriented toward male-typical occupations.
   b. were less likely to engage in same-sex erotic contact.
   c. were more feminine as children.
   d. were more likely to want to have children.

32. Which of the following statements regarding sexual orientation is TRUE?
   a. Gay men are more likely to be bisexual than lesbians.
   b. Lesbians make up a larger proportion of the population than do gay men.
   c. Gay men and lesbians are usually bisexual to a certain degree.
   d. Many more people engage in homosexual behavior than are considered homosexual.

33. Which of the following is TRUE about sex, gender, and sports?
   a. Sports organizations have successfully established a definition for gender in its rules.
   b. Currently physical examination and chromosome testing are acceptable measures for determining gender.
   c. Sports organizations have regarded women with strong athletic performance and a male physique with suspicion.
   d. none of the above

34. Gender nonconformity includes
    a. early heterosexual experiences.
    b. a childhood preference for friends of the other sex.
    c. a preference for activities usually associated with the other sex.
    d. b and c

35. Figure 7.16 refers to which of the following phenomena?
    a. gender nonconformity
    b. imprinting
    c. bioluminescence
    d. intersex

36. Homosexuality in other species
    a. occurs only under controlled laboratory conditions.
    b. results only from the manipulation of hormones during development.
    c. sometimes resembles heterosexuality (e.g., pair bonding, parenting).
    d. is never observed.

37. LeVay's study of brain anatomy showed that the INAH3 is largest in
    a. heterosexual males.
    b. homosexual males.
    c. heterosexual females.
    d. homosexual females.

38. Homosexual and transsexual males respond more strongly to which of the following presumed pheromones?
    a. TET
    b. EST
    c. AND
    d. PRO

39. Which of the following in homosexual women is most male-like?
    a. refractory periods after the resolution phase
    b. increases in testosterone in the MPOA and SDN
    c. weaker evoked otoacoustic emissions
    d. smaller INAH3 volumes

40. According to the text, why haven't people with gender identity differences been classified as minorities according to civil liberties statutes?
    a. Because civil liberties are based on the Christian faith in the United States.
    b. There is not enough funds in the budget to cover the cost of changing federal paperwork to include other gender identities.
    c. Minorities by definition are "defective" labels that are used to medically remove those characteristics from the population.
    d. A minority is classified as a group with a predefined set of inborn characteristics.

41. About what percentage of the homosexual population believes that homosexuality is inborn and that they have no choice?
    a. 10%
    b. 25%
    c. 50%
    d. 75%

## Answers

### Guided Review

1. satiation
2. tissue
3. Masters and Johnson
4. excitement
5. plateau
6. orgasm
7. ejaculation
8. resolution
9. women
10. refractory
11. Coolidge
12. greater
13. castration
14. decline
15. androgens
16. testosterone
17. estrus
18. ovulation
19. estrogen
20. testosterone
21. MPOA (medial preoptic area)
22. performance/behavior
23. copulate
24. medial
25. SDN (sexually dimorphic nucleus)
26. ventromedial
27. Dopamine
28. erection
29. $D_2$
30. sympathetic
31. accumbens
32. serotonin
33. odors
34. histocompatibility
35. pheromones
36. nasal
37. olfactory bulbs
38. 10,000
39. vomeronasal
40. genes
41. MPOA
42. amygdala
43. menstrual
44. ovulating
45. anterior hypothalamic
46. dopamine
47. oxytocin
48. vasopressin
49. orgasm
50. recognition
51. gender
52. identity
53. fertilization
54. X
55. female
56. male
57. ovaries
58. Müllerian
59. Wolffian
60. clitoris
61. labia
62. 6
63. testes
64. Müllerian-inhibiting

65. testosterone
66. seminal
67. Dihydrotestosterone
68. scrotum
69. organizing
70. activating
71. puberty
72. genitals
73. ova/eggs
74. critical
75. lordosis
76. testosterone
77. estradiol
78. Macoby and Jacklin
79. verbal
80. mathematics
81. aggressive
82. overlap
83. mathematics
84. cultural
85. gestation/pregnancy
86. spatial
87. verbal
88. spatial
89. testosterone
90. increases
91. hemispheres
92. frontal
93. parietal
94. autism
95. depression
96. transsexual
97. BSTc or INAH-3
98. INAH-3 or BSTc
99. difference of sexual development

100. gonads
101. hydroxysteroid
102. dihydrotestosterone
103. testosterone
104. Dominican Republic
105. culture/environment
106. Androgen Insensitivity
107. testes
108. breasts
109. androgens
110. penis
111. labia
112. Congenital Adrenal Hyperplasia
113. reconstructive
114. intersexes
115. gender
116. testosterone
117. normal
118. verbal
119. spatial
120. female
121. female
122. homosexual/bisexual
123. bisexual/homosexual
124. homosexual
125. sexuality
126. circumcision
127. ablatio penis
128. bisexual
129. 3%
130. homosexual
131. asexuality
132. social
133. bisexual
134. nonconformity

135. concordance

136. X

137. mother's

138. 64

139. Darwinian

140. men

141. imprinting

142. sensitivity

143. sheep

144. development

145. AND

146. anterior hypothalamus

147. suprachiasmatic or SCN

148. vasopressin

149. female

150. index to ring-finger

151. otoacoustic

152. androgen

153. maternal immunity

154. choice

155. biological

156. genetic

157. acceptable

## Short Answer and Essay Questions

1. Sex and hunger are similar in that they are under the regulation of the brain and hormones, and they both involve arousal and satiation. However, there are important differences. Usually, we eat to reduce hunger, but we seek out stimuli that will increase sexual arousal. Hunger is also more controlled by internal conditions, including tissue needs, whereas sexual arousal is relatively more responsive to external conditions.

2. The phases are excitement, plateau, orgasm, and resolution.

3. Testosterone seems to be required for sexual motivation in both men and women, although only a low level appears to be necessary. However, sexual activity also increases testosterone levels, so the picture is somewhat complicated. In both men and women, castration leads to a reduction of sexual functioning. Men who are voluntarily castrated or are given testosterone-blocking drugs show reduced aggression and sexual tendencies. In women, testosterone levels are correlated with initiating sexual activity. When given testosterone, women show more sexual responsiveness.

4. For females and males, the important brain areas are the MPOA and the medial amygdala. For males, the paraventricular nucleus and the sexually dimorphic nucleus (SDN, in the MPOA) are also involved. In females, the ventromedial hypothalamus plays a role in sexual behavior.

5. Pheromones are airborne chemicals released by an animal that affect the behavior and physiology of members of the same species. They exert their effects mostly via the vomeronasal organ, though there is evidence for some pheromone receptors in the olfactory system. Some research shows that pheromones might be involved in menstrual synchrony in women living together in dorms, and both men and women have reported increased sexual activity when exposed to underarm extracts (presumed to contain pheromones). Also, pheromones in women's sweat (the T-shirt study) may be more attractive to men when she is in mid-cycle.

6. Internally, the primitive gonads develop into either ovaries or testes; development of testes is dependent on the presence of the SRY gene on the Y chromosome. Without the presence of dihydrotestosterone, the external genitalia will become a clitoris, outer segment of the vagina, and labia, which is typical for females. If dihydrotestosterone is present, as it is in males, then the external structures become a penis and scrotum.

7. Organizing effects typically occur when the developing individual is first exposed to the hormone, either before or shortly after birth. This exposure leads to permanent changes in bodily structures. One example is how dihydrotestosterone changes the primitive external genital structures into a penis and scrotum, but there are many other examples in the book. Activating effects can occur any time in the life span after the initial exposure when hormone levels change, and they are reversible. An example is the development of breast tissue in females during puberty, but there are other examples in the book as well.

8. Normal female rats typically engage in lordosis, although they will occasionally mount other females. In females that have been masculinized, mounting occurs much more frequently.

9. The book cites a study by Miles et al. that showed transsexual males taking estrogen supplements scored higher on verbal tasks than those not taking estrogen.

10. He uses the term "other" to reflect the fact that males and females are not really opposite. There are some consistent differences, but even in these there is a great deal of overlap between the sexes. Overall, males and females share more similarities than they do differences. (And later in the chapter you will see that the lines between "male" and "female" as sexes are not as clear as you might think.)

11. Because they do not have ovaries, they do not menstruate and they certainly cannot become pregnant. So during adolescence or early adulthood, they will probably discover their condition if they try to determine the source of problems with their reproductive systems. If diagnosis does not occur at that time, it may after the individual engages in sex and realizes she has a shallow vagina.

12. Yes, because the development of the uterus is determined by the absence of Müllerian-inhibiting hormone, which CAH females are not exposed to.

13. They are insensitive to the effects of masculinizing hormones. Even females outperform them on spatial tasks because their brains are capable of responding to the small amount of androgens their bodies produce.

14. After Semenya won the gold medal in a key track event, some people became suspicious about her gender due to her strong performance and masculine appearance. Her sports participation remained in jeopardy for a year while the International Association of Athletic Federations evaluated the results of her gender testing. Eventually, she was cleared to participate as a woman. This case forced the IAAF to create a clearer definition of gender in their gender verification policy.

15. It may influence some women, as evidenced by the fact that more CAH women reported homosexual contact than a control group of women. However, we can't ignore that some of the normal women behaved like the minority of the CAH women who had homosexual contact and that most of the CAH women did not report homosexual contact. Clearly, CAH is not the only factor.

16. Each case involves only a single individual, so generalizing to others is very difficult. Another problem is that these were not experiments, and there was virtually no control over the many factors influencing gender.

17. Studying individuals with different sexual and gender identity from the majority of humans, and in particular the differences in brain function, can help us discover what the determinants are of sexual orientation. Doing so will tell us not only why some people exhibit homosexual behaviors, but also why others are heterosexual, bisexual, or gender-neutral.

18. The social learning hypothesis suggests that people who have early homosexual experiences will be more likely to become homosexual later. There is evidence for this; for

example, individuals who reported having other-sex friends, masturbating in the presence of or being masturbated by a same-sex partner, and having homosexual contact prior to age 18 were more likely to be homosexual as adults. But an alternative interpretation is that these experiences are early manifestations of an underlying homosexual tendency rather than the origin of homosexuality.

19. It seems unlikely that natural selection would favor a trait such as homosexuality that reduces the likelihood of reproduction. Homosexuality may result from an epigenetic process, rather than inheritance of "genes for homosexuality."

20. A problem with studying the brains of older homosexuals is that they have been practicing homosexual behavior for a longer period of time, so it is unclear whether any brain differences found would be the cause of sexual orientation or the result of homosexual experience. Also, gay men who have died from AIDS may have brains that look different as a result of the disease.

21. They are concerned that if a biological basis to homosexuality is discovered, it will be understood in terms of a physical abnormality that can be corrected medically to "cure" homosexuality or genetically to prevent it.

## Post-test

1. c    2. a    3. b    4. e    5. c    6. d    7. a    8. b    9. c    10. c & d    11. c    12. d
13. c    14. a    15. d    16. b    17. c    18. d    19. d    20. a    21. c    22. c    23. a
24. a    25. a    26. d    27. b    28. c    29. a    30. c    31. a    32. d    33. c    34. d
35. b    36. c    37. a    38. c    39. c    40. d    41. d

# 8  Emotion and Health

## Learning Objectives

After reading this chapter, you should be able to answer the following questions.

1.  What occurs during the four phases of the cycle of sexual arousal and satiation? Describe the differences between men and women with respect to what happens after the fourth phase.

2.  How does the case of Jane at the beginning of the chapter demonstrate the importance of emotions in regulating behavior?

3.  How is the autonomic nervous system involved in emotions?

4.  How do the James-Lange and cognitive theories differ in their explanation of emotions? What evidence is there for these positions?

5.  What are the roles of the hypothalamus, insular cortex, basal ganglia, anterior cingulate cortex, prefrontal cortex, and amygdala in emotion?

6.  What are the different contributions of the two hemispheres to emotion?

7.  In what ways is stress an adaptive response?

8.  What are the negative effects of stress?

9.  How are social and personality variables related to immune functioning?

10. Why is pain considered to be an emotion?

11. How are hormones related to aggression?

12. What brain areas are involved in aggression?

13. How is serotonin involved in aggression? (Include in your answer a discussion of serotonin's interactions with alcohol and testosterone.)

14. How do genes and environment interact to influence aggression?

## Emotion and the Nervous System

### Summary and Guided Review

After studying this section in the text, fill in the blanks of the following summary.

Emotions enrich our lives and _____ (1) our behavior. For example, anger intensifies _____ (2) behavior and accelerates flight, whereas happiness encourages the behavior that produces it. Emotions make experiences more _____ (3), so we are likely to repeat behaviors that bring joy and avoid those that produce pain. Jane was unable to _____ (4) from her emotional experiences, due to damage to her _____ (5) cortex. As Damasio would have said about this case, reason without _____ (6) is inadequate for making the decisions that guide our lives.

Emotions involve subjective "feelings," expressions, and behavior, all of which are rooted in the nervous system. For example, the autonomic nervous system is intimately involved in emotional responding; activation of the _____ (7) branch produces arousal, and the _____ (8) branch helps to reduce activity and restore bodily resources. _____ (9) is an important hormone released from the adrenal glands in times of stress, due to activation of the sympathetic nervous system.

In the late 1900s an American psychologist and a Danish physiologist independently proposed what has become known as the _____-_____ (10) theory of emotion, which states that emotional experience results from the physiological arousal that precedes it. In an experiment in which subjects were made angry or frightened, the two emotions were accompanied by _____ (11) patterns of physiological activity. Years later, Schacter and Singer interpreted these results based on _____ (12) theory, stating that the _____ (13) of the emotion is based on cognitive assessment of the situation, and physiological arousal only determines the emotion's _____ (14). This theory is supported by the finding that similar patterns of arousal can be interpreted differently, based on the _____ (15) context. More recently, studies of facial expression in emotion have added support for the James-Lange theory. Ekman found that posed facial expressions could actually produce the _____ (16) of the intended emotion. When a woman's facial muscles are paralyzed with injections of _____ (17) it affects the ability not only to produce facial expressions of emotion, but to experience them as well; this has been verified by fMRI evidence of reduced activation of the amygdala while trying to imitate angry expressions. Feedback from emotional expressions may also help us _____ (18) other people's emotions, which is critical to social communication. Special cells in the brain called _____ (19) neurons may be involved in our ability to show _____ (20) for others, based on the finding that observation of other people's emotions activate our own "emotional brain" pathways. People with _____ (21) have difficulty understanding the emotions of others; they can imitate expressions but the mimicry is delayed.

There are several brain structures that play important roles in emotions. Many of these areas are located in the _____ (22) system, which also contributes to learning, memory, and motivation. In humans undergoing brain surgery, Heath found that electrical stimulation of the _____ (23) elicited autonomic arousal, and patients reported feeling different emotions, depending on the placement of the electrode. Sexual interest seems to be at least in part a result of stimulation of the _____ (24) area. Recent brain imaging studies indicate that the _____ (25) cortex and _____ _____ (26) are involved in disgust. Because it combines emotional, attentional, and bodily information, the anterior _____ (27) cortex is believed to be important for cognitive processing of emotion. This structure is also larger on the right side in people who manifest _____ (28) avoidance, which involves worry about possible problems, fearfulness, and shyness. Although research has linked emotions to particular brain areas, it is important to remember that no emotion can be linked to a(n) _____ (29) part of the brain.

Patients with damage to the prefrontal cortex have difficulty making rational _____ (30). When damage includes the _____ (31) cortex, people show a lack of responsiveness to a gambling task; their skin _____ (32) response is not affected by risk, and they do not learn to avoid making risky choices. In _____ (33) seekers, brain scans have found strong connections in a loop involving the hippocampus, amygdala, and striatum. But as discussed in the Application, _____ (34) dependent individuals have the strongest connections between the striatum and the _____ (35) areas.

The _____ (36), a limbic structure that sends information to the prefrontal cortex, is especially involved in the negative emotions of fear and

_____ (37). Rats with damage to the amygdala display no _____ (38) of cats, and humans with damaged amygdala are very trusting of others and have difficulty identifying fearful _____ _____ (39) in others. Furthermore, they seem incapable of learning to recognize harmful situations or experiencing emotional responses to rewards and _____ (40).

There are hemispheric differences in emotion; the left hemisphere seems to be more involved in _____ (41) emotions, while the right hemisphere is more involved in _____ (42) emotions. Right hemisphere damage has been linked to impairment of emotional responses and perception of emotions in others, perhaps because people with such damage have diminished _____ (43) response. People with right hemisphere damage often speak in an unemotional _____ (44) and have trouble recognizing emotion from a person's speech.

## Short Answer and Essay Questions

Answer the following questions.

1. Many people believe that decision making should be guided by rationality and that emotion leads to bad decisions. After reading this section of the chapter, do you agree with this view? Why or why not?

2. Compare the James-Lange and cognitive theories of emotion.

3. Identify key brain areas involved in emotion. How do the right and left hemispheres differ in the role they play in emotion?

4. Give an example of how emotional experiences are adaptive (how they promote survival).

# Stress, Immunity, and Health

## Summary and Guided Review

After studying this section in the text, fill in the blanks of the following summary.

The term _____ (45) is used to refer to external events that challenge an organism as well as internal responses to the challenge. The internal experience of stress is highly variable; not everyone feels stress under the same conditions.

Usually, the internal changes associated with stress are positive and _____ (46). These include activation of the _____-_____-_____ (47) axis, a mechanism responsible for the release of stress _____ (48) that prepare the body for "fight or flight" via their effects on circulation and energy availability. For example, the stress hormone _____ (49) converts proteins to glucose and increases both fat availability and _____ (50); this provides more energy for a longer period of time than _____ (51) nervous system does, for prolonged stressful situations. Changes also occur in the _____ (52) system, which protects the body against foreign substances that could be introduced during injury. There are several types of _____ (53), including macrophages, T cells, and antibody-producing _____ (54). Another type of immune cell, _____ _____ (55) cells, destroy cancer and viral-infected cells. The final type of immune cell, the _____ (56), acts in a similar fashion as a macrophage,

protecting the central nervous system from invaders that penetrate the blood-brain barrier. In
_____ (57) disorders, such as multiple sclerosis and AIDS, the immune
system improperly attacks the body's own cells.

   If the stress response continues over a long period of time, considerable harm can
occur, including memory_____ (58), motivational changes, mood
changes, and immune system impairment. People in the vicinity of the Three Mile
Island nuclear accident continued to experience reduced immune functioning as long as
_____ (59) years after the event. In another study, volunteers exposed
to cold viruses were more likely to develop _____ (60) if they had
experienced stress for longer than a month. Increased vulnerability to stress may produce
cardiovascular disease, as evidenced by the fact that children who were more reactive to
having their hands placed in _____ _____ (61)
were more likely to have high blood pressure as adults. There is even evidence that acute
stress can lead to sudden _____ _____ (62). For
example, on the day of the 1994 earthquake in Southern California, the number of deaths
due to _____ _____ (63) was five times higher
than average. Stress may also contribute to brain damage in victims of torture or abuse,
particularly in the _____ (64), perhaps due to prolonged exposure or
greater sensitivity to cortisol. Combat veterans as well as victims of childhood trauma have
reduced hippocampal volume are frequently diagnosed with _____
_____ _____ (65) disorder (PTSD). Cardiac
events can even increase during the first few days after the springtime change to
_____ _____ (66) time due to the loss of an hour of
sleep. Keeping odd hours can even make you sick; disrupting our day-night cycle increases
T-cell counts, which may be the cause for _____ (67) diseases like heart
disease, asthma, chronic pain, and autoimmune disease. Removing stress, on the other hand,
can improve health.

   Social, _____ (68), and genetic factors are linked to stress-related
health problems as well. For example, people who are _____ (69)
are more likely to suffer from heart disease, and among _____ (70)
patients, those who lose hope or accept their disease have a lower survival rate than those
who display a fighting spirit. Individuals with greater left prefrontal activity (associated with
positive emotion) developed more antibodies following _____ (71)
vaccination. Introverted HIV-positive men had _____ (72) viral loads
than extroverts, presumably because of elevated neurotransmitter levels. However, these
studies are correlational, so personality may not be the sole reason for immune response
differences. Vulnerability to stress is heritable, and researchers have implicated two genes in
the stress response: individuals with a low-functioning version of _____
_____ (73) reported more negative emotions when anticipating
unpleasant events. Stress may trigger _____ (74) changes to these genes,
which could be inherited by their offspring.

   Like stress, _____ (75) is in many ways an adaptive response.
People with congenital _____ (76) to pain have difficulty learning
to avoid injuries and may die from untreated injuries. Pain can be considered a(n)
_____ (77) response as well as a sensation. How people experience
pain varies on an individual and cultural basis. For example, in the United States
_____ (78) is considered more painful than it is in some other cultures.
A study of World War II soldiers wounded in combat revealed that 68% refused morphine,
compared with only 17% of civilian patients receiving similar _____ (79)
procedures. While the soldiers still felt pain, they were better able to cope with it since it was
a signal that they were still alive.

Pathways that carry pain messages connect to the _____
(80) area, the cortex dealing with body sensations, and the _____
_____ (81) cortex, which is involved in the emotional component of pain.
The _____ (82) cortex is also involved in emotional responses to pain;
it is presumably where pain is evaluated and a response to it is planned. This area is also
implicated in cases of pain _____ (83) disorders, where individuals feel
pain but are not bothered by it.

## Short Answer and Essay Questions

Answer the following questions.

5. List the four types of immune cells discussed in the book, and explain the function of each.

6. Discuss the role of personality factors in cancer survival. Why is it difficult to determine if factors such as introversion are directly responsible for reduced immune functioning?

7. Why is pain considered to be adaptive? What would your life be like if you could not feel, or were not bothered by, pain?

8. Discuss the role of the anterior cingulate cortex in pain. How do researchers know that it is involved in the emotional response to, but not the sensation of, pain?

# Biological Origins of Aggression

## Summary and Guided Review

After studying this section in the text, fill in the blanks of the following summary.

_____ (84) is defined as a behavior intended to do harm. It
is sometimes, but not always, an adaptive response, involving both motivation and
_____ (85). There are several different forms of aggression. The cold,
emotionless form is _____ (86) aggression, when an animal attacks
and kills prey, or when a person commits a premeditated, unprovoked attack on another
individual. Another form is _____ (87) aggression, which is characterized
by its impulsiveness and emotional arousal. Researchers have frequently separated this latter
form into offensive (attacking another) and defensive (responding to threat) aggression.

The sex hormones seem to be especially involved in offensive affective aggression,
particularly in rats. Studies suggest that increased aggression is linked to low
_____ (88) and progesterone levels found in women suffering
from _____ (89) syndrome, and violent criminals have higher
_____ (90) levels. However, the causal relationship between
hormones and aggression is not clear, because it has been shown that testosterone
_____ (91) while watching one's team win a sports event, and even after
receiving a college degree.

Defensive and predatory aggressions in cats involve different brain pathways
in the amygdala, hypothalamus, and _____ (92) gray (PAG).
_____ (93) aggression travels from the medial amygdala to the medial
hypothalamus, and then to the dorsal PAG. In contrast, _____ (94)
aggression travels from the central and lateral amygdala to the later hypothalamus, and then
to the ventral PAG.

People who exhibit affective and impulsive aggression also show persistently reduced _____ (95) activity in the prefrontal cortex and anterior cingulate gyrus. Evidence for serotonin's causal role in aggression comes from a study in which men deprived of _____ (96), a serotonin precursor, displayed more aggression in a mock competition than controls. In a study performed on monkeys, those with high _____ (97) levels and low serotonin levels were most likely to be impulsive and aggressive to others. In humans, there also is a similar relationship seen, particularly in violent offenders when _____ (98) is involved. In fact, low serotonin levels and alcohol consumption create a deadly cycle of _____ (99) alcohol and aggression. Drugs that inhibit serotonin reuptake at the synapse, such as the _____ (100) fluoxetine, reduce alcohol intake and aggressiveness.

Although there is a genetic basis for aggression, _____ (101) % of the variation among people in aggression is genetic, the environment also plays a role. For example, inadequate _____ (102) as well as psychological and social _____ (103) may contribute to violent criminality in both men and women. Several studies suggest that genes and environment interact. The MAO-L _____ (104) of the MAOA gene results in low levels of the enzyme; this allele was discovered in a Dutch family with a large number of violent males. The allele has also been found to predict males' membership in _____ (105) and their use of weapons in fights. The interaction of genes and environment in aggression is demonstrated by the finding that the MAO-L allele only produced violence in males who had been subjected to childhood physical abuse. A new field of research, called _____ (106), uses our knowledge of the neural, genetic, and environmental influences on violent behavior to understand and prevent criminal behavior. One factor for human aggression is a deficiency in _____ (107) area function; reduced gray matter is seen in individuals with _____ _____ (108) disorder, characterized by reckless, self-fulfilling behaviors and an absence of empathy for others. The _____ (109) is also involved in aggression: individuals with seizures in this area are more violent, and individuals with damage are less so.

Three neurotransmitters are most frequently implicated in studies on aggression. The first, _____ (110), are high in the prefrontal cortex and accumbens in animals before, during, and after an aggressive encounter. In humans, decreasing the neurotransmitters also decrease violence in psychiatric patients. Research suggests that the second, _____ (111), plays a role in inhibiting violence and aggression; low levels are found in aggressive rodents and men. Psychiatric patients taking _____ (112), which raises neurotransmitter levels, also were less likely to have violent outbursts. The last, serotonin, increases a person's appetite for both nutrients as well as sex and drugs, presumably due to its role in stimulating dopamine release. An individual prone to _____ (113) and psychopathic behavior tends to have elevated dopamine levels for more than an hour after a confrontation.

## Short Answer and Essay Questions

Answer the following questions.

9. Distinguish between predatory and affective aggression, and defensive and offensive aggression. Give an example of each.

10. Identify the specific nuclei of the amygdala, hypothalamus, and periaqueductal gray involved in defensive and predatory aggression.

11. Describe how Moeller and colleagues demonstrated a causal relationship between low serotonin levels and aggression in humans. From this study, can we say for sure that low serotonin causes aggression in humans? Why or why not?

12. Describe some environmental influences in aggression.

13. What are the characteristics of people with antisocial personality disorder? What brain anomaly may account for this disorder?

14. Explain how serotonin, dopamine, and alcohol interact in contributing to aggression.

15. Describe how dopamine and GABA contribute to aggression. How does serotonin affect dopamine levels? Be sure to include drugs that can reduce violent behaviors when each is out of balance.

## Post-test

Use these multiple-choice questions to check your understanding of the chapter.

1. Sympathetic arousal involves all of the following EXCEPT
   a. increased heart rate.
   b. increased blood pressure.
   c. increased respiration.
   d. increased digestion.

2. According to the James-Lange theory, emotional experiences occur in which order?
   a. stimulus-arousal-emotion
   b. stimulus-emotion-arousal
   c. stimulus-appraisal-emotion
   d. stimulus-arousal/appraisal-emotion

3. Which of the following is NOT true about mirror neurons?
   a. They respond both when we engage in a specific act and when we observe the same act in others.
   b. They show increased activity in autism.
   c. They most likely play a role in the emotion of empathy.
   d. They were discovered when researchers noted that the same neurons responded when monkeys reached for food and when they saw the researcher pick up food.

4. Studies of physiological changes during negative emotions indicate that
   a. there are no differences in autonomic arousal patterns for different negative emotions.
   b. blood pressure increases more during anger.
   c. heart rate increases more during sadness than fear.
   d. fear involves less motor activation than sadness.

5. Facial expressions
   a. are probably less important in emotional feedback than autonomic arousal.
   b. are all learned from one's family. ——
   c. can evoke emotions consistent with the expression.
   d. none of the above

6. Which of the following structures is NOT considered part of the limbic system?
   a. amygdala
   b. cingulate gyrus

c. hippocampus
d. medulla

7. In the gambling task described in this chapter, individuals with ventromedial prefrontal damage
   a. produced a strong skin conductance response to the risky piles, but did not learn to avoid choosing from the risky card piles.
   b. did not produce a strong skin conductance response to any pile, but learned to avoid choosing from the risky card piles anyway.
   c. did not produce a strong skin conductance response to any pile, and did not learn to avoid choosing from the risky card piles.
   d. produced a strong skin conductance response to the risk piles, and learned to avoid choosing from the risky card piles.

8. In an early study by Heath with humans, stimulation of the septal area evoked
   a. pleasure.
   b. fear.
   c. anxiety.
   d. sadness.

9. In an MRI study, investigators found that the right ___ was larger in people with high scores on ___ avoidance.
   a. hippocampus; pain
   b. amygdala; predator
   c. anterior cingulate; harm
   d. prefrontal cortex; alcohol

10. Someone with heightened activity in the amygdala would be MOST likely to experience
    a. pleasure.
    b. anxiety.
    c. anger.
    d. sadness.

11. People with damage to the amygdala
    a. are completely fearless.
    b. often exhibit fits of rage.
    c. have difficulty learning to avoid harmful situations.
    d. suffer from antisocial personality disorder.

12. People with prefrontal damage can probably do all of the following EXCEPT
    a. experience any emotion at all.
    b. learn to avoid venomous snakes.
    c. experience negative emotions.
    d. learn to avoid risky investments.

13. People with right hemisphere damage have difficulty with all of the following EXCEPT
    a. recognizing facial expressions in others.
    b. recognizing emotion in others' voices.
    c. understanding verbal expressions of emotion.
    d. displaying nonverbal signs of emotion.

14. Cortisol is released by the
    a. hypothalamus.
    b. pituitary gland.

    c. adrenal glands.
    d. all of the above

15. Cortisol is responsible for all of the following EXCEPT
    a. increased oxygen transport to muscle cells.
    b. conversion of protein to glucose.
    c. increase in fat availability.
    d. increase in metabolism.

16. Immune system cells that work by ingesting foreign substances and then displaying their antigens are called
    a. T cells.
    b. B cells.
    c. macrophages.
    d. natural killer cells.

17. Which of the following is not a leukocyte?
    a. T cells
    b. B cells
    c. macrophages
    d. natural killer cells

18. Following the Three Mile Island accident, nearby residents displayed
    a. a reduced number of immune cells.
    b. a higher cancer rate.
    c. a reduced ability to concentrate.
    d. a and c

19. Children who showed the greatest amount of reactivity (in terms of blood pressure increase) when placing their hands in cold water were MORE likely to develop
    a. cancer as children.
    b. cancer as adults.
    c. high blood pressure as children.
    d. high blood pressure as adults.

20. Sudden cardiac death may be linked to
    a. stress.
    b. earthquakes.
    c. sports.
    d. all of the above

21. Which of the following structures is not one of the ones that helps the body cope with stress?
    a. hypothalamus
    b. hippocampus
    c. pituitary gland
    d. adrenal glands

22. Brain damage in posttraumatic stress may be due to increased sensitivity to
    a. cortisol.
    b. norepinephrine.
    c. epinephrine.
    d. all of the above

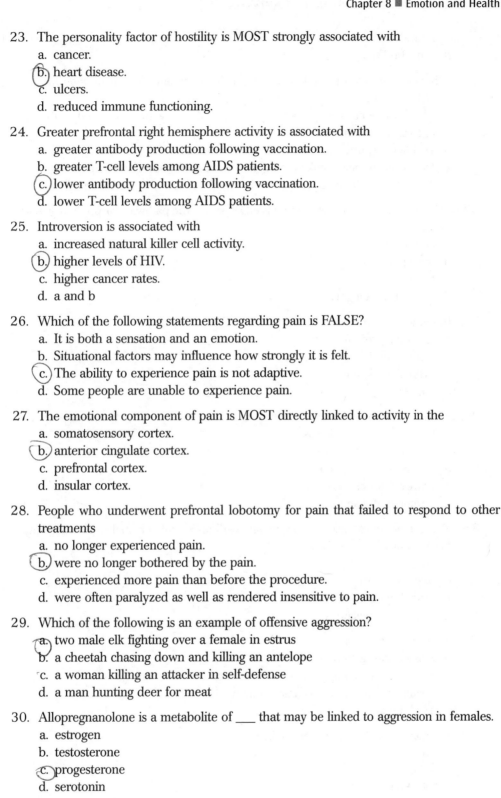

23. The personality factor of hostility is MOST strongly associated with
    a. cancer.
    b. heart disease.
    c. ulcers.
    d. reduced immune functioning.

24. Greater prefrontal right hemisphere activity is associated with
    a. greater antibody production following vaccination.
    b. greater T-cell levels among AIDS patients.
    c. lower antibody production following vaccination.
    d. lower T-cell levels among AIDS patients.

25. Introversion is associated with
    a. increased natural killer cell activity.
    b. higher levels of HIV.
    c. higher cancer rates.
    d. a and b

26. Which of the following statements regarding pain is FALSE?
    a. It is both a sensation and an emotion.
    b. Situational factors may influence how strongly it is felt.
    c. The ability to experience pain is not adaptive.
    d. Some people are unable to experience pain.

27. The emotional component of pain is MOST directly linked to activity in the
    a. somatosensory cortex.
    b. anterior cingulate cortex.
    c. prefrontal cortex.
    d. insular cortex.

28. People who underwent prefrontal lobotomy for pain that failed to respond to other treatments
    a. no longer experienced pain.
    b. were no longer bothered by the pain.
    c. experienced more pain than before the procedure.
    d. were often paralyzed as well as rendered insensitive to pain.

29. Which of the following is an example of offensive aggression?
    a. two male elk fighting over a female in estrus
    b. a cheetah chasing down and killing an antelope
    c. a woman killing an attacker in self-defense
    d. a man hunting deer for meat

30. Allopregnanolone is a metabolite of ___ that may be linked to aggression in females.
    a. estrogen
    b. testosterone
    c. progesterone
    d. serotonin

31. Among prisoners, testosterone would probably be LOWEST in those convicted of which of the following crimes?
    a. drug offenses
    b. rape

c. murder

d. armed robbery

32. Which of the following statements regarding hormones and aggression in humans is FALSE?

a. The hormonal changes accompanying PMS may be associated with increased aggression in women.

b. Winning a sporting event increases testosterone.

c. High testosterone is linked to aggression in men but not women.

d. Their peers rate male prisoners with higher testosterone as tougher.

33. Which of the following structures is NOT part of the pathway for predatory aggression in cats?

a. amygdala

b. hypothalamus

c. thalamus

d. periaqueductal gray

34. In humans, aggression is linked to

a. excessive prefrontal activity.

b. seizures in the amygdala.

c. hypothalamic tumors.

d. b and c

35. Monkeys who are impulsive, reckless, and prone to aggressive behavior probably have high ___ and low ___ levels.

a. serotonin; testosterone

b. testosterone; serotonin

c. estrogen; testosterone

d. serotonin; dopamine

36. The impulsiveness displayed by people with antisocial personality disorder may result from abnormalities of the

a. amygdala.

b. prefrontal cortex.

c. medial hypothalamus.

d. lateral hypothalamus.

37. Proactive aggression

a. is associated with psychopathy.

b. is premeditated, unprovoked, and lacks emotional intensity.

c. is similar to predatory aggression in animals.

d. all of the above

38. Tryptophan is a(n) ___ of serotonin.

a. precursor

b. antagonist

c. metabolite

d. agonist

39. Men who drank a substance that inhibited tryptophan

a. were more likely to physically attack their opponents.

b. were more likely to lose points to their opponents.

c. were more likely to take points away from their opponents.

d. showed elevated 5-HIAA levels.

40. Prozac (fluoxetine) reduces all of the following EXCEPT
    a. alcohol cravings.
    b. serotonin levels.
    c. aggression.
    d. alcohol consumption.

41. Alcohol appears to influence aggression only in people who have
    a. high testosterone levels.
    b. low GABA levels.
    c. low dopamine levels.
    d. low serotonin levels.

42. Heredity accounts for about ___% of the variability in aggression.
    a. 50
    b. 75
    c. 25
    d. 15

43. Benzodiazepines, which ___ GABA activity, ___ impulsive, violent outbursts in psychiatric patients.
    a. reduces; reduces
    b. reduces; increases
    c. increases; reduces
    d. increases; increases

# Answers

## Guided Review

1. motivate
2. defensive
3. memorable
4. learn
5. prefrontal
6. emotion
7. sympathetic
8. parasympathetic
9. cortisol
10. James-Lange
11. different
12. cognitive
13. identity
14. intensity
15. environmental
16. experience
17. Botox
18. recognize/understand
19. mirror
20. empathy
21. autism
22. limbic
23. hypothalamus
24. septal
25. insular
26. basal ganglia
27. cingulate
28. harm
29. single
30. judgments
31. ventromedial
32. conductance
33. novelty
34. reward
35. prefrontal
36. amygdala
37. anxiety
38. fear
39. strangers
40. panic attacks
41. positive
42. negative
43. autonomic
44. monotone
45. stress
46. adaptive
47. hypothalamus-pituitary-adrenal
48. hormones
49. cortisol
50. metabolism
51. sympathetic
52. immune
53. leukocytes
54. B cells
55. natural killer
56. microglia
57. autoimmune
58. impairment
59. 6
60. infections
61. cold water
62. cardiac death
63. heart attacks
64. hippocampus

65. posttraumatic stress disorder
66. daylight savings time
67. inflammatory
68. personality
69. hostile
70. cancer
71. influenza (flu)
72. higher
73. neuropeptide Y
74. epigenetic
75. pain
76. insensitivity
77. emotional
78. childbirth
79. surgical
80. somatosensory
81. anterior cingulate
82. prefrontal
83. insensitivity
84. aggression
85. emotion
86. predatory
87. affective
88. estrogen
89. premenstrual

90. testosterone
91. increases
92. periaqueductal
93. Defensive
94. predatory
95. serotonin
96. tryptophan
97. testosterone
98. alcohol
99. craving
100. antidepressant
101. 50%
102. parenting
103. deprivation
104. allele
105. gangs
106. neurocriminology
107. prefrontal
108. antisocial personality
109. amygdala
110. dopamine
111. GABA
112. benzodiazepines
113. violence

## Short Answer and Essay Questions

1. Answers may vary on this question. However, the author makes a compelling argument against the distinction between rationality and emotion. In particular, the studies of people whose emotional capacities are impaired suggest that without emotion, we would not make very good decisions. For example, people with prefrontal damage seem to be unable to learn from the emotions that normally accompany rewards and punishment, and so their behavior is often impulsive.

2. The James-Lange theory states that emotional experience results from the physiological arousal that precedes, and different emotions are the result of, different patterns of arousal. The cognitive theory of emotion stated that the identity of the emotion is based on the cognitive assessment of the situation, and physiological arousal contributes only to the emotion's intensity.

3. The important systems are the parts of the limbic system, including the hypothalamus, septal area, insula, anterior cingulate cortex, amygdala, and prefrontal cortex. The right hemisphere seems more important in negative emotions, whereas the left hemisphere is more active during positive emotions.

4. There are many possible answers, but a correct response should refer to the role of emotions in decision making, communication, preparation or motivation for a response, or learning.

5. Macrophages are a type of leukocyte that engulf and ingest invading microorganisms, then display the antigens of the invader, attracting T cells. The T cells than multiply and destroy the invaders. B cells produce antibodies that fight off specific intruders. Natural killer cells target cancer cells and virus-infected cells; they are less specific than T and B cells.

6. Cancer survival is higher among patients with a fighting spirit and lower among those who are depressed. However, this research is correlational, which makes cause and effect difficult to determine. A good example comes from the association between introversion and HIV levels in AIDS. The introverted patients had high levels of sympathetic activity. Increased sympathetic activity is caused by epinephrine and norepinephrine, both of which are high in introverted individuals, and norepinephrine increases HIV virus multiplication in the laboratory. Thus, norepinephrine may be responsible for both the introversion and the HIV virus proliferation in the subjects; personality characteristics and emotional states may be more of a marker for physiological activity that results in the health condition rather than a causal influence.

7. Pain is adaptive because it lets us know when we have done something that is harmful, and therefore we can learn to avoid such behaviors. People who are insensitive to or are not bothered by pain do not respond to the warning signals of pain and are subject to greater injury; lacking the emotional deterrent, they have difficulty learning to avoid behaviors that can lead to injury.

8. The anterior cingulate cortex appears to mediate the emotional aspect of pain. When a painful stimulus is presented several times and participants feel increasing unpleasantness (but the stimulus remains the same), there are changes in the anterior cingulate cortex, but not the somatosensory cortex. Also, when participants under hypnosis are instructed that a painful stimulus is becoming more unpleasant (again, without any change in the stimulus), the same result occurs.

9. Predatory aggression involves a premeditated, unprovoked attack on another individual, such as when a male lion kills the offspring of a rival male. This type of aggression generally lacks the emotional components seen in the other forms of aggression. Affective aggression involves a response to a threat or attack and is motivated by fear. An example of this is when an animal fights back when cornered by another animal. This form is usually impulsive and motivated by emotion, usually fear or anger. There are two different subtypes of affective aggression. Offensive aggression occurs when an animal makes an unprovoked attack upon another due to a perceived threat. An example of this is when a person, after many acts of abuse, kills his or her abuser before another assault is committed. Defensive aggression is when an animal fights back when being attacked, such as a snake biting an attacking mongoose.

10. Defensive aggression: medial nucleus of amygdala to the medial hypothalamus to the dorsal periaqueductal gray. Predatory aggression: lateral and central nuclei of amygdala to the lateral hypothalamus to the ventral periaqueductal gray.

11. In this study, one group of men drank a mixture that reduced tryptophan and, it was assumed, would also reduce serotonin, because tryptophan is a precursor for this neurotransmitter.

The control group drank another mixture that had no effect. The men in the first group displayed more aggression by subtracting more points from a competitor's score. The first limitation of this study is that no mention is made of whether 5-HIAA was measured; it is assumed that lowered tryptophan would reduce serotonin. Another problem is the nature of the aggression measure. This is not physical aggression, so even if the men deprived of tryptophan indeed had lower serotonin levels, all we can say from this study is that they displayed one form of aggression more than the control subjects, but it is not clear if this would occur with other forms of aggression.

12. These include the following facts: inadequate parenting, psychological and social deprivation in childhood, influence of alcohol, and epigenetic influences on genes such as SLC6A4, HTR2B, and MAOA-L.

13. People with antisocial personality disorder tend to display impulsive behavior and generally have difficulty getting along with others, because they do not follow the "rules" of social conduct. Furthermore, they apparently lack the capacity for remorse or guilt over their disruptive and destructive behavior. People with antisocial personality disorder are more likely to have smaller prefrontal areas. Furthermore, people with damage to this area (e.g., due to injury) show many of the same characteristics.

14. Both alcohol and low levels of serotonin are associated with increased aggression. Furthermore, alcohol reduces serotonin. Therefore, alcohol probably enhances aggression through its reduction of serotonin.

15. Dopamine levels are high before, during, and after aggressive encounters and are found in the prefrontal cortex and accumbens. Dopamine antagonists decrease violence in psychiatric patients. GABA is an inhibitory neurotransmitter and is low in aggressive, impulsive rodents and men. The anti-anxiety drug class of benzodiazepines can decrease violence in psychiatric patients but sometimes can increase aggression—this perhaps is due to subcategories of GABA receptors having different roles. Finally, serotonin activity is low in aggression and triggers high dopamine release during fights. So high dopamine release during aggressive acts correlates strongly with violent, antisocial, and psychopathic traits.

## Post-test

1. c   2. d   3. a   4. b   5. b   6. c   7. d   8. a   9. c   10. b   11. c   12. d
13. c   14. c   15. a   16. c   17. c   18. d   19. d   20. d   21. b   22. a   23. b
24. c   25. b   26. c   27. b   28. b   29. a   30. c   31. a   32. c   33. c   34. d
35. b   36. b   37. d   38. a   39. c   40. b   41. d   42. a   43. c

# 9 Hearing and Language

## Learning Objectives

After reading this chapter, you should be able to answer the following questions.

1. How is sensory information transmitted to the nervous system?

2. What are the characteristics of sound stimuli?

3. What are the components and functions of the outer ear, middle ear, inner ear?

4. What brain areas are involved in processing sound?

5. How is sound frequency analyzed by the nervous system?

6. How are we able to locate the source of a sound?

7. What brain areas are involved in language? How does damage or impairment of these areas account for different types of language deficits such as aphasia and dyslexia?

8. In what ways is the brain specialized for language?

9. How does echolocation work? Describe evidence that both animals and humans can "see" with sound.

10. What language capabilities do nonhuman animals possess, and what does this indicate about the evolution of language in humans?

## Emotion and the Nervous System

### Summary and Guided Review

After studying this section in the text, fill in the blanks of the following summary.

When we encounter environmental stimuli, our _____ (1), often-specialized neurons, respond to specific types of stimuli and convert sensory information such as light or sound into neural signals. These cells pick up very specific environmental information, called a(n) _____ _____ (2), and nothing else. _____ (3) is the first step in information processing that allows us to interact with the external environment. Then the sensory information is interpreted, a process known as _____ (4). It is the amplitude and timing, or _____ (5), of the neural impulses that makes sensory information meaningful. For hearing, the process of sensation occurs in the _____ (6).

Our sense of hearing is highly complex. The auditory stimulus is the vibration of molecules in a(n) _____ _____ (7), which may be air, water, and even the skull. These vibrations can be represented graphically as number of cycles or _____ (8) per second, with their frequency expressed in _____ (9). _____ (10) is our psychological experience of the sound frequency. The range of frequencies that humans are most sensitive to is _____-_____ Hz (11). A sound with a single frequency is a(n) _____ _____ (12). Most sounds are complex, because they contain many frequencies. The sound _____ (13), or height of the signal, represents the physical intensity of sound, which we experience as _____ (14).

To hear, we must get information about the sound; this involves sound reception, _____ (15), and conversion of sound waves into neural impulses. The _____ (16), or outer ear, captures sound waves and amplifies them by directing them into the smaller auditory canal. Then sound waves reach the first part of the middle ear, called the _____ (17) membrane or eardrum. Its vibration transmits the sound energy to the second part of the middle ear, the _____ (18), which are the bones called the hammer, anvil, and stirrup. The next structure involved is the _____ (19) in the inner ear, a small coiled object about 35 mm long in humans containing three fluid-filled canals. The stirrup rests against the oval window, which is the point of entry into the cochlea. This canal connects with the _____ (20) canal at the far end of the cochlea. Activity in these canals bathes the cochlear canal, where the auditory _____ (21) are located. Conversion of sound waves to neural impulses occurs when vibrations reach the organ of Corti, which rests on the _____ (22) membrane. The organ of Corti consists of four rows of _____ (23) cells, their supporting cells, and the shelf-like _____ (24) membrane into which the hairs are embedded. Vibration of this membrane causes the hair cells to bend, which opens _____ (25) channels, depolarizing the hair cell membrane, which sets off impulses in the _____ (26) neuron. The inner hair cells, less numerous than the _____ (27) hair cells, are apparently responsible for most of what we hear, as is evidenced by the observation that mice lacking inner hair cells due to a mutant gene are _____ (28).

Cochlear neurons project to the primary auditory cortex in the _____ (29) lobe via the auditory nerves, passing through the brain stem, inferior colliculi, and the _____ _____ (30) nucleus of the thalamus. Most, but not all, of the fibers from the auditory nerves cross to the opposite hemisphere. Some of the functions of the auditory cortex of each hemisphere are specialized: _____ (31) in the left, and aspects of music in the right. The auditory cortex is also _____ (32) organized, as neurons from adjacent sites on the basilar membrane project to adjacent points on the cortex. Sound information is conveyed to areas beyond the primary auditory cortex; the _____ (33) stream flows through the parietal lobe and processes information about the spatial location of a sound, and the _____ (34) stream processes information about what an object is.

In converting sound waves into neural impulses, the auditory system codes for the intensity and frequency of stimuli. One group of encoding mechanisms is called _____ (35) theories, because the auditory mechanism transmits the actual frequency of a sound to the auditory cortex. The earliest idea for this mechanism was a 19th-century theory of coding advanced by Rutherford, called the _____ (36) theory, and postulated that auditory neurons fire at the same rate as the sound that stimulates them. This idea was tested by Wever and Bray (1930), who found evidence to support it. But they recorded from the auditory _____ (37) rather than a single neuron or axon, and Wever later hypothesized that several neurons cooperatively encoded frequencies, and this pattern was called _____ (38). However, even this cooperation can only reproduce frequencies below about 5200 Hz; some other mechanism must be responsible for coding higher frequencies.

The 19th-century scientist Helmholtz proposed a(n) _____ (39) theory of frequency coding that suggested that vibration of the _____ (40) membrane varies along its length with the frequency of the sound; frequency is encoded according to the place of maximal vibration. This selective responsiveness helps explain why the cortex contains a(n) _____ (41) map corresponding with different

points along the basilar membrane, and why one can hear through _____
(42) conduction. In the auditory cortex, neurons have very selective _____
_____ (43), where individual neurons are selective to a very small
range of frequencies and are sharpened through lateral inhibition. Since place theory falls
apart at low frequencies (below 200 Hz), most researchers believe that the combined
_____-_____ (44) theory is the most accurate account
of auditory frequency processing across the entire spectrum of sound we hear.

Intensity coding is simpler. With low-frequency sounds, more intense stimuli produce
responses in more neurons; for higher-frequency sounds, intensity is coded by the
_____ (45) of neural impulses.

Most of the sounds that we hear are complex, containing multiple frequencies.
Research suggests that the ear performs a(n) _____ (46) analysis
of complex sounds, in which the sound is analyzed using individual frequency bands.
The _____ (47) membrane carries out this analysis by responding
simultaneously along its length to these individual sound frequencies. We must also
explain why we are capable of identifying and following a single _____
_____ (48) among multiple competing sound sources, such as when
we attend to a particular conversation among many different conversations at a social
gathering . This is known as the _____ _____ (49)
effect. Such selective attention involves both selecting parts of the auditory environment
to focus on, and _____ (50) irrelevant background information.
Sound localization also helps us distinguish among auditory objects. Recognizing different
environmental sounds requires _____ (51) temporal and frontal
areas, whereas recognizing individual voices involves the secondary auditory cortex in the
_____ (52) temporal area. For the most part, recognizing a sound requires
the "_____" (53) pathway of hearing.

Much of our ability to locate sounds involves automatic processing of sounds within the
nervous system. Animals with two ears use three different _____ (54)
cues to locate sounds: phase differences, _____ (55) differences, and time-
of-arrival differences at the two ears. The farther apart the ears are, the easier it is to locate
sounds. Phase differences, which help us locate sounds below _____ (56)
Hz, and intensity differences, which help us locate sounds above _____
or _____ (57) Hz, are detected by cells in the _____
_____ (58) nucleus. Time-of-arrival cues have been studied extensively
in the barn owl. Neurons called _____ (59) detectors, which are located
in the *nucleus laminaris* (a structure analogous to the superior olivary nucleus), fire most
when they receive input from both ears at the same time. The most amazing form of sound
localization based on time of arrival and phase cues is found in the bat: these animals
use _____ (60) to find food in total darkness by emitting ultra-high
frequencies of sounds, and interpreting the echoes bouncing off of objects. Aquatic mammals,
some birds, and even humans can also use sound to see.

## Short Answer and Essay Questions

Answer the following questions.

1. Why do we need different terms for the physical properties of sound (frequency, intensity) and for the experience of sound (pitch, loudness)?

2. Describe Rutherford's telephone theory of frequency analysis. How did Wever and Bray
   test this theory? What was wrong with their procedure?

3. How do frequency theory and place theory account for our ability to process low-frequency and high-frequency sounds, respectively? Why is neither theory sufficient to explain all frequency analysis?

4. What is the possible role of the outer hair cells in selective attention?

5. Explain how phase- and intensity-difference cues help in locating the source of a sound.

6. How does the organization of neural input from auditory neurons to coincidence detectors account for the ability to locate sounds based on time-of-arrival cues?

# Language

## Summary and Guided Review

After studying this section in the text, fill in the blanks of the following summary.

Language, which includes spoken, _____ (61), and gestural communication, is of central importance in human behavior. There are many brain areas involved in language, and damage to them impairs different language functions. For example, in the 19th century Broca and Wernicke identified different forms of language impairment, or _____ (62), resulting from damage to different areas of the _____ (63) hemisphere of the brain.

Broca's aphasia, also referred to as _____ (64) aphasia, is the result of damage to Broca's area, which is located on the _____ (65) lobe anterior to the motor cortex. People with Broca's aphasia have difficulty expressing themselves. They often display _____ (66) (halting) speech, _____ (67) (difficulty finding the right word), difficulty with articulation, and _____ (68) speech (lacking function words). They also have problems with reading, writing, and comprehension of complex language.

Wernicke's aphasia, sometimes referred to as _____ (69) aphasia, is the result of damage to Wernicke's area, located on the left posterior _____ (70) lobe. People with Wernicke's aphasia can articulate words, but their utterances, described as _____ _____ (71), have little meaning. As the term receptive aphasia implies, they also have difficulty understanding all forms of language.

According to the Wernicke-Geschwind model, language processing (answering a question) occurs along a pathway from the auditory cortex to Wernicke's area to _____ _____ (72) and then to the facial area of the _____ _____ (73) (for a spoken response), or to the _____ _____ (74) (for a written response). When a person reads aloud, the route is from angular gyrus to _____ _____ (75), then to Broca's areas for speech production. However, damage to areas outside this pathway, including other areas of the cortex and subcortical structures such as the basal ganglia and _____ (76), also results in language impairment, indicating how widely distributed language processing is. However, there does seem to be an association between the location for storing _____ (77) names and the brain structures that would produce the action of using them. Electrical stimulation and brain damage studies have shown language functions are scattered throughout the four lobes, but the Wernicke-Geschwind model is essentially correct in that temporal areas are most important for comprehension, and frontal areas are most important for _____ (78).

Damage to the _____ (79) gyrus, which connects the visual projection area with auditory and visual association areas, can result in _____ (80) (the inability to read) and _____ (81) (the inability to write).

_____ (82), the most common type of learning disorder, also involves reading and listening difficulties. This disorder can be acquired through damage, but for most individuals it is of _____ (83) origin. The public is most familiar with the _____-_____ (84) symptoms of dyslexia, in which words are read backward, letters are confused, and words seem to move around on the page. The _____ (85) hypothesis argues that difficulty with processing phonemes underlies dyslexia, such as the first sound in the words *book, took,* and *cook.* One area of the brain that appears to be different in dyslexics is the _____ _____ (86): the right side is larger than normal, and the left lacks the usual orderly arrangement. This disorganization suggests that those neurons have _____ (87) past their normal destination during development. There is also a cultural effect of language on dyslexia: Countries with phonologically complex languages (such as multiple pronunciations for the same syllable such as dough and tough) have _____ (88) incidences of dyslexia than ones with simpler languages.

Recovery from aphasia is possible, but generally someone affected by _____ (89) aphasia has a greater recovery than the other type. Recovery is due in part from a decrease in _____ (90) that occurs along with the area of focal injury. Reorganization of the brain is also involved but is age-dependent. For example, there is evidence that if the left hemisphere is damaged before the age of _____ (91), the right hemisphere takes over language functions. For left hemisphere damage occurring later in life, language control can shift into the neighboring _____ (92) lobe. The right hemisphere is important in processing _____ (93) (intonation, emphasis, and rhythm) to convey meaning in speech, as well as understanding the _____ (94) rather than the literal meaning of words.

Because language is readily learned by almost all children, including those born deaf who are exposed to sign language, some theorists believe that the brain contains a language _____ (95) device: brain areas whose sole functions are to acquire language. Regardless of the form of language children learn, they all show the same stages of language development, including early _____ (96) through either speech or gestures. Most people show left hemisphere dominance for language, and several left hemisphere structures, including Broca's area, the _____ (97) fissure, and the planum temporale are larger than their counterparts in the right hemisphere. Prenatal and early postnatal differences in structure and function of the left hemisphere have been observed, suggesting that the left hemisphere in most people is designed to support language. In newborns, speech activates the same left hemisphere language areas as in adults, and sentence _____ (98) activates the right hemisphere. Even though it is a visual language, _____ (99) language activates left hemisphere structures similar to those used in spoken language. People who have learned two languages early in life show activation of the same areas for both languages, while those who acquired a(n) _____ (100) language after childhood show activation of somewhat different areas, but still within Broca's and Wernicke's areas. Although it is clear that language involves specific structures, it is not clear if these structures evolved specifically for language or if they originally served a more general purpose and were later taken over by language.

Studying language abilities in other species allows us to speculate on the evolutionary basis of language in humans, although the results of such studies must be interpreted with caution. Language abilities in _____ (101) and bonobos have been studied the most intensively, although because of limitations to the vocal apparatus, they are unable to speak. The chimpanzee Washoe was exposed to American _____ _____ (102) from an early age, and she learned _____ (103) signs in four years. Additionally, Washoe's adopted son Loulis learned 47 signs from Washoe and other adults, and the group of chimps would frequently have sign-language conversations with each other. The Rumbaughs used a different approach involving symbols on a panel. The bonobo Kanzi first began using the symbols as a(n) _____ (104) when his mother was being trained on it. Savage-Rumbaugh claims that Kanzi's use of symbols is about as sophisticated as that of a(n) _____ (105)-year-old child. Remarkable language abilities have also been demonstrated by Alex, an African gray _____ (106), who was able to give the name, color, quantity, and shape of objects.

There is also evidence that the brains of some species are lateralized in ways similar to humans. The lateral fissure and planum _____ (107) are larger in the left hemisphere in chimpanzees. Japanese macaques show a(n) _____ (108) hemisphere dominance for responding to the calls of other Japanese macaques but not to those of other monkey species. Dolphins and chimpanzees demonstrate faster learning of symbols when the symbols are presented to the left hemisphere. _____ (109) with left hemisphere lesions are unable to sing normally. Humans and primates also have similar hand and face _____ (110), such as waving someone away. Researchers believe that prelanguage communication in man also relied more on these hand and face movements to communicate, which supported the expansion of our emerging language areas. _____ (111) neurons, which are found in language areas in humans and animals, may be important in the ability to imitate the movements and sounds of others. One gene that has been implicated in language is the _____ (112). In humans, this gene differs slightly from its counterpart in chimpanzees, and people with a mutated form of the gene show several language-related deficits. Our human version, which is also found in _____ (113), may have contributed to our increased abilities in reading, writing, and speaking.

## Short Answer and Essay Questions

Answer the following questions.

7. Compare the language limitations observed in people with Broca's and Wernicke's aphasias.

8. How does the Wernicke-Geschwind model account for your ability to write a response to an oral question? To read aloud?

9. What is the Wada technique, and what is it used for?

10. In terms of acquisition and brain mechanisms, how are American Sign Language and spoken language similar?

11. What were the criticisms of the claims that Washoe was using language? How did subsequent work with Washoe and Loulis and the project with Kanzi address these criticisms?

## Post-test

Use these multiple-choice questions to check your understanding of the chapter.

1. If you see a particular pattern of dots on a wall but do not realize that the pattern is that of a dog, you have experienced a
   a. perception.
   b. sensation.
   c. conversion.
   d. translation.

2. The range of human hearing is about
   a. 20–200,000 Hz.
   b. 2–20,000 Hz.
   c. 20–20,000 Hz.
   d. 200–2,000 Hz.

3. Sound may be conducted through
   a. air.
   b. water.
   c. bone.
   d. all of the above

4. We experience the frequency of a sound as
   a. pitch.
   b. loudness.
   c. amplitude.
   d. intensity.

   *Pitch*

5. A pure tone is MOST likely to be produced by a(n)
   a. clarinet.
   b. tuning fork.
   c. air conditioner.
   d. flute.

6. Humans are MOST sensitive to sounds with frequencies in the range of
   a. 1,000–3,000 Hz.
   b. 200–400 Hz.
   c. 2,000–20,000 Hz.
   d. 2,000–4,000 Hz.

7. Which of the following causes the eardrum to stretch or relax in response to different levels of sound?
   a. tensor tympani
   b. incus
   c. pinna
   d. tympanic membrane

8. Which of the following does NOT contribute to amplification of sound waves in the ear?
   a. outer ear
   b. eardrum
   c. stapes
   d. malleus

9. Which of the following structures is (are) NOT part of the auditory system?
   a. cochlea
   b. ossicles
   c. pinna
   d. semicircular canals

10. Vibrations are initiated in the cochlea by movement of the ___ against the oval window.
    a. stapes
    b. malleus
    c. incus
    d. helicotrema

11. The organ of Corti is located in the ___ canal.
    a. vestibular
    b. tympanic
    c. cochlear
    d. auditory

12. Hair cells rest within the ___, and have their hairs embedded in the ___
    a. helicotrema; basilar membrane.
    b. tectorial membrane; basilar membrane.
    c. basilar membrane; tectorial membrane.
    d. tympanic membrane; helicotrema.

13. When hair cells bend, ___ channels open, causing depolarization.
    a. sodium and chloride
    b. potassium and calcium
    c. calcium and sodium
    d. chloride and calcium

14. The primary auditory cortex is located in the ___ lobe.
    a. temporal
    b. frontal
    c. parietal
    d. occipital

15. Neurons from the left ear project
    a. exclusively to the right hemisphere.
    b. exclusively to the left hemisphere.
    c. mostly to the right hemisphere.
    d. mostly to the left hemisphere.

16. At low frequencies, sound intensity is coded by
    a. the number of neurons responding.
    b. the volley pattern of neurons.
    c. the point on the basilar membrane responding.
    d. none of the above

17. The volley theory was proposed by
    a. Rutherford.
    b. Helmholtz.
    c. Békésy.
    d. Wever.

18. Békésy discovered that the basilar membrane is stiffer at one end than at the other, and not a series of piano strings as earlier envisioned by Helmholtz. This discovery led directly to the ___ theory of pitch perception
    a. frequency
    b. telephone
    c. place
    d. volley

19. What physiological limitation prevents a single auditory neuron from reliably tracking a high-frequency tone (such as one at 10,000 Hz)?
    a. glucose availability
    b. refractory period
    c. basilar membrane stiffness
    d. temporal harmonics

20. A 15,000-Hz tone will produce the greatest vibrations at which point along the basilar membrane?
    a. near the base
    b. at the apex
    c. near the apex
    d. in the middle

21. Which sound frequency does NOT seem to produce maximal vibration at a specific point on the basilar membrane?
    a. 20,000 Hz
    b. 2,400 Hz
    c. 1,200 Hz
    d. 20 Hz

22. The more numerous outer hair cells may be involved in
    a. increasing the cochlea's sensitivity.
    b. processing high- but not low-frequency sounds.
    c. correlating body movements with sound sources.
    d. all of the above

23. Which of the following animals probably would you expect to have the MOST difficulty localizing sounds using binaural cues?
    a. elephant
    b. alligator
    c. mouse
    d. owl

24. A sound with a frequency of 50 Hz is located by which of the following cues?
    a. phase difference
    b. intensity difference
    c. time-of-arrival difference
    d. a and c

25. In humans, binaural cues for localizing sound are processed by cells in the
    a. planum temporale.
    b. nucleus laminaris.
    c. superior olivary nucleus.
    d. medial geniculate nucleus.

26. Differences in time of arrival are processed using ___, which only fire when sounds from both ears reach it at the same time.
    a. sound shadows
    b. coincidence detectors
    c. reflector plates
    d. binaural cells

27. Broca's area lies anterior and adjacent to the
    a. motor cortex.
    b. auditory cortex.
    c. somatosensory cortex.
    d. visual cortex.

28. In MOST people, Wernicke's area is found on the ___ lobe.
    a. left frontal
    b. right frontal
    c. left temporal
    d. right temporal

29. Which of the following is NOT a characteristic of Broca's aphasia?
    a. impairment in writing
    b. word salad
    c. agrammatic speech
    d. difficulty with articulation

30. People with Wernicke's aphasia
    a. have difficulty saying words.
    b. have difficulty understanding others.
    c. produce utterances that have no meaning.
    d. b and c

31. Frank had a mini-stroke while driving home, but he did not realize it until later that afternoon when he found he couldn't write a shopping list down. He also was surprised that he couldn't read the newspaper either. Since he could still hear and speak normally, what part of his brain was affected by the stroke?
    a. planum temporale
    b. Broca's area
    c. Wernicke's area
    d. angular gyrus

32. The angular gyrus connects the visual projection area with the
    a. auditory association areas.
    b. visual association areas.
    c. motor cortex.
    d. a and b

33. According to the Wernicke-Geschwind model, when we give a spoken response to an oral question, what is the sequence of brain activation?
    a. auditory cortex to Broca's area to Wernicke's area
    b. Broca's area to Wernicke's area to auditory cortex
    c. auditory cortex to Wernicke's area to Broca's area
    d. Wernicke's area to Broca's area to auditory cortex

34. The most likely developmental anomaly in the language centers of the brain that give rise to dyslexia is a lateralized difference in the size of the
    a. arcuate fasciculus.
    b. planum temporale.
    c. Wernicke's area.
    d. Broca's area.

35. A phonological symptom of dyslexia is
    a. difficulty distinguishing speech sounds from each other.
    b. confusing mirror-image letters like b and d.
    c. reading words backward.
    d. difficulty tracking words on a page.

36. Dyslexia has a higher incidence rate in languages
    a. with symbolic, not letter, representation.
    b. with a higher number of possible words in them.
    c. with different pronunciations of the same spelling.
    d. that differ from other languages by only a few sounds.

37. Someone with damage to the premotor cortex would MOST likely have difficulty
    a. naming tools.
    b. using verbs.
    c. imagining hand movements.
    d. all of the above

38. There is evidence that the right hemisphere may assume left hemisphere language functions
    a. in adults who have suffered strokes or other brain injuries.
    b. in adults who learn a second language.
    c. in children under five who suffer brain injury.
    d. in children who acquire two languages simultaneously.

39. Babies exposed only to American Sign Language
    a. will babble in gestures, but only if they are deaf.
    b. babble in gestures, but at a later age than that at which babies exposed to spoken language begin babbling in sounds.
    c. babble in gestures at about the same age as babies exposed to spoken language babble in sounds.
    d. are at a disadvantage for language learning, because sign language is not a true language.

40. Which of the following is TRUE?
    a. Left-handed people are more likely to show left hemisphere dominance for language than right hemisphere dominance for language.
    b. All right-handed people show left hemisphere dominance for language.
    c. Left- and right-handed people are both more likely to show left hemisphere dominance for language.
    d. The hemisphere dominant for language has no relationship to whether someone is left- or -right handed.

41. Based on information in the text, which language capability in animals is most questionable?
    a. Use signs and symbols to communicate with humans.
    b. Produce grammatically correct sentences.

   c. Use signs and symbols to communicate with each other.

   d. Teach their offspring signs and symbols.

42. Which of the following species has NOT demonstrated a possible capacity for language?

   a. dog

   b. African gray parrot

   c. bonobo

   d. dolphin

43. One interesting genetic finding is that humans share the ___ gene with chimpanzees, though the genes differ by two amino acids. However, our version is identical to those found in ___.

   a. FOXP2; gorillas

   b. COMT; songbirds

   c. FOXP2; Neanderthals

   d. GEN3C; bonobos

44. Mirror neurons ___; this might explain why we find them in ___.

   a. are found only in humans; the motor cortex

   b. are active only during language use; the angular gyrus

   c. are found only in nonhuman animals; chimpanzees and not humans

   d. are active during observation and imitation; Broca's and Wernicke's areas

# Answers

## Guided Review

1. receptors
2. adequate stimulus
3. Sensation
4. Perception
5. patterning
6. cochlea
7. conducting medium
8. waves
9. hertz (Hz)
10. Pitch
11. 2,000–4,000
12. pure tone
13. amplitude
14. loudness
15. amplification
16. pinna
17. tympanic
18. ossicles
19. cochlea
20. tympanic
21. receptors
22. basilar
23. hair
24. tectorial
25. potassium
26. auditory
27. outer
28. deaf
29. temporal
30. medial geniculate
31. language

32. topographically
33. dorsal
34. ventral
35. frequency
36. telephone
37. nerve
38. volleying
39. place
40. basilar
41. tonotopic
42. bone
43. tuning curves
44. frequency-place
45. rate
46. Fourier
47. basilar
48. auditory object
49. cocktail party
50. suppressing
51. posterior
52. superior
53. what
54. binaural
55. intensity
56. 1,500
57. 2,000–3,000
58. superior olivary
59. coincidence
60. echolocation
61. written
62. aphasia

63. left

64. expressive

65. frontal

66. nonfluent

67. anomia

68. agrammatic

69. receptive

70. temporal

71. word salad

72. Broca's area

73. motor cortex

74. angular gyrus

75. Wernicke's area

76. thalamus

77. tool

78. articulation

79. angular

80. alexia

81. agraphia

82. Dyslexia

83. developmental

84. visual-perceptual

85. phonological

86. planum temporale

87. migrated

88. higher

89. Broca's

90. swelling

91. five

92. parietal

93. prosody

94. figurative

95. acquisition

96. babbling

97. lateral

98. melody

99. sign

100. second

101. chimpanzees

102. Sign Language

103. 132

104. infant

105. two

106. parrot

107. temporale

108. left

109. canaries

110. gestures

111. Mirror

112. *FOXP2*

113. Neanderthals

## Short Answer and Essay Questions

1. While pitch varies with frequency and loudness varies with intensity, neither relationship is precise. Our sensitivity is not the same across the range of sounds; for example, we are more sensitive to sounds between 2,000 and 4,000 Hz, and we can detect smaller changes in amplitude in that range. Thus, a sound of a particular intensity and frequency will not have the same loudness at another frequency, and it will not have the same pitch at a different intensity.

2. Rutherford proposed that auditory neurons fire at the same frequency as sounds that stimulate them, so that the brain received signals that matched or followed the frequency of sounds in the environment. Wever and Bray tested this theory by recording from the auditory

nerve of a cat while it was exposed to sounds and amplifying the signal so that it could be heard; the result was very faithful to the original sound. However, this wasn't an adequate test of the theory, because Wever and Bray were not recording from a single neuron. Individual neurons cannot fire fast enough to follow the frequency of most environmental sounds; they found frequency following only because the combined firing of many neurons was able to follow the frequency of the sounds used.

3. Frequency theory accounts for low-frequency sounds, as neurons do fire at the same rate as low-frequency sounds. Place theory accounts for higher-frequency sounds, as different points along the basilar membrane are most responsive to particular frequencies and many auditory neurons are frequency specific. However, neither theory alone is sufficient to account for all frequency analysis. Frequency theory is limited by the physical property of neurons that prevents them from firing more than a few hundred times per second, and place theory cannot account for processing low-frequency sounds, because sounds below 200 Hz cause the entire basilar membrane to vibrate equally.

4. The outer hair cells may be involved in a mechanism for selective attention. Messages along the descending auditory pathway suppress activity in the inner hair cells, but this may occur via the outer hair cells. When the length of the outer hair cells changes, the rigidity of the organ of Corti changes. This may allow the organ of Corti to zero in on a particular sound source (with a particular mix of frequencies) and tune out others with different frequencies. (Note: Be sure to check the Web link for the "Dancing Hair Cell" video.)

5. Phase-difference cues involve the point at which a sound wave stimulates the ear. If a sound is coming from any direction such that it reaches each ear at different points in the wave, this difference will be detected by cells in the superior olivary nucleus. Intensity-difference cues work because the head produces a sound shadow. The ear closer to the source of sound will receive a more intense sound than the other ear; this difference is also detected by specialized neurons in the superior olivary nucleus.

6. Coincidence detectors receive input from neurons from both ears. However, the length of the input neurons connected to a specific coincidence detector from each ear differs. When a sound occurs, it will reach the closer ear first and the farther ear later, but the two signals will arrive at a particular coincidence detector simultaneously because the length of the neuron from the closer ear compensates for the delay in the sound reaching the distant ear. Which coincidence detector is responding most indicates the sound's location relative to the two ears.

7. In Broca's aphasia, people have difficulty recalling the appropriate words, their speech is halting and impaired in articulation, and function words are missing. Their understanding is also impaired by their inability to process function words. Reading and writing are disrupted as well. People with Wernicke's aphasia, on the other hand, often speak fluently, but their utterances make little sense, and they have difficulty understanding what others are saying to them.

8. According to this model, when you write an answer to an oral question, the pattern of activation begins in the auditory cortex, then moves to Wernicke's area, and then to the angular gyrus to elicit the visual pattern. When reading out loud, the visual system sends input through the angular gyrus to Wernicke's area, and then to Broca's area.

9. The Wada technique involves administering an anesthetic to one hemisphere of a person's brain to suppress its activity and then giving the person tasks to perform. This is used along with electrical stimulation to determine the location of different functions (such as language) prior to surgery.

10. Babies exposed to sign language seem to progress in language development along the same lines as babies exposed to speech. Both babble at about the same time, and the babbling seems to have the same function in each case (although it is of a very different form). Furthermore, similar areas of the left hemisphere are involved in both spoken language and sign language.

11. Terrace claimed that chimpanzees do not form sentences, that the utterances lacked grammatical structure and were simply strings of words. Loulis acquired signs from Washoe and other chimps and used these signs to communicate with other chimps, suggesting that the signs are being used like language. The Rumbaughs' work with Kanzi indicates that chimpanzees are capable of spontaneously making complex utterances and understanding complex directions.

## Post-test

1. b  2. c  3. d  4. a  5. b  6. d  7. a  8. b  9. d  10. a  11. c  12. c  13. b
14. a  15. c  16. a  17. d  18. c  19. b  20. a  21. d  22. a  23. c  24. d
25. c  26. b  27. a  28. c  29. b  30. d  31. d  32. d  33. a  34. b  35. a
36. c  37. d  38. c  39. c  40. c  41. b  42. a  43. c  44. d

# 10 Vision and Visual Perception

## Learning Objectives

After reading this chapter, you should be able to answer the following questions.

1. What are the characteristics of electromagnetic energy, particularly for the portion of the spectrum that is visible to humans?

2. What are the functions of the components of the eye? How does light affect cells in the retina?

3. What is the pathway for visual information beyond the retina?

4. What is the significance of retinal disparity?

5. How do the trichromatic and opponent process theories differ in their explanations for color vision?

6. How does the visual system produce the experience of color?

7. What cures are being developed for individuals who are blind?

8. What are the characteristics of color blindness?

9. In what way is the visual cortex a retinotopic map?

10. What is lateral inhibition, and how does it explain contrast enhancement and edge detection?

11. What are the functions of simple and complex visual cells?

12. How does spatial frequency theory account for form perception?

13. What are the functions of the magnocellular and parvocellular systems?

14. What are the functions of the ventral and dorsal streams?

15. What are some disorders of visual perception, and what do they reveal about the functions of different brain areas?

16. What are the possible solutions to the problem of final integration?

## Light and the Visual Apparatus

### Summary and Guided Review

After studying this section in the text, fill in the blanks of the following summary.

The adequate stimulus for the visual system is visible light, which makes up a very small portion of the _____ (1) spectrum. Other forms of electromagnetic energy that humans cannot detect without special devices are X-rays, _____ (2) energy (which some animal species use to detect prey at night), and radio and television waves. Light is measured not in terms of frequency like sounds, but in terms of _____ (3), the distance oscillating energy travels before reversing directions; the portion of the electromagnetic spectrum humans are capable of detecting is _____-_____ (4) nanometers. (A nanometer is 1 _____ (5) of a meter.) Within this range, light rays of different wavelengths are perceived as different _____ (6).

The eye is filled with fluid, and with the exception of the transparent
_____ (7), its outer covering, or sclera, is opaque. Behind the cornea,
the flexible _____ (8) allows us to focus on objects at different
distances. The circular _____ (9) is a muscle that partially covers the
lens, and the opening in its center is the _____ (10), which changes
its size to accommodate different levels of light. The visual receptors are located in the
_____ (11) at the back of the eye; these cells contain light-sensitive
_____ (12). The different types of receptors, _____
(13) and _____ (14), are specialized for different aspects of vision,
due to the fact that they contain different types of photopigments and have different
neural connections. Rods, which are more numerous, contain _____
(15), which is highly sensitive to light; this accounts for our ability to see under low
light conditions. Cones, which contain _____ (16), function best in
bright light. There are different types of this photopigment, each responding most to
different ranges of wavelengths; this is what allows us to see color. In the retina, cones are
concentrated in the _____ (17) in the center, whereas rods are more
numerous in the periphery. Foveal cones show less convergence on the ganglion cells
than cones outside the fovea, which accounts for better visual _____
(18) for images falling on the fovea. Many rods converge on a single ganglion
cell, which contributes to _____ (19) light but not acuity. The
_____ (20) fields of foveal cells are smaller than those in the periphery.
In the dark, photoreceptors release _____ (21), which inhibits bipolar
cells. When stimulated by light, sodium and _____ (22) channels close,
thus disinhibiting the bipolar cells and increasing the firing rate in the ganglion cells they
are connected to. Horizontal and _____ (23) cells interconnect the
receptor cells and ganglion cells, and respectively, producing a complex web of information
processing.

The ganglion cells' _____ (24) form the optic nerve and exit the
retina at the _____ _____ (25); the optic nerves
join for a short distance at the _____ _____
(26), where axons from the nasal side of the eyes cross over to the opposite side of
the brain. Neurons from the _____ (27) side of the eyes project
to the same side of the brain. Nerves next project to the _____
_____ (28) nuclei of the thalamus and then to the cortex. The partial
crossover of information is organized such that, for example, stimuli detected by the right
half of each retina, which receives light from the _____ (29) visual
field, are projected to the _____ (30) hemisphere. We are able to
perceive objects in three-dimensional space due in part to _____
_____ (31), in which each eye receives a slightly different version
of a visual scene. The degree of disparity triggers activity in different cells in the cortex.
The ViewMaster, 3-D movies such as *Avatar*, and the Nintendo 3DS all capitalize on
retinal disparity to produce an illusion of three dimensions. Three principles are helpful in
understanding how the visual system works: _____ (32), which allows
for more detailed information processing than excitation alone; _____
_____ _____ (33), which means that more basic
elements of visual stimuli are processed in lower areas of the nervous system, and this
information is then analyzed by higher areas of the cortex; and _____
(34), which reflects the fact that much of visual processing is segregated in different brain
locations.

## Short Answer and Essay Questions

Answer the following questions.

1. Briefly describe the "adequate stimulus" for vision.

2. How are the receptive fields of ganglion cells that receive input from cones in the fovea different from those receiving input from rods? How do these differences contribute to the visual specializations of each system?

3. What is the blind spot? Why do we not notice it (most of the time)?

4. How are researchers able to present a visual image to only one hemisphere in people whose brains are intact?

5. How is the Nintendo 3DS able to produce such convincing three-dimensional effects using a single screen and no special glasses?

# Color Vision

## Summary and Guided Review

After studying this section in the text, fill in the blanks of the following summary.

Just as _____ (35) refers to our perceptual experience of the frequency of a sound, color refers to our perceptual experience of the _____ (36) of light, but does not correspond perfectly with it. Thus, color is not a property of an object, but an experience produced by the brain. The _____ (37) theory of color vision, proposed separately by Young and _____ (38), explained that our ability to see color is due to three different color processes that are sensitive to red, green, and _____ (39) light. All colors are the result of mixing different combinations of these colors of light; this principle is used in the design of televisions and computer displays. The competing _____ _____ (40) theory, proposed by Hering, explained color vision as the result of receptors whose _____ (41) are broken down by one type of light and regenerated by another. This theory is based on the observation of complementary colors, that is, colors that when mixed in equal amounts produce _____ _____ (42) or white. Also, over-stimulating the eye with one color of light increases sensitivity to its complement. This theory explains complementary colors as well as the phenomenon of _____ _____ (43) aftereffect: When you stare at a green object and then look at a white piece of paper, you will experience the same image in _____ (44). It is important to remember that mixing lights is _____ (45), whereas mixing pigments is subtractive. Hering's theory was not well accepted because of his notion that a single photochemical could be affected in opposite ways by different wavelengths of light.

In 1957, Hurvich and Jameson proposed a theory of color vision that included elements of both the trichromatic and opponent process theories; this theory suggests that our ability to see color depends on two different levels of processing in the cells of the _____ (46). The first level of color processing occurs in the

_____ (47), which contain one of three different photopigments, each of which is maximally sensitive to different wavelengths of light. These red-, green-, and blue-sensitive cones are interconnected to _____ (48) cells in such a way as to produce opponent process effects. For example, long-wavelength light stimulates the _____ (49)-sensitive cones and _____ _____ (50) ganglion cells, whereas medium-wavelength light stimulates the green-sensitive cones and _____ (51) the red-green ganglion cells. Short-wavelength light excites blue cones and _____ (52) the yellow-blue ganglion cells, leading to a sensation of blue. Staring at a red stimulus eventually _____ (53) the red-green ganglion cells, resulting in inhibition and the experience of green. This explains the phenomenon of negative _____ (54). Physical evidence for this theory was produced by studies involving shining different wavelengths of light onto the retinas of human eyes and measuring which wavelengths were absorbed. This finding shows that there are _____ (55) distinct color response curves; each receptor has a sensitivity peak but its response range _____ (56) with that of its neighbors. The _____ (57) for photopigments in red and green cones are probably the most recently evolved and may have emerged around the time in primate evolution when visual signals became important to differentiate _____ _____ (58) and to locate young, tender leaves. Color-opponent _____ (59) cells have been located in the retina and _____ _____ (60) nucleus of the thalamus in monkeys. This theory was considered successful because it was able to demonstrate that it was (1) _____ with the known facts, (2) could _____ those facts, and (3) could _____ (61) new findings.

The study of color blindness can also reveal information about how the visual system works. People who are completely color blind lack functional cones and are limited to vision from _____ (62). This is a rare condition. There are two more common types of color blindness. A person who is red-green color blind sees both colors but is unable to _____ (63) between them. People in the second color blind group do not perceive _____ (64) so they see their world in variations of red and green. Many people who are partially color blind are not even _____ (65) that they see the world differently from other people.

## Short Answer and Essay Questions

Answer the following questions.

6. How does Figure 10.6 demonstrate that our perception of color does not perfectly correspond to the wavelength of light we sense?

7. Why is it that when yellow and blue paints are mixed, green is produced, whereas when yellow and blue lights are mixed, they produce gray?

8. How does the opponent process theory explain the negative afterimage effect?

9. Explain the three ways in which Hurvich and Jameson's combined theory has demonstrated that it is successful as a theory; include a specific example for each.

10. What can we conclude about the color receptors in a person who cannot distinguish between red and green but is especially sensitive to green light?

# Form Vision

## Summary and Guided Review

After studying this section in the text, fill in the blanks of the following summary.

The visual cortex contains a(n) _____ (66) map, which means that the spatial relationships among visual stimuli are conserved from retina to cortex. Form vision allows us to detect the boundaries of objects and is the first step in _____ (67) perception.

In order to perceive a form or object, we must first be able to detect its boundaries. The visual system is designed to respond to boundaries so that they stand out from the rest of the visual field. This fact is demonstrated by the _____ _____ (68) illusion, in which contrast between bands that differ in brightness appears greater at their edges. This illusion, and the visual system's ability to detect contrast in general, is explained by _____ _____ (69) of activity in ganglion cells. In mammals, the ganglion cells have concentric circular receptive fields. _____-_____ (70) cells respond by increasing the rate of firing when light stimulates the receptors in the central portion of the receptive field and _____ (71) their rate of firing when light stimulates the surround portion. Other ganglion cells have an off-center and an on-surround. Cells with opposed centers and surrounds are particularly responsive to the _____ (72) of objects because edges typically have a high contrast in lighting.

While cells in the lateral geniculate nucleus also have _____ (73) receptive fields, those in the cortex respond quite differently, as discovered by Nobel laureates _____ and _____ (74). They identified different types of cells in the cortex that respond to different aspects of these stimuli. _____ (75) cells respond to a line or edge at a specific orientation in a specific portion of the visual field. A simple cell receives input from several _____ (76) cells with adjacent receptive fields arranged in line. _____ (77) cells receive input from several simple cells with adjacent fields; these complex cells are responsive to lines in a particular orientation over a larger area of the retina; some complex cells can also detect _____ (78).

Hubel and Wiesel's theory accounts for the detection of edges, but it cannot account for other surface details by which we identify objects such as texture. Edges represent _____-_____ (79) changes in brightness, whereas subtle shading represents low-frequency changes; according to De Valois, complex cells are responsive to low-frequency as well as high-frequency changes. His _____ (80) theory suggested that sensitivity to a range of spatial frequencies accounts for our ability to make out the varied details of a visual stimulus. In other words, visual cortical cells perform a(n) _____ (81) frequency analysis of luminosity variations in a scene.

## Short Answer and Essay Questions

Answer the following questions.

11. What is lateral inhibition, and how does it explain the Mach band illusion?

12. What will happen to an on-center, off-surround ganglion cell when light stimulates the entire receptive field? Only the surround? The center and only part of the surround?

13. Compare the receptive fields of simple and complex cells. Explain their differences in function and how this comes about.

14. What would our vision be like if we were able to detect only high-frequency visual information, such as from edges?

# The Perception of Objects, Color, and Movement

## Summary and Guided Review

After studying this section in the text, fill in the blanks of the following summary.

The text takes the position that visual processing of objects, color, and movement is both modular and _____ (82), while acknowledging that the representation of some functions in multiple areas means that the modularity is tempered somewhat by the fact that any visual function is _____ (83) across a relatively wide area of the brain.

Beginning in the _____ (84), visual information processing is divided, to some extent, between two systems. The _____ (85) system includes ganglion cells located in the fovea whose circular receptive fields are small and color opponent. These cells are sensitive to the _____ (86) and fine detail of objects. The _____ (87) system includes cells whose receptive fields are large, circular, and brightness opponent. This system is involved in our perception of movement and _____ (88) contrast. Under poor lighting conditions, the _____ (89) system is most active, and we are particularly sensitive to movement in our _____ (90) visual field. Reading and determining the color of objects, functions of the _____ (91) system, become difficult or impossible.

The first cortical area for vision is the primary visual cortex, also known as _____ (92). In the cortex, the parvocellular system makes up the majority of the _____ (93) stream of information that projects to the _____ (94) lobes; along this route, color perception and object recognition occur. The magnocellular system forms the majority of the _____ (95) stream that projects to the _____ (96) lobes; along this route, spatial information about visual stimuli is processed. Movement perception involves the areas V5/MT and _____ (97); these are active even when viewing photos implying action. Activity of cells in these areas is _____ (98) during eye movements, so that stationary objects do not appear to move. The dorsal and ventral streams converge on the _____ _____ (99), where the information is used, for example, in planning actions. The ventral/dorsal distinction can be observed in the effects of brain damage in the different pathways. People with damage to the _____ (100) stream can identify objects but have trouble orienting and reaching toward them. People with damage to the _____ (101) stream have trouble identifying objects, but they can move toward and reach for them accurately.

Damage to one or more areas of the cortex involved in vision can lead to a specific type of _____ (102), which is an impairment of some type of visual perception. For example, people with object agnosia have difficulty recognizing objects; object agnosia usually involves difficulty recognizing faces of familiar people, or _____ (103), which can occasionally occur alone. However, evidence that prosopagnosics respond to familiar faces emotionally suggests that there are separate pathways for recognition and _____ (104) in the brain. An interesting example of this distinction is

_____ (105), a condition in which cortically blind individuals can track object movements and discriminate colors they cannot see. The brain region implicated in object agnosia and prosopagnosia is the _____ _____ (106) cortex, which contains individual cells that respond to specific types of objects, including geometric forms, animals, and faces. In addition, there is evidence that the _____ _____ (107) area in the inferior temporal cortex is especially important for recognition of faces; cells in this area are more active when presented with familiar faces. A nearby area of the inferior temporal cortex is called the _____ (108); it responds to written words as a whole (that is, as objects). Although reduced activity in this area occurs in dyslexia, it does not mean that it is the cause of the disorder.

Another impairment is color agnosia, as characterized by the description of Jonathan in the introduction to the chapter. Our experience of color depends in part on _____ _____ (109), the perceptual process that allows us to perceive the color of an object in the same way despite different lighting conditions. This ability seems to depend on cells in area _____ (110), whose activity Zeki concluded were "color coded." Cortical color blindness, or _____ (111), occurs when people have damage in this area between V1 and the fusiform face area.

_____ (112) agnosia is the impaired ability to detect motion; damage to the MST and parietal cortex may produce an inability to detect _____ (113) movement, which informs us about movement of objects toward or away from us. Individuals with damage to the posterior parietal cortex often display characteristics of _____ (114), such as failing to notice or attend to objects or parts of the body opposite the damage. This is not due to a defect in visual processing but involves a deficit in _____ (115).

How are we able to make sense of all of the visual information we take in? So far, there is no evidence that a single _____ (116) area exists for incorporating visual information into conscious experience. The most likely answer is that our awareness of visual stimuli is the result of _____ (117) activity throughout the brain. The _____ _____ (118) is the question of how the brain combines information from different areas into a unitary whole. One way to approach this problem is to study a condition called _____ (119), in which stimulation in one sense triggers an experience in another sense or a concept evokes an unrelated sensory experience (for example, emotions might have colors). People with this condition seem to "overbind" sensory information, either due to excess connectivity between the brain areas involved or inadequate inhibition in otherwise normal pathways. This is yet another example of how anomalies in brain functioning can help us understand the normal function of the brain.

## Short Answer and Essay Questions

Answer the following questions.

15. What aspects of vision are the parvocellular and magnocellular systems specialized for? Give an example of each.

16. How does the modular nature of the visual system account for specific agnosias (such as object or movement agnosia)?

17. What is blindsight? What is the possible anatomical basis for it?

18. Describe the procedure used in the "Greeble" study. What do the results of this study suggest about the function of the fusiform face area?

## Post-test

Use these multiple-choice questions to check your understanding of the chapter.

1. Electromagnetic energy includes
   a. visible light rays.
   b. gamma rays.
   c. infrared rays.
   d. all of the above

2. The range of visible light for humans is
   a. 40–80 nm.
   b. 4,000–8,000 nm.
   c. 400–800 nm.
   d. 40,000–80,000 nm.

3. Light with a wavelength on the lower end of the spectrum (e.g., 450 nm) is normally perceived as
   a. blue.
   b. green.
   c. yellow.
   d. red.

4. The ___ is a flexible tissue that allows us to focus on objects at different distances.
   a. cornea
   b. lens
   c. pupil
   d. iris

5. The ___ is actually muscle tissue that responds to different levels of light.
   a. cornea
   b. lens
   c. pupil
   d. iris

6. The conversion of light energy into energy the brain can use begins in the
   a. receptors.
   b. bipolar cells.
   c. ganglion cells.
   d. amacrine cells.

7. Photoreceptors
   a. contain photopigments that increase in quantity when stimulated by light.
   b. connect directly with ganglion cells.
   c. are found at the back of the eye.
   d. all of the above

8. Which of the following statements is NOT true?
   a. Iodopsin is the cone photopigment.
   b. Rods function better in dim light.
   c. Cones are responsive to light but cannot distinguish between wavelengths of different colors.
   d. Rhodopsin is the rod photopigment.

9. All of the following types of cells are found in the retina EXCEPT ___ cells.
   a. bipolar
   b. horizontal
   c. amacrine
   d. complex

10. The ganglion cells with the smallest receptive fields receive input from
    a. rods in the periphery of the retina.
    b. rods 20 degrees from the fovea.
    c. cones in the fovea.
    d. cones outside the fovea.

11. When light reaches the photoreceptors
    a. they release more glutamate.
    b. sodium channels open.
    c. calcium channels open.
    d. none of the above

12. The blind spot contains
    a. rods only.
    b. cones only.
    c. both rods and cones.
    d. neither rods nor cones.

13. Visual information from the ___ side of each retina crosses to the other hemisphere at the ___.
    a. right; optic chiasm
    b. nasal; optic chiasm
    c. right; lateral geniculate nucleus
    d. nasal; lateral geniculate nucleus

14. An object's image falls on slightly different parts of the two retinas, depending on the distance of the object. This is called
    a. hierarchical processing.
    b. modularity.
    c. neural inhibition.
    d. retinal disparity.

15. Color televisions produce color in accordance with the principles of
    a. the opponent process theory of color vision.
    b. the trichromatic theory of color vision.
    c. the combined theory of color vision.
    d. none of the above

16. If you stare at a yellow image for a long time and then look at a piece of white paper, you will see the image in
    a. blue.
    b. green.
    c. red.
    d. yellow.

17. Which of the following is NOT true of Hering's original opponent process theory?
    a. It is consistent with principles of mixing light.
    b. It is consistent with the negative color aftereffect.
    c. It proposed four types of color receptors.
    d. It proposed four primary colors.

18. With respect to the cones, yellow light produces
    a. less response in the yellow/blue ganglion cell.
    b. more response in the yellow/blue ganglion cell.
    c. less response in the red/green ganglion cell.
    d. more response in the red/green ganglion cell.

19. With respect to the evolution and genetic basis of color vision
    a. genes for short-wavelength cones evolved relatively recently from a common precursor gene.
    b. red and green genes are adjacent to one another on the Y chromosome.
    c. the development of trichromacy and the use of vision to separate fruit from leaves occurred at the same time.
    d. all of the above

20. Which of the following statements regarding people who lack cones is NOT true?
    a. They have poor visual acuity.
    b. They can distinguish only very bright colors.
    c. They are very sensitive to light.
    d. They are more rare than people with red-green color blindness.

21. People with red-green color blindness
    a. are usually aware of their unusual condition.
    b. can see neither red nor green.
    c. may have red photopigment in their green cones.
    d. are less common than those with complete color blindness.

22. Which of the following is NOT a part of form vision?
    a. formation of tonotopic maps
    b. edge detection
    c. contrast enhancement
    d. detection of orientation

23. The Mach band illusion is a result of
    a. object recognition.
    b. lateral inhibition.
    c. retinal disparity.
    d. modular processing.

24. Light in the ___ of an off-center receptive field will result in ___.
    a. center; excitation
    b. surround; excitation
    c. surround; inhibition
    d. center and entire surround; inhibition

25. Which of the following types of cells have bar-shaped receptive fields?
    a. retinal ganglion cells
    b. lateral geniculate cells
    c. simple cells
    d. horizontal cells

26. Which of the following types of cells have the largest receptive field?
    a. retinal ganglion cells
    b. lateral geniculate cells
    c. simple cells
    d. complex cells

27. Movement is detected by
    a. simple cells.
    b. complex cells.
    c. lateral geniculate cells.
    d. ganglion cells.

28. Hubel and Wiesel's theory accounts for the ability to detect
    a. texture.
    b. edges.
    c. movement.
    d. b and c

29. According to spatial frequency theory,
    a. low-frequency contrast in objects is detected by different cells than high-frequency contrast.
    b. the visual system is capable of detecting only medium- to high-frequency contrast.
    c. the visual system is capable of detecting only low- to medium-frequency contrast.
    d. the brightness of an object is irrelevant.

30. The BEST description of visual processing is that it is
    a. modular.
    b. distributed.
    c. both modular and distributed.
    d. neither modular nor distributed.

31. Which of the following is a characteristic of cells in the parvocellular system?
    a. They have small receptive fields.
    b. They are brightness opponent.
    c. They are responsive to movement.
    d. Their input comes mainly from rods.

32. The magnocellular system dominates the ___ stream, which flows into the ___ lobes.
    a. ventral; temporal
    b. ventral; parietal
    c. dorsal; temporal
    d. dorsal; parietal

33. Magnocellular cells in area V1 are responsive to all of the following EXCEPT
    a. orientation.
    b. movement.
    c. retinal disparity.
    d. color.

34. Movement perception is a function of area
    a. V2.
    b. V4.
    c. V5.
    d. V8.

35. The ventral and dorsal streams converge on the ___ cortex.
    a. posterior parietal
    b. prefrontal
    c. anterior occipital
    d. inferior temporal

36. Object agnosia is often a result of damage to the ___ cortex.
    a. inferior temporal
    b. prefrontal
    c. posterior parietal
    d. posterior occipital

37. People with prosopagnosia
    a. fail to recognize familiar faces.
    b. fail to recognize familiar voices.
    c. fail to respond emotionally to familiar faces.
    d. all of the above

38. Specialized face-recognition cells have been located in the
    a. dorsal stream.
    b. fusiform face area.
    c. V1 area.
    d. parietal lobe.

39. The ability to perceive that an object is the same color despite different lighting conditions is known as
    a. visual constancy.
    b. color agnosia.
    c. retinal disparity.
    d. color constancy.

40. Zeki concluded that light wavelength is coded in ___, and color is coded in ____.
    a. V4; V1
    b. V4; V4
    c. V1; V1
    d. V1; V4

41. Someone with damage to the right posterior parietal cortex would probably exhibit
    a. right-side neglect.
    b. left-side neglect.
    c. movement agnosia.
    d. color agnosia.

42. Neglect probably occurs because of
    a. a lack of attention to the space on one side of the body.
    b. an inability to perceive objects on one side of the body.
    c. both a and b
    d. neither a nor b

43. Which of the following is NOT true about people with synesthesia?
    a. The condition tends to affect the left hemisphere.
    b. V4 has been implicated.
    c. Individuals see what they dream about.
    d. Synesthetes may "underbind" sensory information, due to decreased connectivity of brain areas.

44. According to the text, visual awareness is probably due to
    a. master visual cells in the superior temporal gyrus.
    b. master visual cells in the parietal cortex.
    c. many processes distributed across the brain.
    d. master cells in some part of the cortex that has not yet been identified.

# Answers

## Guided Review

1. electromagnetic
2. infrared
3. wavelength
4. 400–800
5. billionth
6. colors
7. cornea
8. lens
9. iris
10. pupil
11. retina
12. photoreceptors
13. rods
14. cones
15. rhodopsin
16. iodopsin
17. fovea
18. acuity
19. sensitivity
20. receptive
21. glutamate
22. calcium
23. amacrine
24. axons
25. blind spot
26. optic chiasm
27. temporal
28. lateral geniculate
29. left
30. right
31. retinal disparity
32. inhibition
33. hierarchical processing
34. modularity
35. pitch
36. wavelength
37. trichromatic
38. Helmholtz
39. blue
40. opponent process
41. photochemicals
42. neutral gray
43. negative color
44. red
45. additive
46. retina
47. cones
48. ganglion
49. red
50. red-green
51. inhibits
52. inhibits
53. fatigues
54. aftereffects
55. three
56. overlaps
57. genes
58. ripe fruit
59. ganglion
60. lateral geniculate
61. consistent, explain, predict
62. rods

63. distinguish
64. blue
65. aware
66. retinotopic
67. object
68. Mach band
69. lateral inhibition
70. On-center
71. decreasing
72. edges
73. circular
74. Hubel and Wiesel
75. Simple
76. ganglion
77. Complex
78. movement
79. high frequency
80. spatial frequency
81. Fourier
82. hierarchical
83. distributed
84. retina
85. parvocellular
86. color
87. magnocellular
88. brightness
89. magnocellular
90. peripheral
91. parvocellular

92. V1
93. ventral
94. temporal
95. dorsal
96. parietal
97. MST
98. suppressed
99. prefrontal cortex
100. dorsal
101. ventral
102. agnosia
103. propagnosia
104. identification
105. blindsight
106. inferior temporal
107. fusiform face
108. VWFA (visual word form area)
109. color constancy
110. V4
111. achromatopsia
112. Movement
113. radial
114. neglect
115. attention
116. master
117. distributed
118. binding problem
119. synesthesia

## Short Answer and Essay Questions

1. The adequate stimulus for vision is visible light, which makes up a very narrow portion of the electromagnetic spectrum. It is an oscillating form of energy that travels in waves like sound energy but is described in terms of its wavelength. Visible light ranges from 400 to 800 nanometers. Different wavelengths correspond to different colors of light, though inexactly.

2.   Ganglion cells receiving input from foveal cones have smaller receptive fields than those receiving input from rods. Some cones in the fovea have a one-to-one correspondence with ganglion cells (meaning that a ganglion cell receives input from a single cone). This arrangement allows us to make fine discriminations of the details of objects in our visual field. Ganglion cells receiving input from rods have large receptive fields, because they receive input from several rods. They are highly sensitive to light and movements but are not useful for distinguishing fine details.

3.   The blind spot is the portion of the retina where the ganglion cell axons forming the optic nerve exit the retina, and there are no receptors in this area. We do not notice it because when we see with both eyes, the portion of the visual field that falls on the blind spot in the left eye is different from the portion that falls on the blind spot in the right eye. This way, one eye gets the information that the other one misses. In addition, the brain will "fill in" information.

4.   An object that is presented very briefly to one side of the visual field (left or right) is typically processed only in one hemisphere. This is because the image falls only on the left or right halves of the retinas (and is then processed in the right or left hemisphere, respectively). As a result of the brief presentation, the person does not have time to reorient the eyes toward the object. (Also, the neural activity does not last long enough to transfer across the corpus callosum.)

5.   They take advantage of retinal disparity. The slides project a slightly different image to each eye, reproducing what normally happens when we look at a scene with both eyes. The disparity, or difference, between the two images produces the sensation of depth, giving the scene three dimensions rather than two.

6.   In this figure, the circles reflect the same wavelengths of light, but the background color of each leads to the perception that the circles are different colors.

7.   Yellow and blue paints contain pigments. The principle of color subtracting applies here: Pigments absorb some wavelengths of light and reflect others. Mixing yellow and blue paint produces green because these pigments absorb all of the wavelengths except those that correspond to green. When yellow and blue lights are mixed, the effect is additive. Gray or white is produced because these two wavelengths cancel each other out (in their effects on the Y-B cells).

8.   Opponent process theory states that there are only two color receptors: one for red and green, and one for blue and yellow. This theory attempts to explain color vision in terms of opposing processes. Hering believed that the photochemical in the red-green receptor is broken down by red light and regenerates in green light. A similar process would work in the blue-yellow receptor. If someone stares at a red stimulus for a minute and then looks at a white wall or sheet of paper, the person will see a green version of the original object. This happens because overstimulating the eye with one light (red) will make it more sensitive to its complement (green). This is consistent with opponent process theory, which states that two wavelengths affect the same receptor in opposed directions.

9.   The combined theory is consistent with what was previously known about color, including the principles of light mixing as well as complementary colors. The theory also explains these facts, whereas the trichromatic theory could not explain complementary colors or negative color afterimages. Finally, the theory was used to predict the different cone types and the connections among the ganglion cells before there was physical evidence for them, and these predictions have been confirmed.

10.  If someone cannot distinguish red from green, but is highly sensitive to green, then she or he probably has the photopigment for green in the red cones.

11. Lateral inhibition is the result of the way in which receptors and ganglion cells are interconnected. A receptor will have an excitatory effect on one ganglion cell while it inhibits activity in adjacent ganglion cells. This produces the Mach band illusion, which is the perception that at areas of contrast, dark edges are darker and light edges are lighter. This occurs because ganglion cells receiving stimulation from the edge of the dark region are receiving more inhibition (from the receptors stimulated by the light edge) than those farther from the border, and ganglion cells receiving stimulation from the light edge receive less inhibition (from the receptors stimulated by the dark edge) than those farther away.

12. In an on-center, off-surround cell, light falling on the entire receptive field will produce no change in the rate of firing, because the effects of light on the two areas cancel each other out. When the surround is illuminated, the cell will be inhibited, whereas when the center and a portion of the surround are illuminated, the net effect will be excitation.

13. A simple cell receives input from several ganglion cells with adjacent receptive fields oriented in a line. It detects an edge of light contrast that is aligned with its receptive field because the edge stimulates all (or almost all) of its ganglion cells. A complex cell receives input from several simple cells with receptive fields that have the same orientation and are adjacent to each other. Thus, as the edge moves across the receptive fields of these simple cells, the complex cell will continue responding, as long as the orientation doesn't change. This means that, compared to simple cells, complex cells have a larger receptive field, that is, they can detect edges over a wider area of the retina.

14. Objects would appear very simple, like line drawings without gradations of shading and texture (as in Figure 10.23b).

15. The parvocellular system is specialized for seeing in color and fine detail; reading is dependent on this system. The magnocellular system is specialized for perceiving movement and depth; detecting movement in the periphery of the visual field is dependent on this system.

16. The different agnosias (object, color, movement) exist because different parts of the brain are responsible for processing these aspects of visual stimuli. When a specific area is damaged, such as the inferior temporal cortex, the person may experience object agnosia and prosopagnosia but will not experience movement agnosia. Because these functions are handled in relatively distinct areas of the brain, they are disrupted only by damage to specific areas.

17. Blindsight is a phenomenon in which people with damage to the primary visual area perform as if they can see objects, even though they have no awareness of them. This may occur because of connections with parts of the cortex not involved in conscious awareness (connections that bypass V1).

18. In the Greeble study, people were presented with different novel facial stimuli. After several trials, they could tell them apart. The "experts," those who could recognize individual Greebles, showed activity in the fusiform face area, whereas the novices did not. This suggests that this area is used in recognizing familiar people (or members of another species), and that it is affected by our experiences.

## Post-test

1. d   2. c   3. a   4. b   5. d   6. a   7. c   8. c   9. d   10. c   11. d   12. d
13. b   14. d   15. b   16. a   17. c   18. a   19. c   20. b   21. c   22. a   23. b
24. b   25. c   26. d   27. b   28. d   29. a   30. c   31. a   32. d   33. d   34. c
35. b   36. a   37. a   38. b   39. d   40. d   41. b   42. a.   43. c   44. c

# 11 The Body Senses and Movement

## Learning Objectives

After reading this chapter, you should be able to answer the following questions.

1. What are the different types of skin receptors? Identify what general type of receptor each one is, and describe the stimuli to which each responds.

2. What are the structures and functions of the vestibular sense?

3. How do the somatosensory cortex and posterior parietal cortex contribute to body senses and perception?

4. How is information about pain transmitted in the nervous system? What are the internal and external ways to control the experience of pain?

5. How can the experience of pain differ from normal perceptions of pain?

6. What are the types of muscles found in the body? How do skeletal muscles work to produce movement?

7. What role does the spinal cord play in generating movement (such as reflexes and patterns of movement)?

8. What brain areas are involved in movement? How does each contribute?

9. What are some disorders of movement? What are the current and future treatments for each?

## The Body Senses

### Summary and Guided Review

After studying this section in the text, fill in the blanks of the following summary.

Unlike vision and _____ (1), which tell us about things and conditions external to ourselves, the body senses convey information about things we are directly in contact with as well as our own internal conditions. Because the body senses provide information about spatial position, posture, and balance, they are intimately tied in with _____ (2), behavior that allows us to interact with the environment.

We get information about the body from the _____ (3) system and from the vestibular system. _____ (4) refers to our sense of position and movement of our limbs and body. These messages originate in the muscles and joints. The commonly accepted skin senses include touch, _____ (5), cold, and _____ (6), and as such they provide information about both internal and external events. An additional sense might be _____ (7), because it appears to have its own receptors and pathways.

There are several types of encapsulated receptors, each of which is sensitive to different aspects of _____ (8). _____ (9) corpuscles and _____ (10) disks in the superficial layers of skin detect the texture and fine detail, as well as movement, of objects against the skin. In the deeper levels, _____ (11) corpuscles and _____ (12) endings detect stretching of the skin and contribute to our perception of the shape of grasped objects. Free nerve endings are sensitive to temperature and _____ (13). The free nerve ending receptors for temperature are members of the _____ (14) family of protein ion channels. Detection of pain also requires several receptors; these sources are characterized as thermal, _____ (15), and mechanical. Thermal and chemical pain receptors are also members of the TRP family; the best known is the _____ (16) heat pain receptor, which also responds to capsaicin in chili peppers.

The _____ (17) sense, whose receptors are located in the vestibular organs, is involved in maintaining balance as well as providing information about head

position and movement. The three _____ _____
(18), located near the cochlea, are oriented differently in space, providing sensitivity to
acceleration in different planes. When we accelerate, this force displaces the gelatinous
mass or _____ (19), which in turn changes the firing rate of
_____ (20) cells. The utricle and _____ (21) contain
a jellylike substance and hair cells (in horizontal and vertical patches, respectively); they
monitor head position in relation to gravity. In general, proprioception and the vestibular
sense provide coordinated information about the movement and _____
(22) of our bodies. The vestibular system sends projections to the _____
(23), brain stem, and parieto-insular-vestibular cortex (the last of which makes us nauseous
when we get dizzy).

     Each spinal nerve receives sensory information from a different _____
(24); the body areas served by these nerves overlap, so if a nerve is injured the dermatome
retains some sensation. Body sensory information is carried by spinal and cranial nerves
to the _____ (25) and then to the somatosensory cortex, mostly
on the _____ (26) side of the brain. There are many similarities
in the organization and function of the somatosensory systems and the other sensory
systems. The somatosensory cortex contains a(n) _____ (27) map
of the body, with adjacent body parts represented by adjacent parts of the cortex. The
_____ (28) somatosensory cortex plays a role in processing sensory
information from the body and sends information to the _____ (29)
somatosensory cortex that integrates information from both sides of the body. The latter
structure is particularly responsive to stimuli that have acquired meaning, and it sends
information to the _____ (30), contributing to memory formation
when somatosensation is involved. Another target area is the _____
_____ (31) cortex, where information from several sensory
modalities is integrated, and output allowing for coordinated movements is sent to the
_____ (32) areas of the brain.

     A unified _____ (33) image is critical to our ability to function and
even to our self-concept. Damage to the somatosensory system can produce conditions such
as neglect or denial that a particular limb exists; individuals with _____
_____ _____ (34) disorder lack superior parietal
activation when a paralyzed limb is touched and will sometimes ask that it be amputated.
The entire body can be incorporated into an illusion called the _____-
of-_____ (35) experience, during which the person sees his or her body
from another location. This can be caused by either traumatic injury or epilepsy affecting the
junction between the temporal and parietal lobes.

     Painful stimuli such as intense _____ (36) or temperature, damage
to tissue, and exposure to various chemicals are detected by free nerve endings. Pain
neurons and nonneural cells release a wide array of signaling molecules referred to as the
_____ _____ (37). This process produces swelling and
redness, and _____ (38) excitability of the pain neurons so much that they
respond even to _____ (39). This effect is adaptive because it encourages
one to protect the injured area.

     Pain information first travels to the spinal cord. The immediate sharp pain
sensed following an injury is a result of information traveling via large, myelinated
_____ (40) fibers, whereas the more delayed and persistent
_____ (41) pain experienced is the result of activity in smaller C fibers.
In the spinal cord, pain neurons release glutamate and _____ (42), a
neuropeptide that increases pain sensitivity.

Reduction of pain can be accomplished by using local _____
(43) that block _____ (44) channels in the pain neurons and reduce
their ability to fire. General anesthetics may be injected or inhaled, rendering the person
_____ (45). The most frequently used drugs for pain are aspirin,
_____ (46), and acetaminophen (Tylenol). Anti-inflammatory drugs work
by blocking the synthesis of _____ (47) that are released in response to
injury. However, _____ (48) has a weak effect on the enzymes, so it does
not produce anti-inflammatory effects. More powerful drugs are often required for intense
pain, such as _____ (49), the gold standard for pain reduction. Because
this drug causes rapid tolerance and addiction, researchers are studying alternatives such as
Tanezumab, an antibody for _____ _____ (50) factor
that has shown promise for treating arthritis and back pain. There also is promising success
with _____ _____ (51); individuals treated with a
gene that increased endorphin production saw an 80% reduction in cancer pain.

People sometimes feel little or no pain following traumatic injury. For instance
_____ _____ (52) felt no pain despite having been
mauled by a lion. This is because under some conditions, the body releases internal, or
_____ (53), substances to deal with pain. These substances are called
_____ (54) and act on _____ (55) receptors in many
parts of the nervous system. Several kinds of stimulation trigger a result in releasing these
substances, which include _____ (56) stress, acupuncture, and vaginal
stimulation, which might play a role in reducing pain during _____
(57) or intercourse. Pain relief from a placebo may also involve endorphins, as revealed by
_____ (58) blockage of opiate receptors.

According to Melzack and Wall's _____ _____
(59) theory, pressure signals cause the brain to send a(n) _____ (60)
message down the spinal cord, where it closes a neural "gate" in the pain pathway. This is one
of the pathways by which endorphins reduce pain. Pain causes the release of endorphins in
the brain stem structure called the _____ _____ (61)
or PAG; the endorphins inhibit the release of _____ (62) in the spinal
cord and "close" the pain gate.

Fortunately, _____ _____ (63) to pain is a rare
condition, because those who are afflicted unknowingly hurt themselves and often engage
in risky and dangerous behavior. This condition may be genetic. A mutation in the SCN9A
gene renders one type of _____ (64) channel nonfunctional, disabling
pain neurons. A mutation in the gene for nerve growth factor results in considerable loss of
neural fibers.

Chronic pain is defined as pain that persists after _____ (65)
has occurred, or would be expected to have occurred. Chronic pain patients frequently
show signs of being clinically _____ (66) prior to injury, which
tend to cause them to exaggerate the intensity and extent of pain. There also may be
maladaptive responses to stressful events triggered by strong connections between the
_____ _____ (67) and the frontal cortex, which are
found in chronic pain patients one year after injury. Many changes occur in the nervous
system during chronic pain, such as increased sensitivity of pain pathways and an increase
in the amount of the _____ (68) cortex devoted to the painful area.
Although many cortical areas are activated in patients with chronic back pain, there is a loss of
_____ _____ (69).

Sensations from _____ (70) limbs are real for amputees and,
despite the fact that signals are no longer being sent to the brain from the amputated

limb, about _____% (71) of amputees report feeling pain in the missing limb. Anesthetizing the problematic nerves relieves this pain in no more than _____ (72) of the patients. As described in the Application, more successful strategies have involved techniques that reduce _____ _____ (73), such as using a functional prosthesis or a(n) _____ (74) illusion to replace sensations from the missing limb.

## Short Answer and Essay Questions

Answer the following questions.

1. Melanie is driving along the interstate at 55 mph. She crosses into a 70-mph zone and accelerates up to 70. She can feel the difference in speed as she accelerates, but once she reaches 70 and sets the cruise control, her only sensation of movement is from the passing landscape. How does the activity in the vestibular system explain her sensations?

2. List the different forms of encapsulated nerve endings and the types of touch to which they are sensitive.

3. Describe four similarities that somatosensation shares with other senses such as vision.

4. Anatomically, what are the bases of sharp and dull pain? How is each adaptive?

5. Describe the pathway by which endorphins are thought to control pain.

6. What is the probable anatomical basis of phantom pain?

# Movement

## Summary and Guided Review

After studying this section in the text, fill in the blanks of the following summary.

Movement involves striated, or _____ (75), muscles. The two other types of muscles are _____ (76) muscles found in the heart, and _____ (77) muscles found in the internal organs. Striated muscle cells are controlled by motor neurons at the _____ (78) junction (NMJ) via the neurotransmitter _____ (79). A single neuron may control a few or many muscle cells; the ratio of muscle fibers per neuron determines the _____ (80) of movement possible. Each muscle fiber is made up of _____ (81) filaments that slide along the _____ (82) filaments to shorten the fiber and contract the muscle. _____ (83) connect muscles to bone, and movement occurs when muscles contract, pulling against the bone. In the limbs, muscles are paired in a(n) _____ (84) way so that they produce opposing movements at a joint. Most muscle tension adjustments occur due to fast reflexes at the level of the _____ _____ (85).

An example of a spinal reflex occurs when the _____ (86) tendon is tapped; this stretches the quadriceps muscle, where stretch receptors called _____ _____ (87) send a signal up the sensory nerve into the spinal cord. The sensory neurons form synapses with _____ (88) neurons inside the spine, and a motor message is sent back to the quadriceps, causing it to _____ (89). This allows for quick, automatic postural adjustments, and prevent muscle or tendon damage due to over-contraction or forces acting on the tendon. Muscle contractions are detected by _____ _____ (90) organs, which respond by inhibiting motor neurons and limiting the contraction so that damage from over-contraction does not occur. The spinal cord also contains _____ _____ _____ (91), which are networks that produce a rhythmic pattern of motor activity such as walking or swimming. These networks free the brain for more important activities.

There are several cortical and subcortical brain areas involved in movement, organized in a hierarchical manner. The _____ _____ (92) integrates auditory and visual information about the world with information about the body. This has been extensively tested using the delayed _____-to-_____ (93) task, where an individual sees an object, then later must select it out of multiple objects. Information then proceeds to secondary motor areas for conversion to motor commands. The _____ _____ (94) starts planning a movement by combining information received from the prefrontal cortex and the posterior parietal cortex. The primary motor cortex has two secondary areas, the _____ (92) motor area and the _____ (93) cortex. The _____ (94) cortex is an important center in the planning of movement, because it receives, integrates, and briefly stores information about the body and the environment. Studies of brain activity in monkeys during different stages of a delayed _____-to-_____ (95) task indicate that certain cells in the prefrontal cortex become active when a stimulus is presented and continue firing after its removal.

Other cells start firing before activity begins in the premotor areas; this indicates that the _____ (96) cortex selects the target of behavior and the appropriate motor response. The _____ (97) cortex programs an activity by combining information from the prefrontal cortex and the posterior parietal cortex. One interesting demonstration of the activity of these neurons is called the _____ _____ (98) illusion, where a rubber hand is stimulated at the same time as the person's hidden hand. Soon, the person reports a sense of ownership of the rubber hand itself, due to activity in this cortex. Sequences of movement such as eating or playing a musical instrument are coordinated by the _____ _____ (99) area; activity of different cells in this area produces different types of movements. The _____ _____ (100) cortex receives input from secondary motor areas and is responsible for the organizing and executing _____ (101) movements. Cells in this area are relatively unspecialized; each cell may contribute to a range of related behaviors.

Two brain areas do not produce motor actions themselves but do modulate the activity of the motor systems they connect. The first, called the _____ _____ (102), includes the caudate nucleus, putamen, and globus pallidus, which fine-tune and smooth out movements. It is also involved in learning _____ (103) of movement so the sequence can be performed as a unit. This area is also severely affected by _____ (104) disease, which can cause learning disabilities, postural changes, and involuntary movements. The cerebellum receives input from the motor cortex regarding planned movements, and it integrates body posture and movement information from the _____ (105) system. As a result, this area is involved in several functions related to balance and the control of _____ (106) movements. It coordinates the different components of complex movements and provides corrections as movements are being executed. It is also involved in motor learning, nonmotor learning, as well as making time and speed estimates about visual and auditory objects.

There are several neurologically based movement disorders. Parkinson's disease affects 0.3% of the population in industrial nations and 1% of individuals over the age of 60. This disorder is caused by deterioration of the _____ _____ (107), the source of dopaminergic neurons projecting to the _____ (108) composed of part of the basal ganglia and the nucleus accumbens. Symptoms of Parkinson's disease include tremor, rigidity, and problems with balance, coordination, and the initiation of movement. Some of the genes involved in Parkinson's disease control the production of deviant proteins in neurons called _____ _____ (109), which may contribute to cognitive deficits and depression. Brain injury and environmental _____ (110) found in industrial chemicals and pesticides may be involved in causing Parkinson's disease, and some people may inherit a reduced ability to metabolize these chemicals. The risk of Parkinson's disease is reduced by 50% in _____ (111) and 80% in _____ (112) drinkers. One theory is that the active chemical in the beverage, _____ (113), reduces the effects of toxins by blocking adenosine receptors, resulting in increased dopamine and acetylcholine release. Treatment of Parkinson's disease has traditionally involved administration of the dopamine precursor _____ (114). The use of embryonic stem cells has not produced clinically significant improvement, although treatment using _____ (115) stem cells has shown more promise. Other alternatives to drug treatment include strategically placed _____ (116) in the basal ganglia, performed in individuals unable to take dopaminergic drugs, but this approach can lead to deficits such as weakness. There has been better success with _____ _____ (117) stimulation, which improves motor functioning and increases levodopa for up to 10 years, though cognitive deficits remain.

Huntington's disease occurs as a result of progressive cell loss in the cortex and _____ (118), producing movement impairments that become more pronounced with time, as well as psychological changes. The disease is eventually fatal from extensive cell death, presumably from a build-up of the protein _____ (119); the gene responsible for this protein has been located, and a person inheriting the dominant mutated form of the gene will eventually develop Huntington's disease. A number of drugs have been used to treat symptoms, but only one drug has received FDA approval. It works by reducing excess _____ (120) that causes the abnormal movements. Drugs that silence the mutated gene also have shown short-term promise in animal studies.

Several autoimmune diseases also involve the disruption of movement. _____ (121) occurs as a result of a decrease in the number or sensitivity of acetylcholine receptors, and it is characterized by muscular weakness that, if untreated, may cause death. A study using a snake venom that binds to acetylcholine receptors revealed that people with the disease have significantly fewer of these receptors. Treatment normally involves _____ (122), or AChE, inhibitors, but a more permanent treatment involves removal of the _____ (123) gland, the body's major source of antibody-producing lymphocytes. _____ _____ (124) involves the loss of myelin in CNS cells, producing scarring and reducing or eliminating the functioning of affected neurons. Weakness, tremor, and impaired coordination result. Evidence suggests that myelin is destroyed by the _____ (125) system, perhaps as a result of exposure to a virus such as measles, mumps, or the Epstein-Barr virus. One drug treatment that has just been approved for multiple sclerosis blocks _____ (126) channels and improves motor performance, particularly walking. New stem cell treatments also show promise; injecting stem cells from a patient's _____ _____ (127) reduced brain inflammation and improved brain function.

## Short Answer and Essay Questions

Answer the following questions.

7.  In terms of precision of movement, what are the consequences of the fact that a single motor neuron projecting to the biceps muscle serves 100 muscle cells, whereas a single motor neuron projecting to the eye muscles serves only three cells?

8.  How might central pattern generators be useful in treating spinal cord injuries?

9.  Explain the delayed match-to-sample task. How does activity in the prefrontal cortex correspond with different components of this task?

10. How do researchers know that the primary motor cortex, and not other motor areas, is responsible for the execution of movement?

11. Compare Parkinson's and Huntington's diseases in terms of what is known about the genetic basis of each. For which disease does the environment seem to play a more important role? Why?

12. Why is myasthenia gravis considered to be an autoimmune disease?

## Post-test

Use these multiple-choice questions to check your understanding of the chapter.

1.  The receptors in the body that convey information about muscle tension and limb position are part of which sensory system?
    a. vestibular sense
    b. somatosensation
    c. proprioception
    d. none of the above

2.  Pacinian corpuscles are found ___ the surface of the skin and detect ___.
    a. near; touch and shape
    b. far from; touch and shape
    c. near; warmth and cold
    d. far from; warmth and cold

3.  Which of the following areas of the body probably contains the FEWEST touch receptors?
    a. tongue
    b. upper arm
    c. thumb
    d. foot

4.  Which of the following senses is NOT detected by free nerve endings?
    a. warmth
    b. cold
    c. touch
    d. pain

5.  The body segment served by a specific spinal nerve is called a
    a. dermatome.
    b. spinal area.

      c. cupula.
      d. Ruffini area.

6. Information about touch from the right side of the body projects
      a. only to the left hemisphere.
      b. only to the right hemisphere.
      c. to the left and right hemispheres equally.
      d. mostly to the left hemisphere.

7. The primary somatosensory cortex is located in the
      a. anterior parietal lobe.
      b. posterior frontal lobe.
      c. central sulcus.
      d. superior temporal lobe.

8. Capsaicin
      a. acts on the TRPV1 receptor.
      b. is an ingredient of chili peppers.
      c. can alleviate joint pain.
      d. all of the above

9. In the vestibular system, hair cells are found in the
      a. utricle.
      b. saccule.
      c. semicircular canals.
      d. all of the above

10. Which of the following informs the brain about body position and movement?
      a. proprioception
      b. vestibular sense
      c. skin senses
      d. interoceptive system

11. As part of a classroom exercise, you spin around on an office chair for numerous rota-
    tions, and then stop. You feel like you are still spinning because you are still bending
    the hair cells inside your ___. You still know which way up is , because you didn't affect
    your ___.
      a. semicircular canals; cochlea
      b. cochlea; utricle or saccule
      c. semicircular canals; utricle or saccule
      d. utricle and saccule; semicircular canals

12. The vestibular system projects to the ___ cortex, which is responsible for the disgust
    and nausea you feel when you are dizzy.
      a. premotor
      b. parieto-insular-vestibular
      c. somatosensory
      d. posterior parietal

13. The ___ receives input from both sides of the body through the left and right pri-
    mary somatosensory cortices, and are particularly responsive to stimuli that have
    acquired ___.
      a. primary somatosensory cortex; pain
      b. secondary somatosensory cortex; meaning
      c. posterior parietal cortex; emotions
      d. amygdala; reinforcement

14. Patients suffering from one of the weirdest disorders, called ___, are convinced that a particular limb doesn't belong to them and sometimes ask to have it amputated.
    a. out-of-body disorder
    b. mismatched limb disorder
    c. body integrity identity disorder
    d. somnolescence disorder

15. A-delta fibers are ___ and are responsible for our experience of ___ pain.
    a. myelinated; sharp
    b. myelinated; dull
    c. unmyelinated; sharp
    d. unmyelinated; dull

16. Mice that lack receptors for substance P appear to experience
    a. no pain.
    b. only mild pain.
    c. only intense pain.
    d. moderate pain all of the time.

17. Which of the following pain medications acts by reducing inflammation in tissues?
    a. caffeine
    b. morphine
    c. acetaminophen
    d. ibuprofen

18. Endorphins are LEAST likely to be released in response to which of the following?
    a. physical stress
    b. vaginal stimulation
    c. placebo
    d. escapable shock

19. Pain causes the release of endorphins in the ___, which in turn causes inhibition of the release of substance P in the ___.
    a. PAG; spinal cord
    b. spinal cord; PAG
    c. PAG; amygdala
    d. spinal cord; cingulate cortex

20. Which of the following is NOT true about pain disorders?
    a. Most amputees do not experience phantom limb pain.
    b. Congenital pain insensitivity is a rare disorder, most likely genetic in origin.
    c. Chronic pain can cause loss of gray matter in the brain.
    d. Successful treatment of phantom limb pain reverses cortical reorganization.

21. Movements of the stomach and intestines are produced by
    a. smooth muscle.
    b. skeletal muscle.
    c. striated muscle.
    d. cardiac muscle.

22. Which of the following muscles probably has the MOST individual muscle cells controlled by a single motor neuron?
    a. triceps muscle
    b. eye muscle
    c. index finger muscle
    d. tongue muscle

23. Which of the following statements regarding antagonistic muscle pairs is FALSE?
    a. Each muscle has opposing effects on a limb.
    b. Both muscles may be contracted simultaneously.
    c. Maintaining the balance between opposed pairs of muscles requires conscious, voluntary activity.
    d. Coordination of antagonistic muscles is controlled by the spinal cord.

24. Muscle tension (extent of contraction) is detected by
    a. Golgi tendon organs.
    b. muscle spindles.
    c. Lewy bodies.
    d. a and b

25. Central pattern generators
    a. are found in lower animals but not in humans.
    b. are present in young infants, but they atrophy by adulthood.
    c. work even when the spinal cord is severed.
    d. none of the above

26. In producing movement, the last cortical area to be activated is the
    a. premotor area.
    b. association cortex.
    c. supplementary motor cortex.
    d. primary motor cortex.

27. The "memory" of a stimulus used in the delayed match-to-sample task seems to be held in the
    a. primary motor cortex.
    b. supplementary motor cortex.
    c. premotor cortex.
    d. prefrontal cortex.

28. Selection of arm movement needed for reaching a specific target seems to occur in the
    a. primary motor cortex.
    b. supplementary motor cortex.
    c. premotor cortex.
    d. prefrontal cortex.

29. Sequences of movements, such as those involved in typing on a computer keyboard, are coordinated by cells in the
    a. primary motor cortex.
    b. supplementary motor cortex.
    c. premotor cortex.
    d. prefrontal cortex.

30. The actual execution of a movement is triggered by activity in the
    a. primary motor cortex.
    b. supplementary motor cortex.
    c. premotor cortex.
    d. prefrontal cortex.

31. Which brain areas contribute to the smoothness of movement?
    a. cerebellum and premotor cortex
    b. supplementary motor cortex and basal ganglia
    c. prefrontal cortex and premotor cortex
    d. cerebellum and basal ganglia

32. The cerebellum is involved in
    a. the order and timing of complex movements.
    b. the learning of motor skills.
    c. judging the speed of objects.
    d. all of the above

33. Parkinson's disease results from a loss of ___ neurons originating in the ___.
    a. dopaminergic; striatum
    b. dopaminergic; substantia nigra
    c. cholinergic; striatum
    d. cholinergic; substantia nigra

34. Currently, which of the following treatments for Parkinson's disease has been shown to have the FEWEST side effects?
    a. brain stimulation
    b. brain lesions
    c. L-dopa
    d. fetal tissue transplant

35. Which of the following statements is (are) TRUE of Huntington's disease?
    a. It is a degenerative disease, becoming progressively worse over time.
    b. Cognitive and emotional deficits always occur.
    c. Researchers know which gene is involved and how it works.
    d. all of the above

36. People with myasthenia gravis have fewer or less sensitive ___ receptors.
    a. dopamine
    b. serotonin
    c. endorphin
    d. acetylcholine

37. Myasthenia gravis is MOST effectively treated by
    a. acetylcholinesterase inhibitors.
    b. thymectomy.
    c. fetal tissue transplant.
    d. brain stimulation.

38. Multiple sclerosis involves
    a. loss of myelin in the central nervous system.
    b. loss of myelin in the peripheral nervous system.
    c. loss of myelin in both the central and peripheral nervous systems.
    d. none of the above

## Answers

### Guided Review

1. hearing/audition
2. movement
3. somatosensory
4. Proprioception
5. warmth
6. pain
7. itch
8. touch
9. Meissner's
10. Merkel's
11. Pacinian
12. Ruffini
13. pain
14. TRP (transient receptor potential)
15. chemical
16. TRPV1
17. vestibular
18. semicircular canals
19. cupula
20. hair
21. saccule
22. position/orientation
23. cerebellum
24. dermatome
25. thalamus
26. opposite
27. somatotopic
28. primary
29. secondary
30. hippocampus
31. posterior parietal
32. frontal
33. body
34. body integrity identity
35. out-of-body
36. pressure
37. inflammatory soup
38. enhanced
39. touch
40. A-delta
41. dull
42. substance P
43. anesthetics
44. sodium
45. unconscious
46. ibuprofen
47. prostaglandins
48. acetaminophen
49. morphine
50. nerve growth
51. endorphin
52. David Livingston
53. endogenous
54. endorphins
55. opiate
56. physical
57. (child)birth
58. naloxone
59. gate control
60. inhibitory
61. periaqueductal gray
62. substance P

63. congenital insensitivity
64. sodium
65. healing
66. depressed
67. nucleus accumbens
68. somatosensory
69. gray matter
70. phantom
71. 75
72. half
73. cortical reorganization
74. mirror
75. skeletal
76. cardiac
77. smooth
78. neuromuscular
79. acetylcholine
80. precision
81. myosin
82. actin
83. Tendons
84. antagonistic
85. spinal cord
86. patellar
87. muscle spindles
88. motor
89. contract
90. Golgi tendon
91. central pattern generators
92. prefrontal cortex
93. match-to-sample
94. prefrontal
95. match-to-sample

96. prefrontal
97. premotor
98. rubber hand
99. supplementary
100. primary motor
101. voluntary
102. basal ganglia
103. sequences
104. Parkinson's
105. vestibular
106. eye
107. substantia nigra
108. striatum
109. Lewy bodies
110. toxins
111. smokers
112. coffee
113. caffeine
114. L-dopa or levodopa
115. adult
116. lesions
117. deep brain
118. striatum
119. huntingtin
120. dopamine
121. acetylcholine
122. acetylcholinesterase
123. thymus
124. Multiple sclerosis
125. immune
126. potassium
127. bone marrow

## Short Answer and Essay Questions

1. When your body accelerates, the increase in speed displaces the gelatinous masses (cupulas) in the vestibular organs, causing the hair cells to bend and change the rate of firing in their neurons. Once you reach a stable speed, the cupulas return to normal, and the hair cells return to their normal rate of firing, so we do not notice movement.

2. Meissner's corpuscles and Merkel's disks are located near the surface of the skin, and they can detect texture, fine detail, and movement of objects across the skin. Pacinian corpuscles and Ruffini endings are located deeper, and because they detect stretching of the skin, they can detect the shape of objects that are grasped.

3. The visual and somatosensory areas are similar in the following ways: They contain a map of their respective receptive fields (the body and the retina, respectively); the receptive fields of some of the cells are arranged with an excitatory center and inhibitory surround; processing is hierarchical, with certain subareas of the somatosensory cortex passing information along to other areas (similar to the sequential processing seen in the visual system); and both systems contain cells that are feature detectors.

4. Information about sharp pain is carried along large-diameter A-delta fibers; as a result, these pain messages travel to the brain quickly. They signal the onset of a painful stimulus that triggers an almost immediate withdrawal or avoidance response (such as pulling your hand away from a hot burner). Dull pain is encoded along smaller-diameter C fibers, and this message travels more slowly, but the pain is more persistent. Dull pain probably reminds us that we have been injured; it may prevent further injury and also motivates us to seek treatment.

5. When pain messages are received in the periaqueductal gray, endorphins are released onto neurons that project down the spinal cord; there these neurons inhibit the neurons responsible for releasing substance P, reducing the flow of pain.

6. When a limb is amputated or no longer sends sensory input to the brain because of a spinal cord injury, the area of the somatosensory cortex served by that limb may be "taken over" by neurons from adjacent areas. Activation of these neurons produces a painful sensation that feels as if it is in the amputated limb.

7. When the ratio of motor neurons to muscle cells is low, as in the case of eye muscles, it allows for a great deal more precision of movement than when the ratio is high, as in the biceps muscle.

8. Central pattern generators contain "instructions" for producing rhythmic movements such as walking. When the spinal cord is severed, no cortical control of the pattern generators exists. However, they can be stimulated electrically to produce rhythmic stepping movements, and researchers are attempting to use them in therapy with spinal cord patients.

9. In this task, the subject is shown a stimulus, and then the stimulus is removed. After a delay, two stimuli are shown, the original and another one, and the subject must select the original in order to receive reinforcement. During the initial presentation and the delay period, some cells in the prefrontal cortex become active and continue to fire throughout the delay, suggesting that they are "holding" the stimulus in memory. When the opportunity to respond occurs, another group of cells becomes active; because this activity precedes activity in the premotor cortex, it suggests that the prefrontal cortex selects the target and the appropriate response.

10. Activity in the prefrontal and premotor cortices occurs prior to the onset of movement, whereas activity in the primary motor cortex corresponds with movement. This suggests that

although the prefrontal and premotor areas are involved in planning movements, the primary motor cortex executes the movement.

11. Huntington's disease is due to a single gene; the individual will develop the disease if the gene has more than 37 repetitions of the bases cytosine, adenine, and guanine, with more repetitions correlated with earlier development. The genetic basis of Parkinson's is not well understood. It is familial (inherited) in only a minority of cases. In familial Parkinson's disease, several different genes appear to be involved. Implicated genes are involved in the death of dopamine neurons, production of Lewy bodies, and ability to metabolize toxins that may cause Parkinson's. In the latter cases, exposure to the toxins is probably necessary in order for the disease to develop, so both environment and genetics are important.

12. Myasthenia gravis is treatable by removing the thymus gland, the body's major source of the lymphocytes that produce antibodies. Almost 80% of patients treated with thymectomy recover and most of the remainder improve.

## Post-test

1. c    2. b    3. b    4. c    5. a    6. d    7. a    8. d    9. d    10. b    11. c    12. b
13. b    14. c    15. a    16. b    17. d    18. d    19. a    20. a    21. a    22. a    23. c
24. a    25. c    26. d    27. d    28. c    29. b    30. a    31. d    32. d    33. b    34. a
35. d    36. d    37. b    38. a

# 12 Learning and Memory

## Learning Objectives

After reading this chapter, you should be able to answer the following questions.

1.  How do anterograde and retrograde amnesia differ?

2.  What brain areas seem to be involved in memory consolidation and retrieval?

3.  How do declarative and nondeclarative learning differ?

4.  What is working memory?

5.  What is the significance of LTP and related phenomena for learning?

6.  What synaptic changes occur during LTP?

7.  What factors contribute to memory consolidation?

8.  What normal brain processes contribute to forgetting?

## Learning as the Storage of Memories

### Summary and Guided Review

After studying this section in the text, fill in the blanks of the following summary.

In order to be useful for future behavior, experiences or learning must somehow be stored within the nervous system; without _____ (1), we would be capable of only very simple forms of behavior. This point is demonstrated by the case of HM described in the introduction to the chapter. HM, who underwent removal of much of his _____ (2) lobes to reduce his debilitating seizures, suffered from both anterograde and retrograde _____ (3). Consequently, he had great difficulty forming new memories as well as remembering past events (although he could recall some events that occurred before the age of 16). Because of the extent of damage to HM's brain, it is not known exactly which structures were responsible for his amnesia, although the _____ (4) and associated areas were certainly involved. Moderate anterograde amnesia and minimal retrograde amnesia occur following bilateral damage to the hippocampal area known as _____ (5). Damage to the entire hippocampus produces severe _____ (6) amnesia, and severe retrograde amnesia occurs if the hippocampal _____ (7) is damaged as well. HM's story is considered one of the most important cases in the study of learning and memory. Although he died in 2008 at the age of 82, he continues to make a contribution; researchers at the University of California at San Diego have_____ (8) his brain and are making a 3-D digital _____ (9) available online.

Until information stored in memory undergoes _____ (10), which is the process of forming a permanent physical representation, it is subject to disruption. New memories are easily disrupted, and even old memories may be lost as a result of trauma. Evidence from studies on rats placed in a murky water maze suggests that this process in the hippocampus requires the neurotransmitter _____ (11). The process

by which stored memories are accessed, or _____ (12), also appears
to involve the hippocampus. In humans, this process has also been shown to involve the
hippocampus using _____ (13) scans during long-term free recall of
information. However, because very old memories are less affected by hippocampal damage,
there must be some other mechanism responsible for maintaining and retrieving them. The
fact that learning and effortful attempts at retrieval also activate the _____
(14) area suggests that it might also serve these functions.

    The hippocampus is not the actual storage site of memories. Researchers believe
that _____-_____ (15) memory depends on the
hippocampus but that long-term memory depends on an interaction between the hippocampus
and the _____ (16). For example, when subjects recalled recent news
events, fMRI activity was highest in the _____ (17), but when asked to
recall events over the past 30 years, activity increased in several _____
(18) areas. Consolidated memories are stored in the areas of the cortex where specific
types of information are processed; for example, memories for pictures are stored in
the _____ (19) region, whereas verbal memories are stored in the
left _____ (20) lobe. A "map" of a rat's environment is stored in the
hippocampus, where specialized_____ (21) cells are located; in humans
these cells are involved in not only spatial memory but also context.

    The fact that HM displayed some forms of _____ (22) without being
consciously aware of his newly acquired skills suggests that the brain forms at least two kinds
of memory. _____ (23) memory refers to information about facts, people,
and events that we can verbalize, whereas nondeclarative memory refers to memory for
_____ (24) (including skills learning, emotional learning, and stimulus-
response conditioning). Put simply, declarative memories involve the "what" in memory
whereas nondeclarative memories concern the _____ (25). Studies with
rats demonstrate that different brain areas are involved in each form of memory; declarative
or relational memory is disrupted by damage to the _____ (26), whereas
nondeclarative memory is disrupted by damage to the _____ (27). In
humans, this latter form of learning is disrupted in people with _____
(28) and Huntington's diseases. The _____ (29) is involved in
nondeclarative emotional learning. A subject with bilateral amygdala damage responded to
a loud sound with a skin conductance response but could not be conditioned to respond to
a colored slide that was paired with the sound. Activity in the amygdala may also strengthen
_____ (30) learning about emotional events, through its connections with
the hippocampus.

    Both new and old information are held temporarily in _____
(31) memory while it is being used; this is somewhat similar to a computer's RAM, although
the capacity of working memory is very small and it fades quickly. The neurological
basis of working memory can be studied using the delayed _____-
to-_____ (32) task. Following presentation and removal of
the stimulus, cells continue firing in the cortical area appropriate for that stimulus;
but if this activity is disrupted, the animal still makes a correct choice, so these are
not the location of working memory. Working memory apparently is located in the
_____ (33) cortex; cells there continue firing during the delay, even
in spite of a distracting stimulus, and they respond selectively to the stimulus and task
conditions. The prefrontal cortex seems to be responsible for managing information in
working memory by acting as a central _____ (34) rather than merely
serving as a storage facility for memory.

## Short Answer and Essay Questions

Answer the following questions.

1. Distinguish between anterograde and retrograde amnesia. Using HM's case, give one example of each form.

2. Riedel and colleagues studied the role of the hippocampus in learning in rats by placing them in a water maze. The rats could escape from the water by learning the location of a submerged platform. How were the researchers able to show that impairment of the hippocampus can disrupt both consolidation and retrieval?

3. Distinguish between declarative and nondeclarative memory.

4. What did Bechara and colleagues discover about the different roles of the hippocampus and the amygdala in learning?

5. What are place cells and why are they unique?

# Brain Changes in Learning

## Summary and Guided Review

After studying this section in the text, fill in the blanks of the following summary.

_____ (35) rule states that if a presynaptic neuron is active while a postsynaptic neuron is firing, the synapse will increase in strength. The synaptic changes are the result of _____-_____ _____ (36); they are similar to the neural plasticity exhibited by neurons early in development as synapses are being formed. Long-term potentiation (LTP) has been studied mostly in the _____ (37) but has also been found in the visual, auditory, and motor cortex. In the laboratory, LTP is usually induced by applying pulses of _____-_____ (38) stimulation to presynaptic neurons. This change may last briefly or for several months. _____-_____ _____ (39) weakens a synapse; it occurs when stimulation of presynaptic neurons is insufficient to activate postsynaptic neurons. LTD may be an important mechanism for modifying memories and _____ (40) old memories to free synapses for new information. Presynaptic stimulation also influences the sensitivity of nearby synapses; if a weak synapse and strong synapse on the same postsynaptic neuron are active simultaneously, the weak synapse will be _____ (41), or strengthened. This effect is called _____ (42) LTP. Researchers believe that this type of potentiation is the basis for _____ (43) conditioning. These three phenomena, LTP, LTD, and associative LTP, all illustrate the expression "cells that fire together _____ (44) together." EEG activity in the 4- to 7-Hz range, called the_____ _____ (45), occurs in the _____ (46) when an animal encounters novel stimuli. Hippocampal stimulation coinciding with the peaks of theta waves can induce LTP in just five pulses. This rhythm may emphasize important stimuli for the brain and facilitate _____ (47) and _____ (48).

LTP induction involves a cascade of events at the synapse involving the neurotransmitter _____ (49), which has several different types of receptors. Initially glutamate activates _____ (50) receptors but not _____ (51) receptors, because they are blocked by _____ (52) ions. Partial depolarization of the membrane causes displacement of these ions, which then allows the _____ (53) receptors to be activated. This results in an influx of sodium and _____ (54) ions, which further depolarizes the neuron and activates _____ (55), an enzyme that is necessary for LTP.

LTP induction is followed by changes in _____ (56) activation and silencing, and synthesis of _____ (57), resulting in changes at the synapse and growth of new connections. Once the postsynaptic neuron is activated it releases _____ _____ (58), a retrograde messenger that causes the presynaptic neuron to release more neurotransmitter. Within 30 minutes after LTP, structural changes occur at the synapse. These include increased numbers of _____ (59) on dendrites that make the neuron more sensitive. Other changes include transport of _____ (60) receptors from the dendrites into the spines. The neurotransmitter _____ (61) unmasks previously silent synapses and initiates the growth of new ones. Furthermore, the birth of new neurons, or _____ (62), occurs in the hippocampus. Over the course of a lifetime these new cells may make up _____ % (63) of the total population of cells. These changes are long term, and they may explain why London cabbies who memorize the layout of the city show an increase in the size of the posterior part of the hippocampus, which is known to be involved in spatial _____ (64).

There is ample evidence that the formation of long-term declarative memories depends on a stage in the _____ _____ (65) lobe, followed by a transition to a more permanent form in the _____ (66). The enzyme _____ (67) appears to be involved in this transfer process. Mice that are homozygous for a mutant gene for this enzyme show no _____ LTP (68). Mice that are heterozygous produce some enzyme, and show hippocampal, but not _____ (69), LTP. Another enzyme,   protein kinase M zeta, seems to be necessary for the _____ (70) of LTP during long-term memory; injection of this substance into the insula 25 days after training eliminates a learned taste aversion. There is evidence that some transfer of information from the hippocampus to the cortex occurs during _____ (71). During this "offline" period, the replay of neural firing that occurred while learning a task provides the cortex the opportunity to undergo _____ (72) at the more leisurely pace that it requires. During sleep, more than 100 genes increase their activity and many have been implicated in protein synthesis, synaptic changes, and memory consolidation.

Finally, it is important to understand that although memories may be long lasting, the brain has mechanisms for eliminating or changing information. _____ (73) is a process in which a learned association appears to be eliminated; the memory is actually still available but has been replaced by new learning, which involves the activation of NMDA receptors. The enzyme protein phosphatase 1 and the gene Drac1(V12) apparently mediate _____ (74). This gene's protein product _____ (75) causes memory to decay after learning. In rats, it has been shown that _____ (76), which normally occurs after a memory has been retrieved, is a very vulnerable period during which memories can be disrupted by _____ (77) shock or by a drug that interferes with protein synthesis. Finally, retrieved memories may be _____ (78), for example, by being blended with other memories; Loftus and colleagues have shown that _____ (79) memories may be implanted by suggestion. As stated in In The News, perhaps the best method for long-term recall of information is to practice

_____ (80) right after first learning it; cramming and prolonged review do not seem to result in good memory performance. This might be useful to students studying the text!

## Short Answer and Essay Questions

Answer the following questions.

6. How does LTP resemble the developmental mechanism for establishing synapses? What is associative long-term potentiation?

7. What is LTD? Why is it thought to be important for learning?

8. What roles do glutamate and nitric oxide play in LTP?

9. Name three different processes that show that memories are malleable or not "fixed in stone."

10. It is 7:00 p.m. on Tuesday, and your roommate has an exam in her first class tomorrow at 8:00 a.m. She is not sure if it would be better to spend the next 3 hours studying for the exam and go to bed around 10:30 p.m., or not study tonight, go to bed at 9:00 p.m., and then get up around 5:00 a.m. to study. Based on what the book says about the role of sleep in learning, what advice would you offer your roommate?

11. Winona witnessed a bank robbery by two men but was able to provide little more than general information in her description. Over the two years since the robbery and following repeated questioning, she has recalled several details. On the witness stand, the defense attorney questions the accuracy of these memories, but Winona insists her memories are vivid and accurate. Based on information in the text, what problems do you see with her testimony?

# Learning Deficiencies and Disorders

## Summary and Guided Review

After studying this section in the text, fill in the blanks of the following summary.

Until recently, it was believed that loss of memory and cognitive skills was a natural consequence of _____ (81); however, studies indicate that these losses are not inevitable (though it is unclear whether successful aging is due to choosing an active lifestyle or is an inherent characteristic of the individual). Another misconception is that when memory loss does occur, it results from cell loss, particularly in the cortex and the _____ (82). What does seem to happen is that, the hippocampus loses synapses and _____ (83) receptors, which is the likely cause of diminished LTP and learning. In addition, reduced activity in the _____ (84) cortex, which is linked to the hippocampus, and loss of _____ (85) are also thought to be involved. Cell loss in the _____ _____ (86) region may contribute to memory deficits in both Alzheimer's disease and normal aging, and _____ (87) lobe deficits may be present in many elderly as well. From the molecular side, there have been 17 genes in the _____ _____ (88) that undergo changed levels of expression with aging; animal models with reduced expression of RbAp48 (a protein made by one of the genes) exhibited similar memory problems.

_____ (89) refers to the loss of memory and cognitive abilities in the elderly. _____ (90) disease, in which the brain progressively deteriorates, is a form of dementia. In the early stages, _____ (91) memory is impaired, a symptom that becomes worse over time.

The brains of people with Alzheimer's contain _____ (92) (Aβ) plaques, which interfere with neuron functioning, and _____ (93) tangles; both are associated with cell death. Over time, deficits in brain tissue and functioning can be observed in most of the brain, especially the frontal lobes and the temporal lobes, where they effectively isolate the _____ (94). Over the past decade, scientists have realized they need to distinguish whether or not the amyloid is _____ (95); if it is, the concentration in the brain increases 70-fold and has been linked to memory failure, loss of synapses, and impaired LTP in the hippocampus.

Because plaques and tangles are also a characteristic of _____ (96) syndrome, Alzheimer's researchers looked for genes on chromosome 21, where they found the _____ (97) gene; mice engineered with a mutation of this gene that increases plaques also had deficits in LTP and learning. Of the four known genes for Alzheimer's disease, the ε4 allele of the _____ (98) gene has been found in at least 50% of cases and is associated with plaques and tangles. Late-onset Alzheimer's also has 20 other genes implicated, and although the particular identity of those loci are unknown, they are involved in inflammation, immune response, cell migration, and other _____ (99) functions. Environmental factors can increase the likelihood of developing Alzheimer's disease: early _____ (100) exposure has been linked to APP gene expression changes later in life, and the pesticide DDT also has been associated with Alzheimer's disease.

There are five drugs currently approved for treatment of Alzheimer's disease, although none of them provides a cure. Alzheimer's patients have a significant loss of neurons that release _____ (101), an important neurotransmitter for the hippocampal theta rhythm, impairing learning and memory. Three drugs that prevent the breakdown of acetylcholine are currently used to relieve cognitive and behavioral symptoms in mild cases of Alzheimer's. Moderate to severe cases may be treated with _____ (102), which reduces neurons' sensitivity to excessive glutamate, which overexcites and kills neurons. There are three current major fronts of developing treatments: removing amyloid, reducing inflammation, and preventing tangles. While the first two have been unsuccessful, there is promise with the tangle-preventing drug _____ (103), which has reduced symptom progression by 90%. An interesting approach has been in the area of _____ (104) supplementation; Souvenaid (one potential supplement) has shown promise in improving memory and brain connectivity in Phase 2 trials. To help with finding a cure, the _____ (105) is partnering with drug companies to assist with the costs associated with the high failure rate of drug candidates.

Diagnosing Alzheimer's disease involves a battery of tests, but one of the most important steps is to rule out other forms of _____ (106) that may be more treatable. One strategy involves using PET scanning and tracers that specifically target _____ (107). This technique might help predict the disease and follow its course over time. Because PET scans only diagnose 1/3 of individuals with mild impairment, a more accurate approach is to test for _____ (108) for the disease found in blood and cerebrospinal fluid. A study of Catholic nuns found that the disease might start long before the diagnosis actually occurs and that individuals who did not develop

Alzheimer's disease had higher _____ (109) density in autobiographical essays written decades before. This was despite similar number of *APOE4* alleles, and healthy women showing signs of neurofibrillary tangles in autopsies following death. According to the _____ (110) hypothesis, lifelong learning (as evidenced in the healthy sisters with high idea densities) increases a person's cognitive reserve, giving him or her increased resistance to the degenerative effects of dementia.

_____ _____ (111) is associated with thiamine deficiency, which is usually related to _____ (112) abuse. This degenerative disorder results in anterograde and retrograde amnesia due to damage to the _____ (113) bodies, medial thalamic area, and _____ (114) lobes. In the early stages, _____ (115) can relieve the symptoms but not reverse the damage. Korsakoff's patients often exhibit _____ (116), or the fabrication of stories, probably as an attempt to fill in information they can no longer recall. This characteristic seems to be related to damage to a specific area of the _____ (117) lobe, rendering patients unable to distinguish current reality and memories of prior events.

## Short Answer and Essay Questions

Answer the following questions.

12. Why is memory loss in the elderly no longer considered to be an inevitable consequence of the aging process?

13. Briefly describe five possible reasons for age-related memory loss (not including Alzheimer's).

14. In their search for a genetic basis for Alzheimer's disease, why did researchers focus on chromosome 21?

15. What treatments for Alzheimer's disease are most commonly used? What treatments have proven promising, and which ones have not?

16. What is confabulation? Give an example.

17. What causes Korsakoff's syndrome? Be sure to describe the disease mechanism, as well as the characteristic effects on behavior and memory.

## Post-test

Use these multiple-choice questions to check your understanding of the chapter.

1. Which of the following was NOT a result of HM's surgery?
   a. lowered IQ
   b. anterograde amnesia
   c. retrograde amnesia
   d. relief from seizures

2. Which of the following deficits is an example of anterograde amnesia?
   a. being unable to recall events occurring just prior to brain injury
   b. being unable to recall events occurring after brain injury
   c. being unable to recall events occurring many years prior to brain injury
   d. none of the above

3. Bilateral brain damage that is limited to hippocampal area CA1 results in
   a. moderate anterograde amnesia and profound retrograde amnesia.
   b. moderate anterograde amnesia and minimal retrograde amnesia.
   c. profound anterograde amnesia and profound retrograde amnesia.
   d. profound anterograde amnesia and minimal retrograde amnesia.

4. Consolidation is the process of
   a. accessing stored information.
   b. altering memories during retrieval.
   c. fabricating information missing from memory.
   d. making memories long lasting or permanent.

5. The hippocampus plays a role in
   a. consolidation.
   b. retrieval.
   c. both consolidation and retrieval.
   d. neither consolidation nor retrieval.

6. Over 25 days of being tested for retention of a spatial discrimination task, researchers found that mice showed
   a. increased activity in the hippocampus and increased activity in the cortex.
   b. increased activity in the hippocampus and decreased activity in the cortex.
   c. decreased activity in the hippocampus and increased activity in the cortex.
   d. decreased activity in the hippocampus and decreased activity in the cortex.

7. Effortful attempts at retrieval are associated with increased activity in
   a. the prefrontal area.
   b. the hippocampus.
   c. both the prefrontal area and the hippocampus.
   d. neither the prefrontal area nor the hippocampus.

8. Researchers believe that in most cases memories are stored
   a. in the hippocampus.
   b. in a single storage area of the cortex.
   c. evenly throughout the cortex.
   d. none of the above

9. Which of the following is NOT a type of declarative memory?
   a. episodic memory
   b. emotional memory
   c. spatial memory
   d. autobiographical memory

10. People with damage to the striatum (as in Parkinson's and Huntington's diseases) have difficulty with
    a. procedural memory.
    b. declarative memory.
    c. relational memory.
    d. b and c

11. Incorporating emotional information into memory probably depends on the
    a. amygdala.
    b. cingulate gyrus.
    c. basal ganglia.
    d. cerebellum.

12. Which of the following statements regarding working memory is FALSE?
    a. It holds information temporarily.
    b. It has an unlimited capacity.
    c. It provides the basis for problem solving and decision making.
    d. It can hold new information as well as memories already stored.

13. The brain area that seems to be MOST important for working memory is the
    a. inferior temporal cortex.
    b. parietal cortex.
    c. prefrontal cortex.
    d. superior frontal cortex.

14. Following stimulation of presynaptic neurons with high-frequency impulses, postsynaptic neurons will
    a. decrease their firing rate.
    b. produce larger EPSPs.
    c. produce smaller EPSPs.
    d. produce larger IPSPs.

15. LTP occurs
    a. only in the hippocampus.
    b. only in the visual cortex.
    c. only in the motor cortex.
    d. none of the above

16. Classical conditioning most likely involves
    a. LTP.
    b. associative LTP.
    c. LTD.
    d. associative LTD.

17. Low-frequency stimulation of presynaptic neurons results in
    a. LTP.
    b. LTD.
    c. more EPSPs.
    d. more postsynaptic action potentials.

18. Suppression of ___ rhythms in the ___ inhibits some forms of learning.
    a. theta; hippocampus
    b. theta; cortex
    c. beta; hippocampus
    d. beta; cortex

19. Which of these follows LTP induction?
    a. growth of new dendrites
    b. gene activation
    c. release of dopamine
    d. all of the above

20. In order for NMDA receptors to be activated, ___ must be dislodged.
    a. glutamate
    b. magnesium
    c. sodium
    d. nitric oxide

21. Presynaptic neurons may increase their release of neurotransmitter when the postsynaptic neuron releases
    a. acetylcholine.
    b. magnesium.
    c. sodium.
    d. nitric oxide.

22. Which of the following is TRUE about neurogenesis?
    a. It occurs only in the cortex.
    b. Over the life span, it produces less than 5% of cells in a particular area.
    c. It has been most studied in the hippocampus.
    d. b and c

23. A study of the brains of London taxicab drivers revealed that
    a. the entire hippocampus is larger than in other people.
    b. all of the spatial areas of the brain are larger than in other people.
    c. the posterior portion of the hippocampus was larger than in other people.
    d. none of the above

24. The presence of which of the following substances would MOST likely lead to reduced LTP?
    a. α protein kinase M zeta
    b. nitric oxide blockers
    c. αCaMKII
    d. a and c

25. Which of the following statements regarding LTP is MOST likely true?
    a. It is only a laboratory (or experimental) phenomenon.
    b. Hippocampal LTP is permanent.
    c. Cortical LTP is responsible for long-term memory.
    d. Only mammals exhibit LTP.

26. Mice heterozygous for a defective CaMKII gene
    a. are better learners than normal mice.
    b. are incapable of retaining information for more than a few hours.
    c. show no LTP.
    d. have more CaMKII than mice homozygous for the gene.

27. What is the most accurate statement about sleep and memory?
    a. During sleep, neurons in the hippocampus are silent.
    b. During sleep, more than 100 genes decrease their activity.
    c. "Offline" replay that occurs during sleep helps the cortex undergo LTP.
    d. Contrary to what researchers expected, sleep has no measurable effect on memory.

28. Memories seem to be vulnerable to change during
    a. reconsolidation.
    b. reconstruction.
    c. extinction.
    d. suppression.

29. Which of the following is not TRUE about the process of forgetting?
    a. It has no apparent benefit; it would be better to remember everything, if possible.
    b. It involves the enzyme protein phosphatase 1.
    c. It is a different process from extinction.
    d. It may involve the protein Rac, which causes a memory to decay after learning.

30. Supporting the reserve hypothesis is the finding that
    a. memory failure is an inevitable, normal consequence of aging.
    b. engaging in mental but not physical activity reduces memory loss in older adults.
    c. there is no relationship between aging and memory loss.
    d. remaining mentally active is associated with better cognitive functioning.

31. In older rats,
    a. there are fewer NMDA receptors in the hippocampus.
    b. there are significantly fewer cells in the hippocampus.
    c. there are significantly fewer cells in the cortex.
    d. there is a steady loss of synapses throughout the brain.

32. Loss of cells in the ___ that release acetylcholine is associated with cognitive decline.
    a. hippocampus
    b. basal forebrain region
    c. medial forebrain bundle
    d. entorhinal cortex

33. The MOST common cause of dementia is
    a. Alzheimer's disease.
    b. Korsakoff's syndrome.
    c. nutritional deficiencies.
    d. Huntington's disease.

34. One of the most reliable ways to diagnose Alzheimer's disease (>90% accuracy) is to test the
    a. brain directly using a biopsy.
    b. cerebrospinal fluid for biomarkers.
    c. skin for degenerative peptides.
    d. level of amyloid using a PET scan.

35. In Alzheimer's patients, plaques and tangles found in the ___ lobes disrupt connections between the hippocampus and other structures.
    a. frontal
    b. parietal
    c. temporal
    d. occipital

36. Which of the following statements regarding Alzheimer's disease is FALSE?
    a. There are at least four different genes that cause it.
    b. People with Down syndrome will develop it if they live past 50.
    c. The amyloid precursor protein gene is found on chromosome 21.
    d. Symptoms of Alzheimer's disease do not appear before the age of 60.

37. Which of the following is the most common treatment for Alzheimer's disease?
    a. gene therapy
    b. cholinesterase inhibitors
    c. injection of amyloid to trigger an immune response
    d. memantine

38. One of the environmental triggers for Alzheimer's disease has been childhood early exposure to ___, which has been associated with changes in APP gene expression.
    a. lead (paint)
    b. smoking (nicotine)

c. alcoholic beverages

d. animal dander (fur, skin)

39. Which of the following structures is NOT damaged in Korsakoff's syndrome?

a. hippocampus

b. mammillary bodies

c. medial thalamic area

d. frontal lobes

40. Korsakoff's patients are believed to engage in confabulation because

a. their sense of right and wrong has deteriorated, and they do not care if they lie to others.

b. they have difficulty distinguishing between current reality and their memories of the past.

c. they are completely out of touch with reality.

d. none of the above

# Answers

## Guided Review

1. memory
2. temporal
3. amnesia
4. hippocampus
5. CA1
6. anterograde
7. formation
8. dissected
9. reconstruction
10. consolidation
11. glutamate
12. retrieval
13. PET
14. prefrontal
15. short-term
16. cortex
17. hippocampus
18. cortical
19. occipital
20. frontal
21. place
22. learning
23. Declarative
24. behaviors
25. "how"
26. hippocampus
27. striatum
28. Parkinson's
29. amygdala
30. declarative
31. working
32. match-to-sample
33. prefrontal
34. executive
35. Hebb's
36. long-term potentiation (LTP)
37. hippocampus
38. high-frequency
39. Long-term depression (LTD)
40. clearing
41. potentiated
42. associative
43. classical
44. wire
45. theta rhythm
46. hippocampus
47. LTP
48. LTD
49. glutamate
50. AMPA
51. NMDA
52. magnesium
53. NMDA
54. calcium
55. CaMKII
56. gene
57. protein
58. nitric oxide
59. spines
60. AMPA
61. dopamine
62. neurogenesis

63. 10–20

64. navigation

65. medial temporal

66. cortex

67. αCaMKII

68. hippocampal

69. cortical

70. maintenance

71. sleep

72. LTP

73. Extinction

74. forgetting

75. Rac

76. reconsolidation

77. electroconvulsive

78. reconstructed

79. false

80. retrieval

81. aging

82. hippocampus

83. NMDA

84. entorhinal

85. myelin

86. basal forebrain

87. frontal

88. dentate gyrus

89. Dementia

90. Alzheimer's

91. declarative

92. beta amyloid

93. neurofibrillary

94. hippocampus

95. soluble

96. Down

97. APP

98. APOE

99. cellular

100. lead

101. acetylcholine

102. memantine or Namenda

103. LMTX

104. nutritional

105. NIH

106. dementia

107. plaques

108. biomarkers

109. idea

110. reserve

111. Korsakoff's syndrome

112. alcohol

113. mammillary

114. frontal

115. thiamine

116. confabulation

117. frontal

## Short Answer and Essay Questions

1. Anterograde amnesia is the failure to form new memories following a brain injury, whereas retrograde amnesia is the failure to retrieve memories for events and information experienced prior to the injury. In the case of HM, there are many examples of anterograde amnesia. For example, he could not find his way home to his parents' new house (they moved after his surgery was done), and he could not recall what type of work he was doing. He also experienced retrograde amnesia; he could not recall several significant events from his late teens and early adult years, such as his high school graduation and the end of World War II.

2. These researchers injected a glutamate blocker bilaterally into the hippocampus of rats. If the drug was given shortly after training, the rats showed poor performance at testing (after the drug had worn off), suggesting that consolidation was impaired. However, trained rats that were given the drug only at the time of testing also failed to perform the task, suggesting that the hippocampus is important in retrieval as well.

3. Declarative memory is memory for information about which we can verbalize, such as memories for events, whereas nondeclarative memory does not require verbalization in order to be used; it includes skills or procedures, emotions, and stimulus-response associations.

4. A patient with bilateral hippocampal damage and one with bilateral amygdala damage underwent a conditioning procedure in which a loud sound was paired with a blue slide. Both patients showed a normal physiological response (SCR) to the sound. The hippocampal patient showed conditioning without being able to verbalize the association. (This patient showed a response to the blue slide but could not state which slide was paired with the sound.) The amygdala patient did know which slide was paired with the sound but did not show an increased SCR to that slide. What this suggests is that the hippocampus is necessary for declarative memory, whereas the amygdala is necessary for emotional learning, a form of nondeclarative learning.

5. Place cells increase their rate of firing when the individual is in a specific location in the environment. These cells are found in the hippocampus whereas other memories are stored in different cortical areas.

6. During early development, synapses are "selected" for survival based on patterns of firing; the synapses that are most likely to survive are those for which pre- and postsynaptic neurons fire together frequently. LTP operates under a similar mechanism, but in the laboratory, it is induced by applying high-frequency stimulation to a group of presynaptic neurons; following LTP, the postsynaptic neurons are more likely to fire when stimulated by the presynaptic neurons. Associative LTP occurs when a weak synapse and a strong synapse on the same neuron are activated simultaneously, which potentiates the weak synapse. Associative LTP may explain the phenomenon of classical conditioning.

7. Long-term depression is the weakening of a synapse as a result of a presynaptic neuron firing when the postsynaptic neuron is not depolarized. It is believed that this is an important mechanism in learning because it prevents LTP from becoming permanent and frees synapses for new associations. LTD may be particularly important for clearing the hippocampal area of old memories so new memories can take their place.

8. In most cases of LTP, glutamate is released and first activates AMPA receptors. The resulting partial depolarization dislodges magnesium ions from the NMDA receptors, which allows them to be activated. Sodium and calcium ions flow in, depolarizing the membrane and activating key enzymes. Nitric oxide is a retrograde messenger released by the postsynaptic neuron; it facilitates the release of neurotransmitter by the presynaptic neuron, which then stimulates the postsynaptic neuron.

9. Extinction, forgetting, and reconsolidation are three such processes.

10. There is some evidence suggesting that sleep facilitates consolidation, so you could advise your roommate to study the night before the exam, and maybe even two nights before, to ensure that sleep-dependent consolidation has a chance to occur.

11. The jury should not consider her current statement to be accurate. Because she did not recall the details until after multiple chances for reconsolidation and reconstruction of the memory, it is likely that her memory for the event has been altered.

12. Not all elderly individuals undergo memory loss or cognitive deficits. For example, the book cites a study in which college professors in their 60s scored about the same as those in their 30s.

13. The hippocampus loses synapses and NMDA receptors, which probably accounts for impaired LTP. There is decreased activity in the entorhinal cortex, which provides connections between the hippocampus and other brain areas. Cells in the brain lose myelin, which interferes with their functioning. The basal forebrain region also undergoes neuron loss; this is an important area because its cells connect to the hippocampus, amygdala, and cortex. Finally, there are deficits in frontal lobe functioning, which suggests damage there.

14. This chromosome was targeted because of its role in Down syndrome. People with Down have three 21st chromosomes, rather than the usual two, and their brains have plaques and tangles like those of Alzheimer's patients. Researchers thus suspected that one or more genes on this chromosome were responsible for these brain abnormalities.

15. One current type of drug inhibits the breakdown of acetylcholine. Another reduces sensitivity to glutamate (which is overactive in affected neurons). Other potential treatments include anti-inflammatory drugs (unsuccessful), anti-amyloid injections (unsuccessful to date), and tangle-preventing drugs (successful in phase 2 trials), injecting stem cells (some improvement), and nutritional supplementation (promising).

16. Confabulation is the tendency of some amnesiacs, especially people with Korsakoff's syndrome, to make up stories about their lives. Several examples are given in the book about a woman living in a nursing home who at various times seemed confused about where she was; in one instance she complained that she was stranded there and needed to get back to her army post, and another time she explained her circumstances by believing she was a prisoner. In both instances she was confusing current reality with earlier memories from her life, which some believe is characteristic of confabulation.

17. Korsakoff's is a disease caused by low thiamine (B1) vitamin, usually due to chronic alcoholism. Largest symptoms include anterograde amnesia, some retrograde amnesia, and more impairment in declarative memory. Reductions of mammillary bodies, thalamus, and frontal lobes are seen in patients. Behavioral problems include confabulation (making up details to forgotten declarative memories), usually due to damage to a specific location in the frontal lobe.

## Post-test

1. a   2. b   3. b   4. d   5. c   6. c   7. a   8. d   9. b   10. a   11. a   12. b   13. c   14. b
15. d   16. b   17. b   18. a   19. d   20. b   21. d   22. c   23. c   24. b   25. c   26. d
27. c   28. a   29. a   30. d   31. a   32. b   33. a   34. b   35. c   36. d   37. b   38. a
39. a   40. b

# 13 Intelligence and Cognitive Functioning

## Learning Objectives

After reading this chapter, you should be able to answer the following questions.

1. How is intelligence defined and measured?

2. What are some of the controversies surrounding intelligence testing?

3. In what ways are the brains of more intelligent people different?

4. What brain areas are associated with specific cognitive skills?

5. What evidence supports the argument that heredity is important for intelligence? That environment is important? Can intelligence be enhanced?

6. What are the effects of aging on the brain and on intelligence or cognitive performance?

7. What are some of the causes of intellectual disability?

8. What are the biological bases of autism?

9. What are some brain differences in ADHD? What are some benefits and concerns related to its treatment?

## The Nature of Intelligence

### Summary and Guided Review

After studying this section in the text, fill in the blanks of the following summary.

_____ (1), defined as the capacity for reasoning, understanding, and benefiting from experience, is challenging to measure. Originally, the intelligence quotient (or IQ) was determined as the ratio of a child's mental and _____ (2) age, multiplied by 100. Currently, a person's IQ represents her or his performance compared with that of the general population; the average IQ score is arbitrarily set at _____ (3) for both children and adults, and most scores fall near this number. Only 2% of the population score above 130 or below _____ (4). The first intelligence test, developed by _____ (5), was used to identify French children with special needs. IQ scores are positively correlated with school grades, level of education, job performance, and income level; and negatively correlated with juvenile _____ (6). Because of the correlation between IQ and both academic success and socioeconomic status, critics argue that IQ tests are designed to reflect these forms of success. The _____ _____ _____ (7) test, a culture-free test, is believed by some to provide a measure of "pure" intelligence. Another criticism of IQ tests is that they do not measure cognitive skills that people use in their everyday lives, or _____ (8) intelligence. _____ (9) argues that intelligence is actually a cultural invention to account for why some individuals are more successful than others.

There is also controversy over the structure of intelligence. _____ (10) are intelligence theorists who assume that there is a unitary capability underlying intelligence, often referred to as the _____ _____ (11), or "g." This argument is supported by the fact that different abilities such as math and verbal skills are correlated. _____ (12) argue that mental abilities are distinct from one another; this perspective is supported by the fact that brain damage often impairs one type of skill and not others.

## Short Answer and Essay Questions

Answer the following questions.

1. What are some factors that influence the results of IQ tests?

2. What are two criticisms of intelligence tests?

3. How do lumpers and splitters differ on their positions regarding the structure of intelligence?

# The Origins of Intelligence

## Summary and Guided Review

After studying this section in the text, fill in the blanks of the following summary.

The search for a biological origin of intelligence led some researchers to ask whether more intelligent people have bigger brains. However, the brain of the genius _____ _____ (13) was rather small and did not differ from other brains in most respects. One exception is that his _____ (14) lobes were larger, which are associated with mathematical skills and visual-spatial processing. Other changes included increased number of _____ (15) cells and other anomalies in that lobe. Scans of brain-damaged individuals support the idea that "g" requires a(n) _____ (16) system, spanning and connecting areas in several lobes of the brain.

If we compare across species, brain size alone is not a good predictor of intelligence. Among humans, who are among the _____ (17) in brain-to-body size ratio, there is some evidence for a relationship between IQ and brain-to-body size ratio, although it is modest. There is a gender difference in the ratio, with males' brains being somewhat _____ (18) in relation to body size than females' brains, although men and women do not differ in intelligence. One possible reason for the gender difference is that women's brains, which have more densely packed neurons and relatively more _____ _____ (19), are more efficient. Another possibility is that the males' advantage in _____ (20) abilities requires a larger brain capacity. How the brain is organized appears to be more important than how big it is. General intelligence is moderately correlated with cortical _____ (21) in association areas. Interestingly, this process reaches its peak at 8 years in children with average intelligence, but the process in those with superior intelligence continues until age _____ (22).

The speed at which people process information may be an indication of general intelligence; in fact, IQ and _____ _____ (23) are correlated. An even stronger correlation exists between IQ scores and _____ _____ (24) velocity, which may lead to more efficient processing. _____ (25), which speeds neural impulses and prevents inappropriate communication between adjacent neurons, is also believed to be

related to intelligence. People who are higher in IQ use less brain _____
(26); people with higher IQs show less _____ _____
(27) while playing Tetris, while people with mild _____
_____ (28) exhibit more brain activity than above average
individuals while performing a mental task. These results suggest that IQ is related to
the _____ (29) of neural processing. One current theory, called the
_____ _____ (30) Theory, suggests that information
processing takes place in four stages. First, sensory information is processed in secondary
areas, then passed to parietal areas for abstraction and integration, then to the frontal
lobes for problem solving and evaluation. In the final step, the _____
_____ (31) cortex selects the response and inhibits alternative responses.
More intelligent individuals have been shown to have more numerous interconnections and
shorter paths between steps.

Individual components of intelligence may be identified by _____
_____ (32), which involves giving people a variety of tests and then
looking for correlations among clusters of related tests. Although performance on all
mental tests tends to be correlated, _____ (33), logical-mathematical,
and _____ (34) components have emerged as major components of
intelligence. One brain-based explanation for these different components is that they evolved
separately and consist of different _____ (35) or networks to support a
particular function. For example, performing calculations from memory depends on activity
in the left _____ (36) cortex, while estimating values involves both
_____ (37) areas. Research involving human infants and nonhuman
_____ (38) suggests that the brain is "wired" for numbers. There are also
many examples of complex behaviors in the animal world that most people assume are unique
to humans, including their ability to make and use _____ (39). Ingenuity
and "planfulness" have also been observed in chimps and in some birds, such as crows and
burrowing _____ (40). In spite of these examples, humans' brains seem
to be unique in possessing specialized structures for tool use, or the ability to develop them
through _____ (41).

Because intelligence is complex, identifying its genetic and environmental components
has proven to be extremely difficult. One interesting finding is that while heritability estimates
for intelligence are around _____ % (42), the influence of heredity
seems to _____ (43) with age. Estimated heritability from twin studies
show high rates for brain functions, including _____ (44) memory and
processing speed, and structural characteristics such as brain _____ (45)
as well as amounts of white and gray matter. Locating specific genes involved in intelligence
has been frustrating due to the failure to _____ (46) a promising finding.
One possibility is the _____ (47) gene, which is related to brain size,
and the PACAP precursor gene, which is involved in _____ (48) and
neural signaling. Researchers are now combining genetic data with brain morphological
measurements to try to identify genes and alleles correlated with brain pathways, cortical
thickness, and IQ results.

The fact that intelligence is highly heritable does not mean that it cannot be influenced
by the _____ (49); rather, genes set a range of potential intelligence
levels, and the environment determines where in that range intelligence will fall. Furthermore,
it has been necessary to adjust IQ test norms to maintain the average at 100 as people's
performance on intelligence tests has steadily _____ (50). Some argue that
twin studies are not a fair assessment of the heritability of IQ, because parents and others may
treat identical twins as being more similar based on appearance, and hence provide similar
learning experiences that could result in more highly correlated IQs (higher concordance

rates). However, studies show that parents' belief as to whether their twins are fraternal or identical has no influence on the twins' intellectual similarity, whereas the twins' true _____ (51) relationship does.

The reasons behind racial differences in IQ scores are hotly debated. Some researchers such as Arthur Jensen argue that IQ differences between ethnic groups are largely _____ (52), while others contend that this is not the case. For example, Scarr and colleagues failed to show any cognitive test difference among blacks with different degrees of African _____ (53), and the American Psychological Association has concluded that there is little evidence for a genetic explanation of the racial differences.

Environmental contributions to intelligence are also difficult to identify, in part because environmental and genetic factors are _____ (54); because children share both genes and environment with their parents, it is difficult to separate their influences. Also, environmental factors are numerous and individually _____ (55). Some forms of environmental intervention have been successful in improving achievement in at-risk children. Although there are long-term educational and career benefits among children participating in the _____ _____ (56) program, the IQ gains disappear over time. The _____ (57) project seems to produce longer-lasting IQ improvement, possibly because this program starts intervention at the time of _____ (58). Children who are _____ (59) show stronger IQ correlations with their biological than their adopted parents, but African American children from impoverished backgrounds adopted into middle-class homes showed IQ score increases from 90 to about _____ (60) points.

Humans have always been interested in improving their cognitive abilities and intelligence. A poll conducted by the journal *Nature* indicated that _____ (61) of 5 respondents had used drugs to improve their concentration or memory. However, there is no miracle drug yet, although many are being used and abused. _____ (62) drugs such as modafinil (that alleviates sleepiness) and _____ (63), which improves working memory, are popular on college campuses to stimulate focus, concentration, and working memory. However, these drugs also have side effects, some severe enough for individuals who need to take them to discontinue their use. One promising treatment, _____ _____ (64) of the scalp over the prefrontal cortex were better at mathematical tasks, and participating in cognitively challenging activities regularly also show improved memory and attention, presumably through increased _____ (65) binding and connections between the frontal and parietal lobes.

## Short Answer and Essay Questions

Answer the following questions.

4. What are two possible explanations for the gender difference in brain-to-body ratio?

5. Identify several features of brain structure and neural processing that are related to intelligence.

6. Describe how factor analysis is used to identify components of intelligence. What components have consistently emerged?

7. Why is it incorrect to assume that because intelligence is highly heritable, it is influenced very little by the environment?

8. What have adoption studies revealed about the genetic and environmental contributions to intelligence?

## Deficiencies and Disorders of Intelligence

### Summary and Guided Review

After studying this section in the text, fill in the blanks of the following summary.

As we age, activity decreases in genes that are involved in _____-_____ _____ (66) and memory storage. Particularly affected are genes responsible for _____ (67) and _____ (68) receptors. However, the degree of loss of cognitive functioning has been _____ (69). When older adults are given tests on material relevant to their lives, they show much less deterioration than on meaningless tasks such as memorizing lists of words. Also, consistent with the Flynn effect, _____ (70) studies of the same people as they age reveal less decline than cross-sectional studies of people of differing ages. Speed of information processing, which is important for _____ (71) memory, does decrease in the elderly. In normal aging there is a loss of coordination in the _____ _____ (72) network (portions of the frontal parietal, and temporal lobes active when the brain is at rest or focused internally). This loss appears to be related to a decline in _____ _____ (73) connections between these areas in the brain. Elderly adults may compensate for less efficient processing by using additional brain areas to complete tasks, or by increasing _____ (74). Elderly individuals can regain lost skills through practice and enhancement of _____-_____ (75). Cognitive decline can be lessened by changing dietary habits, for example, by increasing _____ (76) intake. Vitamin supplements also might help performance; individuals with mild cognitive impairment slowed declines in brain atrophy and cognition by increasing their Vitamin _____ (77) intake. Sex hormones may also play a role. Older women who take estrogen are at lower risk for _____ (78) disease. Many neurons contain _____ (79) receptors, and therefore this hormone may play a role in several cognitive tasks. Men receiving testosterone therapy show improvement in _____ (80) memory; additional skills are improved by dihydrotestosterone, which is converted into _____ (81) by the body.

Retardation is a term that has negative connotations, causing practitioners to use the term _____ _____ (82). This term covers limitations in reasoning, learning, problem solving, and adaptive behavior, originating before age _____ (83). A person is generally considered to have an intellectual disability if the person's IQ is below _____ (84) and has difficulty with self-care. Most cases of intellectual impairment fall into the _____ (85) category, which is characterized by less factual knowledge, lack of strategies for learning and problem solving, and slower mental operations. For most individuals in this group, there is no single attributable cause of retardation. About _____% (86) of all cases can be traced to one of the 200-plus physical disorders that cause intellectual impairment, such as meningitis or prenatal exposure to viruses such as _____ (87). Prenatal exposure to _____ (88) is the most common of all environmental causes.

_____ (89) syndrome, which results from an extra 21st chromosome, is the most common genetic cause of retardation, occurring in 1 in _____ (90) births. The Ts65Dn mouse strain is a model for Down syndrome; these animals are similar to humans with the disorder in that their _____ (91) cells secrete less proteins that support cell survival. Another frequent genetic cause of intellectual disability is _____ _____ syndrome (92), due to a mutation of the X Chromosome FMR1 gene. This gene may be important in the pruning or elimination of excess _____ (93). A genetic disorder that interferes with myelination, _____ (94), may not lead to intellectual impairment if the affected individual avoids foods with phenylalanine, as well as the artificial sweetener _____ (95). The buildup of cerebrospinal fluid in _____ (96) may also lead to impairment, but it can be treated if caught early. However, many affected individuals have surprisingly normal IQs.

Autism Spectrum Disorder (ASD) is a set of neurodevelopmental disorders characterized by social deficits, communication difficulties, and _____ (97) behaviors. ASD includes the previous diagnostic criteria for autism, _____ (98) syndrome, pervasive developmental disorder, and childhood disintegrative disorder. There is some debate over whether the incidence of autism has actually _____ (99) over time; while the prevalence of ASD increased three-fold from 2000 to 2012, it could be due to improved detection and broader diagnostic criteria. In addition, _____% (100) of children with ASD had intellectual disabilities, and 31% had average or above average intelligence. Children with ASD usually prefer to be alone, and when interacting with other people tend to treat them as _____ (101). ASD children perform more poorly on _____ of _____ (102) tasks than younger normal children, and even children with Down syndrome. Researchers have suggested that autistic individuals' difficulty empathizing and learning language through imitation involves impairments with _____ (103) neurons. There is some evidence that people with autism and Asperger syndrome have insufficient activity in the _____ (104) stream connections that provide input to brain areas associated with imitation (inferior frontal cortex and motor cortex).

Some autistics, referred to as _____ (105), are extremely talented in one area, such as music, drawing, painting, computation, or memorizing but whose overall functioning is below normal. The most likely explanation for these skills is that the autistic lacks _____ (106) or integrative functions within the brain, and this gives the savant access to speedy lower levels of processing. The best-known savant was Kim Peek, who was the basis for the character in the movie *Rain Man*. There are also _____-_____ (107) autistics such as Temple Grandin, who have normal or above normal intelligence but who still show autistic characteristics such as poorly developed theory of mind.

Although originally thought to be purely psychological in origin, autism is now considered a disorder of the _____ (108). However, because not all autistics show the same pattern of abnormalities, there are probably several ways in which the disorder can develop. Although the brain of an autistic individual is normal or slightly reduced at birth, it undergoes dramatic _____ (109) during the first year, particularly in the _____ (110) and _____ (111) areas. One of the differences in the autistic brain is an apparent lack of _____ (112) between the _____ (113) and the ventromedial prefrontal cortex (cmPFC). One obstacle for developing social interaction skills is that autistic children often have difficulty looking at people's _____ (114) and show related deficits in tracking a visually moving object. In the brain, ASD individuals tend to have an overgrowth of _____ (115) matter, which then degenerates after adolescence and reduces connections between language, memory, social, and executive function areas.

Several neurotransmitters have been implicated in autism, particularly
_____ (116), because of its contribution to neural development. ASD
children have reduced synthesis of the neurotransmitter, and treatment with reuptake
inhibitors such as _____ (117) decrease repetitive and obsessive behaviors
in some individuals. Additionally, high levels of _____ (118) (decreased by
the antipsychotic risperidal) and glutamate have been found in autistic children. But symptoms
are not just the result of too much neurotransmitter. _____ (119), known
as the "sociability molecule," is reduced in many autistic children. In addition, decreases in
repetitive behavior and fear were seen following treatment.

Many environmental factors have been associated with autism, including
_____ (120) due to agriculture and automobile traffic. Other
influences originate in the mother herself; up to _____% (121) of
women who have an autistic child have immune molecules sensitive to brain proteins.
In addition, the current obesity epidemic is also linked to autism. Mothers of ASD
children were _____% (122) more likely to be obese than mothers
of intellectually average children, though mothers who supplemented their diets with
_____ _____ (123) during pregnancy reduced
the risk to the child by 50%. One factor that has been definitively ruled out as a cause
of autism is the normal procedure of giving children _____ (124)
against common childhood diseases: the original study showing a link was retracted due to
unethical behavior by the authors. Despite the lack of any credible link between vaccinations
and subsequent diagnosis of Autism Spectrum Disorders, immunization rates continue to
_____ (125) in several countries.

Autism has a(n) _____ (126) component, as autistic children have a
much higher chance of having an autistic sibling than normal children, and the concordance
rate for identical twins is 60%. When analyses consider additional abnormal symptoms
found in _____ (127), the concordance rate for identical twins increases
to _____% (128). The genes implicated in ASD individuals tend to
be involved in neuronal development and migration, and in particular they interfere with
the development of _____ (129) between cortical layers. One gene in
particular, the _____ (130) gene, targets more than 2,500 other genes
(some involved in neural development) and is sensitive to sex-specific hormones, which may
explain the gender differences in ASD incidence.

_____ (131) typically develops during childhood; it includes
impulsive and hyperactive behavior as well as problems with attention and learning. Three
subtypes are currently recognized; combined inattention, hyperactivity-impulsivity, or
combined. The sex ratio for this disorder is also skewed: _____ (132)
are more than twice as likely to be diagnosed with attention-deficit/hyperactivity disorder.
While most clinicians use behavioral reports from parents and teachers to diagnose the
disorder, a new diagnostic method (NEBA) measures changes in EEG brain waves; ADHD
children have decreased _____ (133) waves when working on a task
compared to normal children. Those diagnosed with ADHD as children often continue to
have problems as adults, including increased rates of criminal behavior, drug abuse, and
_____ _____ (134) disorder. The link between
ADHD and drug use led to concerns that treating children with _____
(135) drugs such as methylphenidate (Ritalin) and amphetamine was encouraging later
addiction to drugs. However, there is no evidence that these drugs increases the risk
of addiction; if anything, they have a(n) _____ (136) effect. Given
that stimulant drugs used to treat ADHD also increase _____ (137)
activity, it is not surprising that researchers have found _____ (138)

activity in pathways for this neurotransmitter, particularly in the _____ (139) cortex. This cortical area is involved in impulse inhibition and reward, which could account for many ADHD symptoms. For example, people with ADHD have difficulty foregoing _____ (140) rewards for better, but delayed, rewards. While stimulant drugs are the drugs most commonly used to treat ADHD, they do not work for everyone. Two other drugs that are used, modafinil and atomoxetine, block the reuptake of _____ (141).

Regarding brain abnormalities in ADHD, one of the most consistent findings is that there is reduced volume in the right hemisphere and right _____ (142) nucleus, as well as changes in the cerebellum. These and other findings indicate a disruption of the _____-_____ (143) network.

There is strong evidence for a genetic basis to ADHD; the concordance rate for ADHD among identical twins is much higher than among fraternal twins. Heritability averages _____ % (144) across studies. Several genes have been identified as being involved in ADHD and are found in the dopamine, norepinephrine, and serotonin transmission systems. One interesting finding is that a number of copy number variations (CNVs) found in ADHD are also found in individuals with _____ (145), implying that gene changes affect common processes and are not disease-specific.

Environmental factors that play a role in ADHD are often parental in nature, such as maternal _____ (146) and stress during pregnancy, parental abuse of drugs, and parental mood and _____ (147) disorders. Other environmental influences include stroke, pregnancy complications, and exposure to toxins such as _____ (148) and organophosphate pesticides.

## Short Answer and Essay Questions

Answer the following questions.

9. Give a reason that the degree of cognitive impairment in the elderly has been overestimated. What impairments are associated with aging? Are they permanent?

10. Identify common causes of intellectual impairment that occur early in life (other than autism and ADHD). Describe one of them in detail in terms of what is known about cause(s), symptoms, and treatment.

11. What does theory of mind mean? Why are autistic individuals thought to have poorly developed theory of mind? Identify some other key symptoms of autism.

12. What are the possible explanations for autistic savants? Which one seems most likely to be correct? Why?

13. Describe the brain anomalies (structural, developmental, and functional) associated with autism.

14. Why do researchers believe there is a strong genetic component to autism?

15. Describe the controversy about whether there is a link between childhood vaccinations and autism.

16. What evidence points to dopamine as an important factor in ADHD? Address the issue of dopamine's role in treatment.

17. Is there a genetic basis to ADHD? Provide support for your answer. How does the environment play a role in AHDH?

## Post-test

Use these multiple-choice questions to check your understanding of the chapter.

1. The intelligence quotient was originally based on
   a. the ratio of intellectual capacity to the population average.
   b. the ratio of mental age to chronological age.
   c. the ratio of chronological age to mental age.
   d. none of the above

2. What percent of the population has an IQ above 130?
   a. 2%
   b. 12%
   c. 20%
   d. 0.2%

3. IQ scores are correlated with which of the following?
   a. grades earned in school
   b. income
   c. job performance
   d. all of the above

4. The Raven Progressive Matrices test is designed to
   a. be culture free.
   b. measure nonverbal abilities.
   c. measure practical intelligence.
   d. a and b

5. Robert Sternberg argues that
   a. intelligence tests measure a general, underlying factor of cognitive ability that contributes to specific mental skills.
   b. intelligence tests are completely useless.
   c. intelligence is how a culture defines people's ability to succeed.
   d. tests that measure practical intelligence are better than traditional intelligence tests.

6. An intelligence theorist who proposes that there are seven different components of intelligence would BEST be described as a
   a. lumper.
   b. splitter.
   c. general factor theorist.
   d. reaction time theorist.

7. Which of the following is TRUE regarding Albert Einstein's brain?
   a. It had fewer glial cells.
   b. It was larger (heavier) than the average person's brain.
   c. It contained more neurons than the average brain.
   d. Its parietal lobes were larger than those of the average brain.

8. PET studies reveal that tasks requiring general intelligence produce higher activity in the ___ areas of the brain.
   a. frontal
   b. temporal
   c. parietal
   d. occipital

9. Studies of people with brain damage have shown that general intelligence or "g" requires
   a. a distributed network.
   b. a system involving the frontal, parietal, and temporal lobes.
   c. the ability to integrate different types of processing from several areas of the brain.
   d. all of the above

10. Which of the following statements regarding brain size is FALSE?
    a. Species with the highest brain-to-body ratio are the most intelligent.
    b. There is no correlation between brain size and intelligence in humans.
    c. Men's brains are proportionately larger than women's brains.
    d. Elephants' brains are larger than humans' brains.

11. Which of the following is more strongly associated with intelligence than brain size?
    a. a thicker cortex and larger cortical columns
    b. a thicker cortex and many smaller columns
    c. larger processing units and greater surface area
    d. more layers and larger processing modules

12. Which of the following is probably the BEST predictor of IQ score?
    a. brain size
    b. reaction time
    c. nerve conduction velocity
    d. frontal area activity

13. Which of the following statements about myelination is TRUE?
    a. People with more gray matter and less white matter tend to have higher IQs.
    b. Myelination increases from childhood to maturity.
    c. Myelination increases cross-talk between neurons.
    d. Myelination is at its peak in the elderly.

14. People with higher IQs tend to
    a. have faster nerve conduction velocity.
    b. use less energy when processing information.
    c. have a high white matter/gray matter ratio.
    d. all of the above

15. Which of the following is NOT one of the components of intelligence frequently iden-
    tified by factor analysis?
    a. practical intelligence
    b. linguistic intelligence
    c. logical-mathematical intelligence
    d. spatial intelligence

16. Which of the following MOST specifically engages the right parietal lobe?
    a. language functions
    b. mathematical calculations
    c. spatial ability
    d. rote arithmetic tasks, such as using times tables

17. What area(s) of the brain is (are) involved in mathematical abilities such as calculation
    and estimation?
    a. frontal lobe only
    b. parietal lobe only
    c. both the frontal and parietal lobes
    d. none of the above

18. Which of the following is NOT true with respect to intelligence in animals?
    a. Nonhuman primates are able to demonstrate language skills but not mathematical abilities.
    b. Chimps show evidence of intelligence by using tools to acquire food.
    c. Crows and owls show planfulness in their methods for obtaining or "luring" food.
    d. Mirror neurons are activated in monkeys when they watch someone retrieve an object with the hand or a tool.

19. The proportion of variability in intelligence due to heredity is HIGHEST in
    a. infancy.
    b. childhood.
    c. adolescence.
    d. adulthood.

20. Which of the following is TRUE with respect to the genetic basis of intelligence?
    a. The heritability of intelligence is about 70%.
    b. The PACAP precursor gene is a major determinant of brain size.
    c. In a twin study, estimated heritability was highest for brain volume as a structural contributor to intelligence.
    d. There are probably 50 candidate genes that have been linked to some aspect of cognitive ability.

21. IQ scoring standards have been adjusted in the last 50 years to reflect the fact that
    a. people are scoring more poorly on the tests than they have in the past.
    b. the average performance on IQ tests has risen.
    c. fewer people are intellectually impaired now.
    d. our genes are making us more intelligent.

22. Studies of identical and fraternal twins reveal that the STRONGEST correlation for IQ scores is between
    a. identical twins, but only if correctly identified by their parents as identical.
    b. fraternal twins, but only if correctly identified by their parents as fraternal.
    c. identical twins, regardless of whether their parents identified them as identical or fraternal.
    d. identical twins incorrectly identified by their parents as fraternal.

23. Scarr's study of IQ scores among African Americans revealed that
    a. there was no relationship between degree of African ancestry and IQ.
    b. those with more African ancestors had lower IQs than those with fewer African ancestors.
    c. there were no differences between African Americans and whites.
    d. none of the above

24. Which of the following statements regarding environmental contributions to intelligence is FALSE?
    a. Environmental factors may be confounded with genetic factors.
    b. The results from the Abecedarian project suggest that the environment is not as important as genes when it comes to intelligence.
    c. Many environmental factors may contribute weakly to intelligence.
    d. Illness is an important factor in explaining worldwide differences in IQ.

25. Which of the following statements regarding Head Start is FALSE?
    a. There are long-term benefits in IQ scores.
    b. There are long-term benefits in career accomplishments.

    c. There are long-term benefits in mathematics.

    d. There are long-term benefits in educational attainment.

26. Adoption studies reveal that adopted children's IQ scores are

    a. relatively unaffected by the adoptive home.

    b. most strongly correlated with their biological parents' scores in childhood and adulthood.

    c. most strongly correlated with their adopted parents' scores in childhood and adulthood.

    d. initially more similar to their biological parents' scores but become more similar to their adopted parents' scores in adulthood.

27. With respect to aging and intelligence,

    a. the declines are significant and irreversible.

    b. loss occurs, but it has been overestimated.

    c. much of the decline has been attributed to loss of glutamate.

    d. performance speed is not affected as much as verbal memory.

28. Which of the following is FALSE about the default mode network?

    a. It is involved in a person's preparedness for action.

    b. The elderly show loss of coordination in this network.

    c. The network primarily involves gray matter.

    d. It involves activity and communication between the frontal, temporal, and parietal lobes.

29. The elderly could compensate for loss of cognitive function by

    a. eating more fish.

    b. practicing skills.

    c. taking drugs that increase GABA.

    d. all of the above

30. Which of the following is TRUE concerning hormones and cognitive function in the elderly?

    a. Testosterone works better than dihydrotestosterone at improving cognitive abilities.

    b. Estrogen plays a role in increasing cognitive function in females but not males.

    c. Estrogen most likely exerts the majority of its beneficial effects in the parietal lobes of the brain.

    d. Estrogen lowers the risk of Alzheimer's disease in menopausal women.

31. Which of the following has been identified as a possible "smart drug"?

    a. ampakines

    b. modafinil

    c. guanfacine

    d. all of the above

32. What percentage of the population falls in the IQ range for intellectual impairment?

    a. 0.02%

    b. 0.2%

    c. 2%

    d. 5%

33. Most individuals with mild intellectual impairment

    a. come from families of lower socioeconomic status.

    b. are incapable of caring for themselves.

c. are more likely to have a genetic than environmental cause that explains their disability.

d. have an IQ below 50.

34. The leading genetic cause of intellectual impairment is
   a. prenatal exposure to cigarette smoke.
   b. prenatal exposure to alcohol.
   c. Down syndrome.
   d. hydrocephalus.

35. Down syndrome
   a. is caused by the FMR1 gene, according to new studies.
   b. can be studied in a mouse model that has been engineered to produce more norepinephrine.
   c. may be caused by more than just the genes on the 21st chromosome.
   d. cannot be identified until the baby is born.

36. PKU
   a. is typically diagnosed by amniocentesis.
   b. can be controlled by diet.
   c. is caused by a lack of phenylalanine.
   d. if untreated, can lead to mild mental impairment.

37. Which of the following statements regarding hydrocephalus is (are) TRUE?
   a. It is treatable.
   b. If untreated, it usually causes intellectual disability, but not in all cases.
   c. It results from a buildup of cerebrospinal fluid.
   d. all of the above

38. Autism
   a. is caused by poor parenting.
   b. has increased from 1% in the 1960s and 1970s to 5% currently.
   c. is one disorder in the autism spectrum that includes Asperger syndrome.
   d. involves the least intellectual impairment in the spectrum.

39. Which of the following is NOT a common characteristic of autism?
   a. locked in a world of fantasy
   b. delayed language development
   c. repetitive behaviors
   d. limited interactions with others

40. Theory of mind
   a. is lacking in autistic individuals.
   b. may involve activity in mirror neurons.
   c. has been explained by both the "theory theory" and "simulation theory."
   d. all of the above

41. Which of the following statements regarding savants is TRUE?
   a. Their skills usually result from a great deal of concentrated practice.
   b. Their skills typically generalize to other related tasks.
   c. Their skills may involve speedy access to lower levels of cognitive processing.
   d. All savants are autistic.

42. Which of the following is NOT true of Temple Grandin, the high-functioning autistic described in the textbook?
   a. She has a PhD in animal science.
   b. She gives lectures about her condition.

    c. She had normal language development as a child, which explains her high-functioning adult state.

    d. She exhibits a poorly developed theory of mind.

43. Which of the following brain areas was NOT listed in the textbook as being implicated in autism?
    a. occipital lobe
    b. temporal lobe
    c. brain stem
    d. cerebellum

44. What characterizes early brain development in autism?
    a. an initial stage of degeneration, followed by some recovery
    b. a rapid growth in size during the first year
    c. overgrowth in parietal and occipital areas
    d. very small brains that develop to adult size by adolescence

45. Although research has been inconsistent, which of the following has/have been studied as playing a role in autism?
    a. fusiform face area
    b. mirror neurons
    c. functional connectivity in the default network
    d. all of the above

46. With respect to the genetic basis of autism
    a. the fraternal twin concordance rate for autistic individuals is 92%.
    b. the identical twin concordance rate for autistic individuals is at least 60%.
    c. relatives of autistic individuals have a concordance rate of 10%.
    d. the heritability rate is probably overestimated because parents stop having children.

47. The impairment of sociability in autistics has been linked to
    a. oxytocin.
    b. dopamine.
    c. GABA.
    d. a and b

48. What is the most accurate statement about vaccines and autism?
    a. There is strong evidence that childhood vaccinations cause autism.
    b. There is a causal link between autism and the mercury preservative in autism, but not to the vaccines.
    c. The initial study supporting the link between the MMR vaccine and autism has been criticized as being methodologically flawed.
    d. Because most parents of autistic individuals agree that there is no link between immunizations and autism, there has been a worldwide increase in childhood vaccinations.

49. Which of the following is NOT a symptom of ADHD?
    a. attentional problems
    b. impulsiveness
    c. lack of theory of mind
    d. hyperactivity

50. When children with ADHD grow up,
    a. they are usually normal.
    b. they are normal only if they were medicated as children.

   c. they are more likely to exhibit personality disorders.

   d. they are unlikely to have children who are subsequently diagnosed with ADHD.

51. Children with ADHD who are treated with stimulant drugs
   a. are more likely to become addicted to drugs like amphetamine or cocaine.
   b. may be protected from drug abuse.
   c. are more likely to smoke marijuana, because stimulant drugs act as gateway drugs.
   d. are more likely to become addicted to alcohol, but not other drugs.

52. In people with ADHD, dopamine activity is typically
   a. low.
   b. higher than normal.
   c. normal.
   d. lower than normal when the person takes Ritalin.

53. Which of the following show(s) that the prefrontal lobes play a key role in ADHD?
   a. People with ADHD tend to be impulsive.
   b. People with ADHD prefer immediate rewards over delayed rewards.
   c. There is reduced dopamine activity in the area in people with ADHD.
   d. all of the above

54. Studies of people with ADHD have shown reduced brain volume in all of the following areas EXCEPT for the:
   a. thalamus.
   b. prefrontal areas.
   c. caudate nucleus.
   d. cerebellum.

55. Which of the following drugs has NOT been used to treat ADHD?
   a. methylphenidate
   b. modafinil
   c. atomoxetine
   d. risperidone

56. Which of the following genes has been implicated in ADHD?
   a. a serotonin receptor gene
   b. a gene for the serotonin transporter
   c. the LPHN3 gene
   d. all of the above

57. All of the following have been considered as environmental contributors to ADHD except:
   a. thimerosal.
   b. lead.
   c. parental drug abuse.
   d. pesticides.

# Answers

## Guided Review

1. Intelligence
2. chronological
3. 100
4. 70
5. (Alfred) Binet
6. delinquency
7. Raven Progressive Matrices
8. practical
9. Sternberg
10. Lumpers
11. general factor
12. splitters
13. Albert Einstein
14. parietal
15. glial
16. distributed
17. highest
18. larger
19. gray matter
20. spatial
21. thickness
22. 11 (or 12)
23. reaction time
24. nerve conduction
25. Myelin
26. energy
27. glucose metabolism
28. intellectual disabilities
29. efficiency
30. Parieto-Frontal Integration
31. anterior cingulate
32. factor analysis
33. linguistic/spatial
34. spatial/linguistic
35. modules
36. prefrontal
37. parietal
38. primates
39. tools
40. owls
41. experience
42. 50
43. increase
44. working
45. volume
46. replicate
47. ASPM
48. neurogenesis
49. environment
50. increased
51. genetic
52. inherited (genetic)
53. ancestry
54. confounded
55. weak
56. Head Start
57. Abecedarian
58. birth
59. adopted
60. 106
61. 1
62. Narcolepsy
63. d-amphetamine
64. electrical stimulation
65. dopamine
66. long-term potentiation
67. glutamate
68. GABA
69. overestimated
70. longitudinal

71. working
72. default mode
73. white matter
74. metabolism
75. self-esteem
76. fish
77. B
78. Alzheimer's
79. estrogen
80. spatial
81. estrogen
82. intellectual disability
83. 18
84. 70
85. mild
86. 25
87. rubella (German measles)
88. alcohol
89. Down
90. 700
91. glial
92. Fragile X
93. synapses
94. phenyketonuria or PKU
95. aspartame
96. hydrocephalus
97. repetitive
98. Asperger
99. increased
100. 55
101. objects
102. theory of mind
103. mirror
104. dorsal
105. savants
106. executive
107. high-functioning
108. brain
109. growth
110. frontal/temporal
111. temporal/frontal
112. coordination
113. amygdala
114. faces
115. white
116. serotonin
117. Prozac
118. dopamine
119. Oxytocin
120. pollution
121. 10%
122. 40%
123. folic acid
124. vaccinations
125. decrease
126. genetic
127. relatives
128. 92
129. connections
130. RORA
131. ADHD
132. Boys
133. beta
134. antisocial personality
135. stimulant
136. protective
137. dopamine
138. reduced
139. prefrontal
140. immediate
141. norepinephrine
142. caudate
143. attention-inhibition
144. 75
145. schizophrenia
146. smoking
147. anxiety
148. lead

## Short Answer and Essay Questions

1. IQ tests can be influenced by socieconomic status, verbal ability, education, and Western culture. In addition, most have a verbal component that can be influenced by language and comprehension ability. In addition, most of them do not measure forms of more practical intelligence.

2. One criticism of intelligence tests is that they are designed to measure academic and socioeconomic success and thus do not measure important things like practical intelligence. Another criticism is that people who are highly successful sometimes score in the mediocre range on these tests, suggesting that the content of the tests is too narrow. Another is that performance on most intelligence tests is too dependent on familiarity with the culture and language the test was designed for.

3. Lumpers argue that because scores on different tasks such as math and verbal skills are highly correlated, intelligence is a unitary capacity that we apply to many different tasks; a single IQ score is sufficient to represent a person's intelligence. Splitters argue that it is necessary to look at people's scores on different types of tests to get an accurate picture of intelligence, because many people have strengths in some areas and weaknesses in others. Splitters believe that there are actually several types of intelligence.

4. One possibility is that women's brains are more efficient, and another is that men's superiority on spatial tasks requires a larger brain.

5. People with higher intelligence typically have a larger brain and a thicker cortex, and they may have more columns; functionally, they have better short-term memory, shorter reaction times, and higher nerve conduction velocity (possibly related to greater myelination). As a result, people with greater intelligence might be better at transferring short-term memory to long-term memory, and use less energy to do so. In other words, their brains are more efficient at accomplishing cognitive tasks.

6. Factor analysis involves giving people several tests measuring different intellectual abilities and then looking for clusters of abilities that are more strongly correlated with one another than with other abilities. Such clusters are assumed to represent approximately the same types of skills. Separate abilities that have been identified repeatedly are linguistic, logical-mathematical, and spatial skills.

7. If a particular trait is highly heritable, the environment can still have profound influence over it. For example, people's IQ scores have been steadily increasing over the past few generations, most likely as a result of improved environment. In addition, studies have found large IQ increases following adoption into a richer environment. A better way of thinking about how genes influence intelligence is that they provide a range of possibilities, and whatever environment a person is exposed to will then determine where within that range his or her intelligence will fall.

8. Adoption studies have shown that children's IQs are more strongly correlated with their biological parents' IQs than with their adoptive parents' IQs. However, they have also shown that disadvantaged children's IQs can be dramatically improved in an adoptive home.

9. One reason is that the tasks given to elderly research participants may not be interesting or relevant to them. They perform much better on tasks involving meaningful material than on simple word memorization tasks. Another reason is that some studies compare people of different ages, rather than following the same individuals for several years, and the older participants may have had less enriching experiences. Impairments that are noted with aging mostly include speed decreases: perceptual speed, performance speed, and processing speed,

the latter of which also accounts for almost all of the loss in working memory. There is also a loss of coordination in the default mode network, due to a decline in white matter connections among areas. Some reversibility of aging effects has resulted from skills training, increased self-esteem, and dietary improvement. In addition, improved GABA functioning and treatment with testosterone and estrogen are promising.

10. Conditions that cause intellectual impairment early in life are Down syndrome, phenylketoneuria (PKU), hydrocephalus, and fragile X syndrome. Down syndrome is caused by an additional 21st chromosome. Individuals typically have IQs in the range of 40–55. There is currently no treatment although research with animal models is being conducted, but some individuals with Down syndrome can function quite well with support. PKU involves an inability to metabolize the amino acid phenylalanine, which accumulates and destroys myelin, leading to profound intellectual disability. These serious effects can be prevented by limiting the amount of phenylalanine in the diet. Hydrocephalus is a condition in which cerebrospinal fluid builds up in the ventricles of the brain and compresses brain tissue against the skull, producing brain damage that leads to intellectual impairment. This condition can be treated by using a shunt to drain the fluid out of the ventricles. Fragile X syndrome is due to a mutation is the FMR1 gene, resulting in IQs below 75. This gene may play a role in synaptic pruning during development. Males are more likely to have this condition.

11. Theory of mind refers to the ability to infer the mental state of others. Autistic children perform more poorly on theory of mind tasks than normal children and even children with Down syndrome with a lower mental age. Also, many autistics have difficulty "reading" other people, or making inferences about what other people know. Other symptoms of autism include impaired language development, lack of social interaction and communication, repetitive behaviors, and, typically, intellectual impairment.

12. One possibility is that they acquire skills through extensive, focused practice; however, often their skills appear without any apparent practice. Another possibility is that they have more brain area devoted to a particular skill, although no evidence is given for this in the text. A third possibility, one that is more likely to be correct, is that because they lack central executive functions, as a result, they have atypical access to speedy lower levels of processing, but perform poorly on similar tasks that require higher order processing. This hypothesis is supported by the case of a man with dementia who began composing classical music in spite of limited musical training.

13. Brain changes in autism include a rapid period of growth in the first year of life, particularly in the frontal and temporal lobes, followed by some degeneration. Activity deficiencies have been reported in the fusiform face area and mirror neuron system, but this may be due to deficits in synchronization in the default mode network. This lack of functional connectivity is correlated with deficits in social, communication, and task performance in autistic individuals.

14. A genetic basis is confirmed for autism: identical twin concordance rates are about 60%, and when the comparison groups include nonautistic relatives who show symptoms, concordance is 92% for identical twins and 10% for fraternal pairs. Because autism occurs more frequently in males, scientists have examined the X chromosome for candidate genes and a few have been found, but their effects are small. Other genes that have been implicated in autism are involved in neurotransmitter activity, neuron development and migration, and synapse formation.

15. A 1998 study by Wakefield and colleagues suggested that autism was linked to MMR vaccinations or mercury-based preservative. This study was later criticized as being

methodologically flawed and was retracted by the journal that published it. Two reviews of all the available literature have found no credible association. However, many parents remain convinced that the link is "real" and causal, and some are refusing to immunize their children against these serious childhood diseases.

16. Dopamine activity is lower in people with ADHD, particularly in the striatum and prefrontal cortex; deficits in these areas may contribute to the associated impulsive behavior and learning difficulties. The mechanism may be excess transporters, which remove dopamine from the synapse before it has time to work. Stimulant drugs used to treat ADHD, such as methylphenidate (Ritalin) and amphetamine, increase dopamine levels; drugs that affect norepinephrine (such as atomoxetine) are more effective for some individuals.

17. ADHD clearly "runs in families," with a heritability of 75% across studies. Several of the genes that have been implicated in ADHD are involved with dopamine receptors and transporters. The LPHN3 gene, which plays an important role in neural transmission and neuron survival, predicts how well people with ADHD will respond to stimulant medications. Genes that affect serotonin receptors and the serotonin transporter have also been identified as playing a role in the disorder. Parental factors correlated with ADHD that may be environmental or genetic include maternal smoking and stress, parental abuse of alcohol and other drugs, and parental mood and anxiety disorders. Definite environmental contributors include brain injury, stroke, birth/pregnancy complications, and neurotoxins such as lead and pesticides. Chemicals called phthalates found in shampoo and perfumes are now being studied as well.

## Post-test

1. b    2. a    3. d    4. d    5. c    6. b    7. d    8. a    9. d    10. b    11. b    12. c    13. b    14. d
15. a    16. c    17. c    18. a    19. d    20. c    21. b    22. c    23. a    24. b    25. a    26. b
27. b    28. c    29. d    30. d    31. d    32. c    33. a    34. c    35. c    36. b    37. d    38. c
39. a    40. d    41. c    42. c    43. a    44. b    45. d    46. b    47. a    48. c    49. c    50. c
51. b    52. a    53. d    54. a    55. d    56. d    57. a

# 14 Psychological Disorders

## Chapter Outline

## Learning Objectives

After reading this chapter, you should be able to answer the following questions.

1. What are the characteristics of schizophrenia?

2. How are genes thought to be involved in schizophrenia?

3. How do positive and negative symptoms of schizophrenia differ?

4. What is the dopamine hypothesis of schizophrenia? Why is this hypothesis insufficient to fully explain schizophrenia?

5. What brain deficits are associated with schizophrenia?

6. What are the characteristics of affective disorders?

7. What are some of the possible genetic bases for depression? Bipolar disorder?

8. What is the monoamine hypothesis of depression? What evidence supports it?

9. Why is ECT sometimes used as a treatment for depression? How is it believed to work?

10. What is SAD? How is it typically treated?

11. How is bipolar disorder treated?

12. What brain areas seem to be involved in affective disorders?

13. What are some possible biological explanations for suicide?

14. What are the characteristics of anxiety disorders?

15. What are some biological causes of anxiety disorders?

16. What are the symptoms and possible treatments for posttraumatic stress disorder?

17. Why is obsessive-compulsive disorder considered to be an anxiety disorder?

## Schizophrenia

### Summary and Guided Review

After studying this section in the text, fill in the blanks of the following summary.

According to recent estimates, one out of every _____ (1) people in the United States currently suffers from a diagnosable mental disorder, and 46% will suffer from at least one. Schizophrenia is a mental disorder marked by a number of perceptual, emotional, and _____ (2) deficits along with a loss of contact with _____ (3) and an inability to function in life. Schizophrenia is a(n) _____ (4), meaning that there are severe disturbances in reality, orientation, and thinking. It affects about _____% (5) of the population, regardless of gender or socioeconomic status, and about 20% of people hospitalized for psychiatric care suffer from it.

Schizophrenia literally means "split mind" and reflects a distortion of _____ (6) and _____ (7), which are not based in reality. Symptoms include hallucinations, false and unfounded beliefs called

_____ (8), and paranoia. Schizophrenia affects men and women in equal amounts, though _____ (9) typically show symptoms at an earlier age. The use of diagnostic categories based on predominant symptoms, such as paranoia, will most likely change in the future because patients often have _____ (10) symptoms and multiple diagnoses. People exhibiting sudden _____ (11) symptoms generally respond to treatment better than those who suffer from gradually developing chronic symptoms. Although in the early 20th century schizophrenia was believed to have a(n) _____ (12) basis, the technology for determining this did not become available until the 1960s; in the meantime, social explanations held sway for decades.

Twin and adoption studies suggest a strong genetic component to schizophrenia; heritability has been estimated at _____ to _____% (13). Furthermore, being _____ (14) out of a family with a history of schizophrenia provides little or no protection from the disorder's development.

_____ (15) among identical twins for schizophrenia demonstrate that children of "normal" twins are as likely to exhibit schizophrenia as children of the twin with schizophrenia. Twin studies may be difficult to interpret, however, because of the inconsistency of researchers including the _____ (16) disorders into their schizophrenia diagnoses. For example, when identical twins are discordant for schizophrenia, over half of the _____ (17) twins have spectrum disorders. Another problem is that schizophrenia most likely results from the cumulative effects of multiple _____ (18), each of which contributes a relatively small effect.

Researchers have identified over _____ (19) genes suspected of a role in producing schizophrenia, most of which are related to neurodevelopment and plasticity, immune response, and hormonal activity. _____ _____ _____ (20) (CNVs), such as deletions or rearrangements of the information on chromosomes, have larger effects and are largely inherited. The genetic changes associated with schizophrenia go back millennia, as the symptoms have been documented in individuals as long ago as _____ (21) years ago. Explanations for why such a maladaptive behavior has persisted include the ability to cope with rapid cultural evolution, and the disorder fosters creative thinking (exhibited by many Nobel laureates such as Albert Einstein).

It is more accurate to think of genes as conferring risk for schizophrenia rather than as the single cause. According to the _____ (22) model, a person will become schizophrenic if the combined genetic and environmental causal factors reach or exceed a threshold. Environmental factors might be _____ (23), such as job difficulties or divorce, or _____ (24), such as poor nutrition, infection, or exposure to toxic substances. There is evidence that environmental influences work in part by _____ (25) means through altering gene expression.

The symptoms of schizophrenia may be classified as either _____ (26) (including hallucinations and delusions) or _____ (27) (including lack of emotion or motivation). While positive symptoms tend to have a(n) _____ (28) onset and respond well to drug treatments, negative symptoms tend to be _____ (29) and are associated with brain deficits. Crow theorized that there were two different syndromes of schizophrenia: Type _____ (30) schizophrenia involving positive symptoms and increased _____ (31) receptors, and Type _____ (32) schizophrenia associated with poverty of speech, negative affect, and associated with cell loss in the _____ (33) lobes.

Until the mid-1950s, very little could be done to help individuals with schizophrenia. The first effective _____ (34) drugs were introduced at that time,

although researchers did not know why these drugs worked. Later, it was discovered that
_____ (35) overdoses produce psychotic behavior via increased dopamine
activity, suggesting that excess dopaminergic activity was involved. This was supported by the
fact that drugs that _____ (36) $D_2$ dopamine receptors are effective in
reducing positive symptoms of schizophrenia.

However, 30–40% of schizophrenics failed to respond to dopamine-blocking
neuroleptics; some, especially those with chronic symptoms, appeared to have a dopamine
_____ (37). A significant problem with prolonged use of dopamine
blockers is that they often lead to _____ _____
(38), producing involuntary tremors and movement because of increased sensitivity
of dopamine receptors in the basal ganglia. Newer antipsychotic drugs, referred to as
_____ (39), target $D_2$ receptors to a lesser degree and produce fewer
_____ (40) disturbances. _____ (41) has also
been implicated in schizophrenia; hallucinogenic drugs such as psilocybin and LSD trigger
schizophrenic-like responses. On the other hand, PCP induces strong negative symptoms, and
since the drug strongly inhibits the _____ (42) receptor, which has led to
the _____ (43) theory of schizophrenia. _____ (44),
which activates the NMDA receptor, alleviates both positive and negative symptoms where
this neurotransmitter is implicated. The fact that three major neurotransmitters have been
implicated in schizophrenia suggests that focusing on a single one might not be wise. Plus,
there are additional structural and functional _____ (45) in the brain that
can also cause schizophrenia symptoms.

A signature characteristic of the schizophrenic brain is a 2% _____
(46) in the volumes of both white and gray matter. Enlarged _____
(47), indicating loss of brain tissue, are often associated with schizophrenia and other
neurological conditions. Although tissue loss has been found in at least 50 areas, deficits in
the _____ (48) and _____ (49) lobes are particularly
important. Although activity is decreased in the dorsolateral prefrontal cortex, it is increased
in the orbitofrontal cortex, as well as a subregion of the _____ (50).
The symptoms of schizophrenia have been associated with _____ (51),
a condition in which working memory and other functions of the prefrontal cortex are
impaired. This may be due to a deficiency of _____ (52) in the prefrontal
cortex; administering amphetamine increases blood flow in the prefrontal cortex, improving
performance on the _____ (53) Card Sorting Test. The behavioral results
of hypofrontality in schizophrenics include flat affect, social withdrawal, impaired attention,
and problem solving.

Schizophrenia may also involve lack of coordination in activity between the
_____ (54) and the _____ (55) cortex and
across the brain in general. Since linking activity within and across cortical activity
requires _____ (56) firing of neurons, it is no surprise that patients
with schizophrenia have disruptions in this process. In patients with positive symptoms,
these oscillations are enhanced in some areas and reduced in others. For instance,
_____ (57) areas are active during auditory hallucinations, and visual
areas during visual hallucinations. In normal people, these areas are activated during
"inner speech," but in the schizophrenic this activation might result in misperceiving self-
generated thoughts. Another effect associated with altered synchrony is the schizophrenic's
inability to suppress _____ (58) sounds; this is an impairment of
auditory _____ (59). Antipsychotic drugs may improve gating, but
_____ (60) actually normalizes it; while _____ (61) in
the United States has declined by half in the last 50 years to 20%, it remains at 80% among
people with schizophrenia.

Many environmental factors, such as maternal stress and birth complications, have been associated with schizophrenia. The _____ _____ (62) effect refers to the fact that more people who eventually develop schizophrenia are born in January to May. The factor implicated is not the temperature but that mothers are at greater risk for prenatal exposure to viruses in the second trimester of pregnancy. In these cases, the culprit is probably not the virus itself but the _____ (63) reaction that is triggered. While an original study in Netherlands mothers during World War II had some limitations, recent evidence from a study in China confirmed that prenatal _____ (64) may also play a role. A nonmaternal factor that may contribute to schizophrenia is the father's _____ (65) at the time of conception. These factors suggest epigenetic changes are occurring.

Some brain deficits, such as failed _____ (66) of neurons in the frontal and temporal lobes, occur during pregnancy. Evidence comes from studies of children, who later exhibited schizophrenia, demonstrating deficits in physical coordination and positive affect compared to their siblings. By the time a person is diagnosed with schizophrenia, physical changes in the brain have already occurred, probably during _____ (67) and young adulthood. However, some studies of schizophrenic adolescents have found progressive loss of _____ (68) matter following diagnosis.

## Short Answer and Essay Questions

Answer the following questions.

1. In a study described in the text, the offspring of both the schizophrenic and nonschizophrenic members of discordant identical twin pairs were equally likely to become schizophrenic. What does this suggest about the contributions of genes and environmental factors to schizophrenia?

2. What is the vulnerability model of schizophrenia? How does it account for schizophrenia developing in an individual with a low genetic predisposition? How does it account for schizophrenia NOT developing in someone with a high genetic predisposition?

3. Distinguish between Type I and Type II schizophrenia in several ways.

4. How are dopamine, glutamate, and serotonin thought to be involved in schizophrenia? In your answer, consider how antipsychotic medications affect these neurotransmitters.

5. What anatomical and functional brain deficits occur in schizophrenia? Why do some researchers believe that schizophrenia is a disorder of synchrony? When do these deficits develop?

# Affective Disorders

## Summary and Guided Review

After studying this section in the text, fill in the blanks of the following summary.

Major depression, which is more severe than normal _____ (69) depression, is characterized by hopelessness, loss of ability to enjoy life, slowed thought, and sleep disturbances. _____ (70) disorder involves cycling between depression and mania or agitation, which is characterized by periods of excess energy and confidence and development of grandiose schemes. Unipolar depression is more common in

_____ (71), but bipolar disorder is equally common in men and women. Recent data indicate that _____ (72) out of ten individuals will suffer a mood disorder in their lifetime (most likely depression).

While there is an environmental contribution to affective disorders, the concordance rate is 69% for _____ (73) twins and 13% for fraternal twins, and adoption has little effect on this rate. There is a sex difference in heritability (29% for men, 42% for women), as well as the genes implicated in depressive symptoms (seven exclusive to men, nine to women, and only three in both). As in schizophrenia, the genes implicated are many and of small effect individually, which has forced researchers to perform large-scale meta-analyses to identify candidate genes. For instance, individuals with one or two copies of the "short" allele of the 5-HTTLPR _____ _____ (74) gene have an increased vulnerability to depression, along with reduced gray matter in the _____ (75) and part of the cingulate cortex. These changes may also increase susceptibility to chronic _____ (76), which can lead to depression. The effect of this allele may be suppressed by another gene, a process called genetic _____ (77); the protective gene in this case is an allele of the gene for _____ (78), a protein that encourages neuron growth and survival. A common characteristic of depression is disruption of the _____ (79) (day-night) rhythm, and five genes involved in this rhythm have also been associated with depression. Bipolar disorder is also _____ (80), even more so than depression, with heritability estimates of at least 85%. Few genes have been confirmed, though large-scale studies have found common genes across bipolar disorder, major depressive disorder, autism spectrum disorders, and attention-deficit/hyperactivity disorder. One notable difference is that three _____ (81) found in circadian rhythm genes are not found in those other disorders.

Early drugs for depression were discovered accidentally. For instance, iproniazid was a drug developed to treat _____ (82), but it also elevated mood and had a strong antidepressive effect. This drug's ability to raise the levels of the neurotransmitters norepinephrine and _____ (83) led to the _____ (84) hypothesis of depression. Some antidepressant drugs, such as the tricyclic and atypical antidepressants, act by blocking _____ (85) at the synapse, while others block the enzymatic inactivation of neurotransmitters in the terminals (like MAOIs). Atypical antidepressants block only a single neurotransmitter; Prozac increases _____ (86) levels, improving mood, activity level, daily rhythms, eating, sex, and cognition. _____ (87) is related to motivation and responsiveness to the environment. A non-nicotine component of tobacco smoke serves as a(n) _____ _____ _____ (88) or MAOI, which may explain why so many depressed people smoke and have difficulty quitting. The drug _____ (89), which blocks NMDA glutamate receptors, shows some promise as a temporary treatment for depressive symptoms that fail to be alleviated with standard drug treatments. A nondrug treatment that is as effective as drug therapy is _____ _____ (90) therapy (CBT); in patients receiving CBT, there was an almost twofold improvement in depression scores.

Electroconvulsive therapy (ECT) is sometimes used to treat depression in extreme cases of nonresponsiveness to traditional therapy or who exhibit _____ (91) behaviors. This requires applying an electrical current to the brain to produce a brief _____ (92) and is performed under anesthesia and muscle relaxers. It is safer and more effective than many drug treatments, its effects are experienced more quickly, and cognitive improvements can even exceed pre-depression levels. The one disadvantage of ECT is that it conveys often short-term benefits, so its use is often combined with drug treatment over the longer term. ECT is effective with depression, mania, and schizophrenia, suggesting that ECT has complex effects in the brain. Two effects are increasing the _____ (93) of postsynaptic serotonin receptors, while decreasing it on autoreceptors of norepinephrine and dopamine neurons. ECT also seems to _____ (94) neural firing throughout the brain.

ECT and antidepressant drugs may also relieve depression by enhancing _____ (95) in the hippocampus. These new neurons then migrate to their new locations and show more _____ (96) than the existing one, but ECT may increase plasticity independently of neurogenesis. The time required for the new neurons to migrate and assume functions coincides with the delay in symptom improvement that occurs with most antidepressant drugs. As described in the Application, a different kind of brain stimulation with relatively few side effects is _____ _____ _____ (97). TMS has been approved by the Federal Drug Administration for use with depression, and in a recent study it improved depression in 68% of medication-resistant patients. Another interesting treatment involves stimulating the brain with electrodes implanted on the left _____ (98) nerve, where 70% of patients reported reduced depressive symptoms. Finally, a more aggressive strategy is deep brain stimulation, where the _____ (99) cortex is stimulated directly from a pulse generator implanted under the skin; 50% of patients were symptom-free after three years.

People with depression often suffer from _____ (100) rhythm disturbances, including feeling sleepy early in the evening, waking early in the morning, or spending more time in _____ (101) sleep. Readjusting one's circadian rhythm by altering sleep habits may bring relief, as may reducing REM sleep. In many depressed individuals, sleep _____ (102) can temporarily alleviate symptoms, and most antidepressant drugs also reduce the amount of REM sleep. People with _____ _____ _____ (103), or SAD, experience depression either in the summer or winter and improve or experience hypomania in the other season. This disorder accounts for 10% of all affective disorders and is much more common in _____ (104). Depression in SAD is usually characterized by excess sleepiness, increased appetites and _____ (105) intake, and weight gain. Winter depression is associated with a reduced amount of natural _____ (106); moving to or visiting a more tropical region (even for a few days) often brings some relief. Heat is associated with _____ (107) depression; finding ways to stay cool seems to relieve this form of depression. Winter depression is often treated with _____ (108), which involves exposure to high-intensity light for a few hours each day. The light exposure must mimic bright sunlight, and it seems to work by _____ (109) the circadian rhythm. In addition, people suffering from winter depression may self-medicate by eating more carbohydrates, which increases brain _____ (110) levels.

People with _____ (111) disorder exhibit a great deal of variability in their cycling. Stress often triggers the transition from depressive to _____ (112) phases, although over time the switch tends to occur more spontaneously. Bipolar disorder is most often treated with _____ (113), which stabilizes both manic and depressive episodes; it is believed that this is accomplished through normalization of several neurotransmitter and receptor systems. However, one specific effect of lithium, and an alternative drug valproate, is the inhibition of _____ (114), a family of enzymes that regulate neural excitability.

Structural abnormalities in affective disorders include larger _____ (115), which is indicative of decreased tissue volume. Frontal areas show decreases as well as the hippocampus, but the _____ (116) is actually larger. Depression is associated with reduced activity in the _____ (117) nucleus and dorsolateral prefrontal cortex, and increased activity in the ventral prefrontal cortex, which may indicate the state of depression. Mania is also characterized by increased brain activity; the _____ (118) prefrontal cortex may control cycling and could be referred to as a "bipolar switch" that cannot be turned off during emotionally neutral activities. There is also evidence that both depressed and bipolar patients have anomalies in functional brain _____ (119), which return to more normal levels as an individual's symptoms improve.

People with affective disorders, particularly those with bipolar disorder, are at greater risk for suicide than others in the population. According to the _____-_____ (120) model, the individual has a genetic predisposition for suicide, and the stress of a psychiatric disorder may be the environmental "trigger" for suicide. Suicide, even among nondepressed individuals, is associated with low levels of the _____ (121) metabolite 5-HIAA. Low levels of 5-HIAA are linked to suicidal behavior, particularly in _____ (122) suicide attempters. Recently, prescriptions for _____ (123) to teens have decreased over concerns about the drugs' link to suicide; this drop in the prescription rate was followed by an increase in suicide rate among depressed teens in the United States and the Netherlands.

## Short Answer and Essay Questions

Answer the following questions.

6. Distinguish between the mechanisms of monoamine oxidase inhibitors, tricyclic anti-depressants, and atypical (second-generation) antidepressants.

7. What are two ways in which depressed individuals may self-medicate to relieve depression?

8. Describe the similarities and differences between unipolar depression and bipolar disorder in terms of symptoms, genetic basis, and treatment.

9. What are the ways of alleviating the symptoms of winter depression?

10. Why does the author of the text suggest that the ventral prefrontal cortex acts as a depression "switch" and the subgenual prefrontal cortex acts as a bipolar switch?

11. Identify the many ways that brain stimulation can be used to treat depression. How might these treatments exert their therapeutic effects on the brain?

12. Why are people with low serotonin levels thought to be the most at risk for suicide?

## Anxiety Disorders

### Summary and Guided Review

After studying this section in the text, fill in the blanks of the following summary.

Anxiety disorders include generalized anxiety disorder, panic disorder, _____ (124), and phobia. Whereas _____ (125) is an adaptive response to real objects or events in the environment, anxiety involves the anticipation of stressful events and inappropriate reactions to objects and events. Anxiety disorders may be treated with benzodiazepines, which increase sensitivity to _____ (126) though have a high addiction potential. Reduced _____ (127) activity is also implicated in anxiety disorders, and as a result _____ (128) such as SSRIs are now the treatment of choice for anxiety disorders.

Posttraumatic stress disorder, or PTSD, is characterized by recurrent thoughts or images called _____ (129), lack of concentration, and overreactivity to environmental stimuli. PTSD is observed in individuals exposed to combat and other traumatic experiences, and it is four times more likely to occur in _____ (130) when they are exposed to trauma. PTSD has a(n) _____ (131) of about 30%; two of the genes are mutations of FKBP5. PTSD is not easy to treat with traditional approaches; one alternative is _____ (132) therapy, which allows confrontation of the anxiety-provoking stimuli under safe conditions. Another therapeutic technique that capitalizes on reconsolidation is called _____ _____ (133).

Anxiety disorders share a common set of brain anomalies: the _____ (134) and the anterior cingulate are hyperactive in general anxiety, phobia, and panic disorders, while the _____ (135) cortex is overly responsive in phobias and PTSD. In addition, the _____ (136) decreases its activity in PTSD patients, which could explain memory problems associated with the disorder. The key to whether a traumatic event will be followed by PTSD does not appear to be related to the severity of the event or the emotional state of the individual. Rather, it seems to be the person's _____ (137) to PTSD, due to decreases in _____ (138) matter in the orbitofrontal cortex, hippocampus, and anterior cingulate cortex. Researchers are now identifying four faulty networks that contribute to anxiety disorders. One interesting new treatment for PTSD will be simulating a traumatic event using _____ _____ (139) technology; simulating a traumatic event while a patient undergoes relaxation exercises and administration of a drug that increases neuroplasticity and learning has been very successful in reducing PTSD.

Many people with anxiety disorders have other psychiatric problems, especially _____ (140) disorders. The genetic bases for anxiety disorders include mechanisms that influence the activity of the neurotransmitter _____ (141), but other substances such as adenosine, glutamate, and dopamine are also involved. _____-_____ (142) disorder is marked by recurring thoughts (obsessions) and resulting compulsive actions over which the person claims to have no control. These behaviors are often repetitive and _____ (143), such as checking locks or appliances multiple times, or engaging in unnecessary routines. OCD runs in families: about a fourth of OCD patients have a family member with the same condition.

OCD is associated with increased activity in the _____ (144) cortex and the caudate nuclei, which decreases following both successful drug and behavior therapy. OCD occurs with a number of diseases that damage the _____ _____ (145), which is involved in motor activity. Millionaire Howard Hughes displayed OCD later in his life, after a series of _____ (146), and included a crippling obsession with avoiding germs. Serotonin activity is _____ (147) in OCD, since SSRI drugs reduce symptoms in some individuals. Other effective drug treatments include antipsychotics and antiglutamate drugs. One controversial psychosurgical procedure is to remove the _____

_____ (148) cortex, though deep brain stimulation to the same area has had equal efficacy.

OCD is related to _____ _____ _____ (149), a disorder in which dogs and cats overgroom themselves; similar disorders are seen in birds (feather pulling) and primates (hair pulling). The human version of this condition involves nail biting and _____ _____ (150), or trichotillomania. A compulsive collecting behavior found among many people with OCD (but can occur on its own) is _____ (151); this disorder can result in injury, unsanitary living conditions, and even death to individuals trapped in and by their own belongings. Two of the most famous individuals with this disorder were the Collyer brothers, who died in such a cluttered house that they were forced to move through tunnels in the garbage. Apparently this disorder is characterized by high activity levels in areas of the brain that evaluate behavior and a sense of _____ (152); throwing out anything, even garbage, would seem like throwing out parts of the individual. OCD is also related to _____ _____ (153), which is characterized by recurring _____ (154), which are sudden, rapid, non-rhythmic facial expressions, body movements, and noises. Other symptoms include mirroring facial expressions and gestures, though the popularly reported tendency to blurt out profanity and insults is relatively rare (10–15% of all cases). The disorder, which affects approximately 0.3% of the population, typically emerges in _____ (155) and becomes more pronounced over time; _____ (156) are more likely to have this disorder. The heritability for Tourette's is high, with a concordance rate of 53% for identical twins, suggesting a strong _____ (157) basis. Tourette's involves increased activity in the _____ _____ (158), and although the _____ (159) blocker haloperidol is the treatment of choice, other similar drugs are also being used. One report suggests the high levels of neurotransmitter over-stimulates the _____ _____ (160) portion of the basal ganglia in Tourette's patients.

## Short Answer and Essay Questions

Answer the following questions.

13. What are the main symptoms of PTSD? Why doesn't everyone exposed to a traumatic event develop PTSD? How is it treated?

14. Describe the symptoms and brain changes that occur in OCD. What other disorders are linked to OCD? Describe the typical treatment of OCD.

15. How are OCD and Tourette's syndrome similar? Why are they thought to be related?

## Post-test

Use these multiple-choice questions to check your understanding of the chapter.

1. How many people in the United States are estimated to be suffering from a diagnosable mental illness?
   a. 1 out of every 3 people
   b. 1 out of every 4 people
   c. 1 out of every 5 people
   d. 1 out of every 10 people

2. Schizophrenia is typically characterized by all of the following EXCEPT
   a. loss of contact with reality.
   b. perceptual, emotional, and intellectual deficits.
   c. periods of intense excitement.
   d. an inability to function in life.

3. If an individual has severe disturbances of reality, orientation, and thinking, he or she is suffering from a(n)
   a. psychosis
   b. tic
   c. OCD
   d. affective disorder

4. Schizophrenics with ___ symptoms are MORE likely to recover.
   a. chronic
   b. negative
   c. violent
   d. acute

5. Twenty years after first hospitalization, ___ of schizophrenics seem fully recovered, and another ___ were improved.
   a. 12%; 50%
   b. 22%; 43%
   c. 35%; 55%
   d. 56%; 26%

6. In the 1940s, emphasis shifted from biological to ___ causes of schizophrenia.
   a. genetic
   b. emotional
   c. hormonal
   d. social

7. When spectrum disorders are NOT considered, the concordance rate for schizophrenia among identical twins is
   a. 48%.
   b. 17%.
   c. 89%.
   d. 28%.

8. Jerry and Jason are identical twins. Jerry has schizophrenia, but Jason does not. Which of the following statements is correct?
   a. Jerry's children are more likely to develop schizophrenia than Jason's children.
   b. Jason's children are more likely to develop schizophrenia than Jerry's children.
   c. Jerry and Jason's children are equally likely to develop schizophrenia.
   d. Jerry and Jason's children are no more likely to develop schizophrenia than other members of the population.

9. Schizophrenia is a very old disorder, with symptoms having been documented 4,000 years ago and some genes developing over 100,000 years ago. What is one hypothesis for why the genes have persisted despite their negative effects?
   a. They are found alongside highly beneficial genes and therefore are hitchhiking on them.
   b. They are the result of rapid mutation, so when one is eliminated through evolution, another one appears to take its place.
   c. They may help individuals cope with a rapidly developing social culture.
   d. They encode vital proteins and only become damaging when mutated.

10. Which of the following genes have been implicated, according to a large database analysis?
    a. genes involved in hormonal activity
    b. genes that affect the immune response
    c. genes that play a role in neural development and plasticity
    d. all of the above

11. Schizophrenia research indicates that
    a. genes are more important than the environment.
    b. the environment is more important than genes.
    c. most of the genes implicated protect the individual from environmental causes of schizophrenia.
    d. environmental factors work in part by epigenetic means.

12. A person with genes linked to schizophrenia might be normal until an environmental challenge occurs (such as a death, loss of a job, or infection), pushing the person over a threshold that triggers schizophrenic symptoms. This idea is called the
    a. epistasis model.
    b. traumatic model.
    c. depressive model.
    d. vulnerability model.

13. Which of the following symptoms is MOST likely to respond to treatment with antipsychotic medication?
    a. hallucinations
    b. impaired attention
    c. poverty of speech
    d. lack of affect

14. The first effective antipsychotic drugs were
    a. dopamine antagonists.
    b. dopamine agonists.
    c. serotonin antagonists.
    d. serotonin agonists.

15. All of the following support the dopamine hypothesis of schizophrenia EXCEPT:
    a. amphetamines can produce a psychosis that resembles schizophrenia.
    b. schizophrenia can be treated by drugs that block NMDA receptors.
    c. effective drugs block the $D_2$ type of receptors.
    d. schizophrenics have higher dopamine activity in the striatum.

16. Tardive dyskinesia results from
    a. the blocking of serotonin receptors in the prefrontal cortex.
    b. enhancing dopamine release throughout the brain.
    c. compensatory sensitivity of dopamine receptors in the basal ganglia.
    d. activating NMDA glutamate receptors.

17. Enlarged ventricles are associated with
    a. schizophrenia.
    b. Alzheimer's disease.
    c. Huntington's chorea.
    d. all of the above

18. Hypofrontality is a decrease in dorsolateral prefrontal activity caused by ___ deficiency, which impairs performance in the ___ task.

    a. dopamine; Wisconsin Card Sorting

    b. serotonin; delayed match-to-sample

    c. norepinephrine; knee reflex

    d. glutamate; anger avoidance

19. One of the key functions that is disrupted in schizophrenia is
    a. synchrony between the prefrontal lobes and the hippocampus.
    b. coordination of activity between auditory and visual areas.
    c. oscillation synchrony at low frequencies.
    d. none of the above

20. Auditory gating, the filtering out of environmental noise, is normalized in schizophrenics by which activity?
    a. drinking
    b. smoking
    c. breathing the gas from whipped cream containers
    d. laughing loudly

21. All of the following are linked to brain and transmitter anomalies associated with schizophrenia EXCEPT
    a. prenatal exposure to influenza (flu).
    b. maternal stress during pregnancy.
    c. prenatal starvation of the mother.
    d. prenatal exposure to alcohol.

22. Which of the following statements regarding the development of schizophrenia is TRUE?
    a. Gray matter deficits are a result of lack of pruning, caused by glutamate excess.
    b. Cortical neurons fail to migrate to the appropriate locations in the second trimester of pregnancy.
    c. Ventricle enlargement is evident at birth.
    d. Brain damage associated with schizophrenia does not begin until after 40.

23. Edna had to put her cat Fluffy down due to kidney failure, and as a result she felt very sad and depressed. While her depression felt severe, after a few days she remembered happier times with Fluffy, and the dark cloud eventually went away. What form of depression did she suffer from during that low time?
    a. major depression
    b. bipolar disorder
    c. monoamine disorder
    d. none of the above

24. Women are MORE likely than men to suffer from
    a. unipolar depression.
    b. bipolar disorder.
    c. both unipolar depression and bipolar disorder.
    d. bipolar depression and schizophrenia.

25. The concordance rate for depression among identical twins raised apart
    a. is much lower than for those raised together.
    b. is about the same as for fraternal twins raised together.
    c. is about the same as for those raised together.
    d. none of the above

26. If you have tested positive for the short allele of the 5-HTTLPR serotonin transporter gene, what substance created by the VAL66MET allele can protect you against its negative effects?

    a. glutamate

    b. L-dopamine (L-dopa)

    c. Prozac

    d. brain-derived neurotrophic factor

27. The first drug that showed antidepressant effects was
    a. fluoxetine.
    b. iproniazid.
    c. chlorpromazine.
    d. nicotine.

28. Prozac (fluoxetine), because of its effects on a single neurotransmitter, is a
    a. monoamine oxidase inhibitor.
    b. tricyclic antidepressant.
    c. first-generation antidepressant.
    d. selective serotonin reuptake inhibitor.

29. Reduced norepinephrine is associated with
    a. sleep.
    b. lack of motivation.
    c. body temperature dysregulation.
    d. sexual activity.

30. A treatment that produces improvement in treatment-resistant depression in less than 2 hours of administration is
    a. glycine.
    b. nicotine.
    c. phototherapy.
    d. ketamine.

31. Which of the following is NOT true of ECT?
    a. It typically involves profound memory loss.
    b. It must result in a brain seizure in order to be effective.
    c. It must be repeated multiple times.
    d. Its therapeutic effects are equal or better than those of antidepressant drugs.

32. Which of the following brain changes is (are) associated with ECT?
    a. increased sensitivity to serotonin
    b. decreased sensitivity in norepinephrine autoreceptors
    c. widespread synchrony of neural firing
    d. all of the above

33. All of the following are existing or potential treatments for depression EXCEPT:
    a. deep brain stimulation.
    b. ECT administered two to three times a month.
    c. TMS.
    d. stimulation of the vagus nerve.

34. What mechanism(s) may be responsible for the effectiveness of antidepressant treatments?
    a. neurogenesis
    b. migration of new cells in the hippocampus
    c. greater plasticity in new cells
    d. all of the above

35. Unipolar depression is associated with
    a. early onset REM sleep.
    b. REM sleep deficit.
    c. a heightened sense of arousal in the evenings.
    d. late REM onset.

36. Which of the following statements regarding SAD is TRUE?
    a. It is more likely to improve if a person moves away from the equator.
    b. It affects people only in the winter.
    c. It is more common in men.
    d. It can be associated with hypomanic periods during the "good" season.

37. Regarding the role of light in SAD,
    a. the length of exposure to light is more important than the amount or intensity of light.
    b. the amount of light is more important than the length of exposure to light.
    c. phototherapy works only if it is used early in the morning.
    d. phototherapy is more effective than drug therapy because it lowers serotonin levels.

38. People with SAD sometimes self-medicate by
    a. eating a lot of carbohydrates.
    b. smoking.
    c. limiting their intake of junk food.
    d. all of the above

39. All of the following are true about bipolar disorder EXCEPT:
    a. lithium is the medication of choice.
    b. the manic phase usually lasts longer than the depressive phase.
    c. stress is a common trigger for cycling between depression and mania.
    d. effective drug treatments share the effect of inhibiting the PKC family of enzymes.

40. Which of the following brain areas shows heightened activity during depressive episodes?
    a. caudate nucleus and inferotemporal cortex
    b. dorsolateral prefrontal cortex and anterior cingulate cortex
    c. subgenual prefrontal cortex and hippocampus
    d. ventral prefrontal cortex and amygdala

41. Which of the following brain areas has been referred to as the bipolar "switch"?
    a. hippocampus
    b. subgenual prefrontal cortex
    c. amygdala
    d. ventral prefrontal cortex

42. Which of the following groups is MOST at risk for suicide?
    a. people with unipolar depression
    b. people with bipolar disorder
    c. people with substance abuse
    d. people with schizophrenia

43. Trevor becomes anxious whenever he gets around water, so he avoids going to lakes, rivers, and other large bodies of water. What type of anxiety disorder does he MOST likely have?
    a. generalized anxiety disorder
    b. phobia
    c. panic disorder
    d. OCD

44. Which of the following relieve(s) anxiety by enhancing GABA activity?
    a. atypical antidepressants
    b. neuroleptic drugs
    c. lithium
    d. benzodiazepines

45. Which of the following is NOT true about PTSD?
    a. It is characterized by flashbacks and nightmares.
    b. Men are more vulnerable than women.
    c. Its heritability is about 30%.
    d. It has been linked to changes in the hippocampus that might be caused by child-hood abuse.

46. Which of the following treatments is NOT particularly effective with PTSD?
    a. psychotherapy
    b. exposure therapy
    c. therapy involving virtual reality
    d. fear erasure

47. Howard Hughes suffered from
    a. generalized anxiety disorder.
    b. phobia.
    c. panic disorder.
    d. OCD.

48. Ryan was diagnosed with OCD when he was 21. He feels like every surface is contaminated, so when he touches something, he must immediately wash his hands with hot water and soap from a fresh pack to get the "germs" off. In this example, handwashing is the
    a. obsession.
    b. compulsion.
    c. disorder.
    d. MacGuffin.

49. Which of the following brain changes is (are) associated with OCD?
    a. increased activity in the orbitofrontal cortex
    b. a decrease in white matter in the circuit connecting the cingulate gyrus with other brain areas
    c. increased activity in the caudate nucleus
    d. all of the above

50. Which drug is MOST likely to be used in treating OCD and related disorders such as hair pulling and nail biting?
    a. serotonin reuptake inhibitors
    b. benzodiazepines
    c. haloperidol
    d. monoamine oxidase inhibitors

51. Tourette's syndrome probably results from increased ___ activity in the ___.
    a. dopamine; prefrontal cortex
    b. serotonin; prefrontal cortex
    c. serotonin; basal ganglia
    d. dopamine; basal ganglia

# Answers

## Guided Review

1. four
2. intellectual
3. reality
4. psychosis
5. 1
6. thought/emotions
7. emotions/thought
8. delusions
9. men
10. overlapping
11. acute
12. physical/biological
13. 60–90
14. adopted
15. Discordance
16. spectrum
17. nonschizophrenic
18. genes
19. 70
20. immune
21. 4,000
22. vulnerability
23. external
24. internal
25. epigenetic
26. positive
27. negative
28. acute
29. chronic
30. I
31. $D_2$
32. II
33. temporal
34. antipsychotic
35. amphetamine
36. blocked
37. deficient
38. tardive dyskinesia
39. atypical/second generation
40. motor/movement
41. Serotonin
42. NMDA
43. glutamate
44. glycine
45. anomalies
46. decrease
47. ventricles
48. frontal/temporal
49. temporal/frontal
50. hippocampus
51. hypofrontality
52. dopamine
53. Wisconsin
54. hippocampus
55. prefrontal
56. synchronized
57. language
58. environmental
59. gating
60. nicotine
61. smoke
62. winter birth
63. immune
64. starvation
65. age
66. migration

67. adolescence
68. gray
69. reactive
70. Bipolar
71. women
72. 3
73. identical
74. serotonin transporter
75. amygdala
76. stress
77. epistasis
78. BDNF (brain-derived neurotrophic factor)
79. circadian
80. heritable
81. mutations
82. tuberculosis
83. serotonin
84. monoamine
85. reuptake
86. serotonin
87. Norepinephrine
88. monoamine oxidase inhibitor
89. ketamine
90. cognitive behavior
91. suicidal
92. seizure
93. sensitivity
94. synchronize
95. neurogenesis
96. plasticity
97. transcranial magnetic stimulation
98. vagus
99. cingulate
100. circadian/biological
101. REM (rapid eye movement)

102. deprivation
103. seasonal affective disorder
104. women
105. carbohydrate
106. light
107. summer
108. phototherapy
109. resetting
110. serotonin
111. bipolar
112. manic
113. lithium
114. PKC
115. ventricles
116. amygdala
117. caudate
118. subgenual
119. connectivity
120. stress-diathesis
121. serotonin
122. impulsive
123. SSRIs
124. phobias
125. fear
126. GABA
127. serotonin
128. antidepressants
129. flashbacks
130. women
131. heritability
132. exposure
133. fear erasure
134. amygdala
135. insular
136. hippocampus
137. vulnerability

138. gray

139. virtual reality

140. mood

141. serotonin

142. Obsessive-compulsive

143. ritualistic

144. orbitofrontal

145. basal ganglia

146. accidents/crashes

147. high

148. anterior cingulate

149. acral lick syndrome

150. hair pulling

151. hoarding

152. self

153. Tourette's syndrome

154. tics

155. childhood

156. males

157. genetic

158. basal ganglia

159. dopamine

160. caudate nuclei

## Short Answer and Essay Questions

1. Because the children of each twin were equally likely to develop the disorder, genes are clearly involved in the disorder. It is not something one gets exclusively from the environment; otherwise, the children of the normal twin would have a much lower rate of schizophrenia than the offspring of the affected twin. At the same time, because the "normal" twin possesses the same genes as the schizophrenic twin, the differences in environmental factors between the twins must account for the fact that one of them is more affected than the other.

2. The vulnerability model suggests that schizophrenia develops as a result of the combined influence of genetic and environmental factors that reach or exceed some threshold. According to this model, someone with a low genetic predisposition may become schizophrenic if environmental factors, such as stressors, are strong enough to trigger the disorder. It also explains that someone with a high degree of genetic predisposition may not develop the disorder if he or she is exposed to low levels of environmental challenges.

3. Type I schizophrenia is a type of schizophrenia that has an acute onset; is potentially reversible; is characterized by positive symptoms and a lack of intellectual deficit; and responds well to drugs that block dopamine due to excess D2 receptors. Type II schizophrenia is characterized by negative symptoms, often including intellectual deficits; responds poorly to antidopaminergic drugs; and possibly involves irreversible brain changes in the temporal lobes.

4. Drugs that block D2 receptors are effective in some cases of schizophrenia. However, atypical antipsychotics, which increase glutamate levels but block D2 receptors less, are more effective (work in more cases). Glycine, which increases glutamate release, also produces better results when paired with conventional antipsychotics than these drugs alone. Glutamate increases have been linked to an improvement in negative symptoms. Some atypical antipsychotics also block serotonin receptors. It is likely that these three neurotransmitter systems interact to produce schizophrenia.

5. Anatomical deficits include reductions in brain tissue, particularly in frontal and temporal areas, which may lead to enlarged ventricles. In addition, neurons in the frontal and temporal lobes (including the hippocampus) are disordered and mislocated, indicating errors in migration. Functional deficits include increased dopamine and serotonin activity and decreased

glutamate activity; hypofrontality (which apparently contributes to negative symptoms); and disordered connections between prefrontal areas and the hippocampus and between frontal and sensory areas. Some researchers believe schizophrenia is a disorder of synchrony in part because the disordered connections result in lack of synchrony among areas, which is associated with gating problems; in addition, excessive synchrony in sensory areas is associated with hallucinations.

6. Monoamine oxidase inhibitors work by preventing the breakdown of monoamines in the synapse. Tricyclics prevent reuptake of the monoamines. Second-generation antidepressants affect one specific neurotransmitter, rather than all of the monoamines; for example, fluoxetine (Prozac) prevents the reuptake of serotonin.

7. Many depressed people smoke, and an ingredient in tobacco smoke acts as a MAO inhibitor. Also, people with SAD often eat a lot of carbohydrates, which increases their serotonin levels and may produce some relief from their depression.

8. Unipolar depression and bipolar disorder share the symptom of severe depression, but in bipolar disorder the depression alternates with mania. Depression is more common in women than men, whereas there is no sex difference for bipolar disorder. Both disorders have a genetic basis, but the heritability for bipolar disorder is about 85%, compared to 37% for unipolar depression. While it is well accepted that unipolar depression involves some imbalance in the monoamine transmitter, the biological basis of bipolar disorder is less clear. Unipolar depression is typically treated with drugs that increase serotonin and/or norepinephrine. Bipolar disorder has traditionally been treated with lithium, but newer drugs exist (valproate) or are being tested for effectiveness (PKC inhibitors). Tissue loss is characteristic of depression (with the exception of the amygdala, which is larger), along with reduced brain activity; activity is also decreased during bipolar depression but increases during mania. Activity in the ventral prefrontal area comes and goes with depression, and the area may be a "depression switch"; the subgenual prefrontal cortex is active during mania, and appears to be a "bipolar switch."

9. Winter depression may be alleviated by moving to or visiting a region where there is more natural light (in the direction of the equator). Phototherapy also provides relief if the person is exposed to a few hours of bright light during the day in the winter (when days are short and light levels are less intense than in summer). Consuming carbohydrates may also help, because it increases serotonin levels.

10. The ventral prefrontal cortex is thought to be a depression switch, because it is more active during periods of depression and less active when the person is not experiencing symptoms. The subgenual prefrontal cortex may be a bipolar switch because activity levels within it correspond with the manic and depressive states of the disorder; it is more active during mania and less active during depression. Also, it helps regulate the neurotransmitters involved in affective disorders.

11. All of the following involve some sort of brain stimulation: ECT, which causes seizure activity in the brain; TMS, which increases brain activity by exposing the brain to a magnetic field; deep brain stimulation, which involves stimulation by electrodes placed in areas such as the anterior cingulate cortex; and stimulation of the vagus nerve. ECT and drugs used for affective disorders may exert their effects on correcting imbalances in transmitters. They may also affect neurogenesis and plasticity in the brain.

12. Low serotonin is a marker for impulsive behavior, regardless of psychiatric disorder. Studies have found lower levels of the metabolite 5-HIAA in suicide attempters and in impulsive suicide attempters compared to nonimpulsive attempters. However, in individuals with two particular gene alleles serotonin reuptake inhibitors can increase suicide risk.

13. PTSD is characterized by flashbacks, nightmares, lack of concentration, and overreactivity to environmental stimuli. The reason some people develop PTSD while others do not has to do with vulnerability, which seems to be linked to reduced hippocampal volume, genetic factors, and childhood abuse. PTSD is difficult to treat with traditional drug and psychotherapy approaches. One alternative is exposure therapy or a newer procedure called fear erasure.

14. The symptoms of OCD are primarily obsessions (recurring thoughts) and compulsions (repetitive and ritualistic acts). Brain changes in OCD occur in a circuit involving the cingulate gyrus's connections to the basal ganglia, thalamus, and cortex. OCD-like behaviors include acral lick syndrome in animals, hair-pulling or trichotillomania in humans, hoarding, and Tourette's syndrome. Treatments include SSRIs, antipsychotics, glutamate blockers, surgical disconnection of the orbitofrontal cortex from the anterior cingulate cortex, deep brain stimulation, and TMS.

15. OCD and Tourette's syndrome are similar in that the behaviors exhibited are so compulsive. In Tourette's, a person can control the behavior, but only for a while. The reason the two are thought to be related is because they co-occur in families, and both involve increased activity in the basal ganglia. However, they are typically treated using different drugs.

## Post-test

1. b   2. c   3. a   4. d   5. b   6. d   7. a   8. c   9. c   10. d   11. d   12. d   13. a   14. a
15. b   16. c   17. d   18. a   19. a   20. b   21. d   22. b   23. d   24. a   25. c   26. d
27. b   28. d   29. b   30. d   31. a   32. d   33. b   34. d   35. a   36. d   37. b   38. a
39. b   40. d   41. b   42. b   43. b   44. d   45. b   46. a   47. d   48. b   49. d   50. a   51. d

# 15 Sleep and Consciousness

## Learning Objectives

After reading this chapter, you should be able to answer the following questions.

1. What are some possible functions of sleep?

2. What controls circadian rhythms?

3.  What rhythms of brain activity accompany wakefulness? Sleeping?

4.  What are the functions of REM and non-REM sleep?

5.  What brain areas control sleep and arousal?

6.  What are some sleep disorders?

7.  When we sleep, are we unconscious?

8.  What are the biological bases of awareness and attention?

9.  What brain areas contribute to our sense of self?

10.  What are some disorders of the self? What do they tell us about self-awareness?

11.  What do we know about the biological bases of consciousness?

## Sleep and Dreaming

### Summary and Guided Review

After studying this section in the text, fill in the blanks of the following summary.

The study of consciousness within psychology has been controversial. The use of
_____ (1) to study consciousness, popular at the end of the 19th century,
fell out of favor when the _____ (2) attempted to rid psychology of
subjective methods during the first half of the 20th century. When _____
(3) psychology emerged in the mid-20th century, mental experiences were once again
acceptable to study if they could be examined objectively. However, because of lack of
technology as well as lack of consensus concerning the meaning of consciousness, this topic
has remained controversial. Psychologists who do study it often work with researchers from
other disciplines, including _____ (4), philosophy, and computer science;
of the conscious states, _____ (5) is most commonly studied, because it
can be objectively observed and measured.

Although sleep is one of our most basic needs, researchers who study it have been
unable to fully explain its functions. One explanation is that sleep is _____
(6); it allows us to conserve energy and repair our bodies. Because amount of sleep is
correlated with a species' body size, food availability, metabolic rate, and vulnerability,
the _____ (7) hypothesis suggests the amount of sleep is a function of
needs for energy conservation and safety. In a study of 39 species, the factors of body size
and danger accounted for _____ % (8) of the variability in sleep time.
One interesting finding is that when you sleep, that is when the brain increases CSF flow to
cleanse itself of _____ (9). There is also considerable evidence that getting
adequate sleep at the right time is important. People who are _____
(10) workers experience difficulty getting enough sleep during the day. Rates of vehicle
and work-related accidents are higher in the early morning hours than at other times. Also,
_____ _____ (11) baseball teams playing games in
East Coast cities seem to be at a disadvantage if they are not given adequate time to adjust to
the time shift. This difficulty in adjustment while traveling across time zones is often referred
to as _____ _____ (12).

Our sleep/wake cycle is an example of a(n) _____ (13) rhythm,
and the sleep period corresponds with decreases in several physiological measures
such as urine production and body temperature. These cycles are controlled by the

_____ _____ (14); rats with lesions in this region no longer exhibit circadian cycles of sleep. When daylight cues are unavailable, people's circadian rhythms tend to increase to _____ (15)-hour cycles. This suggests that natural light is the critical _____ (16) for entraining the SCN to a 24-hour cycle. Furthermore, being exposed to _____ (17) light during wakefulness and darkness during sleep are important for coordinating the different biological rhythms associated with sleep. The fact that we tend toward a 25-hour cycle may explain why it is easier to adjust to _____ (18) times for falling asleep and waking up. Shift workers whose shifts rotate according to phase _____ (19) are able to adjust more easily than those who must accommodate phase advance changes. Light controls the sleep cycle through its influence on the pineal gland's secretion of _____ (20); in totally blind individuals, a failure to produce this substance in response to changing levels of light is associated with _____ (21). Blind individuals with normal melatonin cycling probably rely on signals from the _____ (22) pathway to the SCN. This pathway may be mediated not by rods and cones but by retinal ganglion cells containing the photopigment _____ (23), which is sensitive to short-wavelength light. The internal clock itself consists of two major groups of _____ (24) and their _____ (25) products. The groups alternate in activity as a group's proteins turn those genes off and turn the other group of genes on. Every day the feedback loop that comprises the circadian clock must be reset by _____ (26). Other clocks in the body are entrained to the day-night cycle by the _____ (27).

Several bodily rhythms in humans follow shorter, _____ (28) cycles. Some examples are hormone production, urinary output, and alertness. The basic rest and activity cycle is a rhythm that is about _____ to _____ (29) minutes long. When the person is awake, the EEG is a mixture of _____ (30) waves, associated with arousal and alertness, and _____ (31) waves, characteristic of relaxed wakefulness. _____ (32) waves occur during Stage 1, or light sleep. During Stage 2, we exhibit _____ _____ (33) and K-complexes. Slow-wave sleep (SWS) in Stages 3 and 4 is associated with _____ (34) waves; movement, including sleepwalking, often occurs during this time. The EEG activity then indicates a reverse progression through the sleep stages until _____ _____ _____ (35) sleep is achieved. This type of sleep is sometimes called _____ (36) sleep, because it is characterized by eye movements, physiological arousal, dreaming, and brain waves that are similar to a waking state. One unusual characteristic of REM sleep is that in spite of these signs of arousal, the body is in a state of paralysis or _____ (37). The length of REM sleep periods increases over the night as the amount of slow-wave sleep _____ (38).

People deprived of REM sleep will enter it more quickly on subsequent nights and spend more time in this stage of sleep, which implies that the brain or the body has a need for REM sleep. The _____ -_____ (39) hypothesis suggests that dreams are the product of spontaneous neural activity during REM sleep and have no function; we merely attempt to make sense of the somewhat random activation. Researchers do not agree on the function(s) of REM sleep. One suggestion is that because REM sleep is more common in infants and children than in adults, it promotes neural _____ (40). Because the amount of SWS is associated with _____ (41) in the brain prior to sleep, it has been suggested that SWS is more important for brain than body restoration. It may be involved in cerebral recovery, particularly in the _____ (42) cortex. Individuals given _____ (43) prior to a nap experienced less SW sleep during the nap and had poorer cognitive performance following the nap than those given a placebo, though they reported feeling vigorous and no sleepier than the control group.

Another possibility is that non-REM sleep is important for _____ (44). Applying slow oscillating potentials to the frontal and temporal lobes improved word association recall, presumably by increasing neuroplasticity. But it's not just the slow waves; _____ (45) is likely a multistep process requiring both slow-wave and REM sleep. Even taking a brief _____ (46) that includes both parts improves visual discrimination performance. Based on recent research, evidence suggests that memories are _____ (47) during non-REM sleep and _____ (48) during REM sleep. One way the brain consolidates memory during REM sleep is the use of the theta rhythm in the _____ (49). Once that occurs, the replay shifts to the troughs of the theta rhythm, resulting in memory deletion consistent with Crick and Mitchison's idea of the _____ -_____ (50) hypothesis. Therefore, REM sleep provides the mechanism by which memories are reconsolidated, made more efficient, or deleted. Animals who do not engage in REM sleep, such as two species of dolphin and the Australian _____ (51), have unusually large brains and therefore might not need to have a cognitive efficiency mechanism. Tononi and Cirelli also postulate that sleep is also an opportunity to eliminate inaccurate connections through synaptic _____ (52), since non-REM sleep corresponds to decreases in AMPA receptors and neuromodulator levels.

Sleep is a homeostatic mechanism. During wakefulness, adenosine builds up in the _____ _____ (53) area, and eventually this inhibits arousal. Cells in the _____ _____ (54) of the hypothalamus are responsive to temperature; warming them increases slow-wave sleep. This finding supports the idea that one function of slow-wave sleep is to _____ (55) the brain after waking activity. Activity in the _____ _____ (56) nucleus inhibits arousal in several brain areas located in the hypothalamus and pons. Activity in the _____ (57) nucleus in the medulla initiates atonia during REM sleep. Caffeine acts on sleep-related areas in the pons through its effect on _____ (58) receptors.

The brain's arousal system is active during waking and to some extent during _____ (59) sleep. There are two major pathways in the arousal system. In the first pathway the PPT/LDT releases _____ (60) during waking. Activation of this pathway also shifts from synchronous EEG activity to _____ (61), high-frequency, low-amplitude waves by inhibiting nuclei in the _____ (62). This pathway is also active during REM sleep. A second pathway activates the cortex. It originates from the locus coeruleus, which releases _____ (63) and the raphé, nuclei which release _____ (64). Neurons in the tuberomammillary nucleus arouse the cortex by releasing _____ (65), and those from the basal forebrain area do so by releasing _____ (66). The arousal pathway also includes neurons in the _____ _____ (67), which send axons to many brain stem and basal forebrain regions. During waking these neurons release _____ (68), or hypocretin, to stabilize the sleep and waking system and prevent inappropriate switching into sleep. Drugs that _____ (69) orexin have proven effective as sleep aids and have few side effects but are being held up due to safety issues. One new use of orexin is as a nasal spray, which has shown promise for combating sleepiness, improving memory performance, and is being tested as a treatment for _____ (70) where a person goes from wakefulness into REM. During REM sleep, _____ (71) waves travel from the pons to the lateral geniculate nucleus of the thalamus and then to the occipital lobe; these waves precede REM by around 80 seconds and may account for the visual aspects of dreaming.

_____ (72) is the inability to sleep or to obtain quality sleep. People who get either too little or too much sleep typically have a shorter life span. Body mass index is higher in people who get too _____ (73) sleep, apparently because several eating-related hormones shift out of balance. Insomniacs apparently suffer from hyperarousal during sleep; their non-REM sleep contains excess _____-_____ (74) EEG, and secretion of excess _____ (75) and adrenocorticotropic hormone indicates disturbance of the hypothalamic-pituitary-adrenal axis. Many factors contribute to insomnia, but the disorder is often found in people with _____ (76) disorders. Surprisingly, many _____ (77) medications can cause insomnia when people decrease the nightly dosage. Another reason for insomnia may be that a person's body temperature cycle is out of sync with the sleep cycle; going to sleep when body temperature is high results in _____-_____ (78) insomnia, while a phase advance in body temperature results in early waking. The ideal time to go to sleep is when the body temperature is low. Whether your _____ (79) is synchronized to the 24-hour day depends on both genes and the environment. A counterintuitive treatment for _____ _____ (80) syndrome involves delaying each sleep cycle by 3 hours over several consecutive days.

Sleepwalking occurs during _____-_____ (81) sleep, as do bedwetting and night terrors. There have been cases in which sleepwalkers committed violent acts, including murder. This condition appears to have a genetic basis; the involvement of one particular gene suggests that in some cases cells important in sleep regulation have been attacked by the _____ (82) system. A sleep disorder that usually results in weight gain as well as daytime fatigue is _____-_____ _____ (83) disorder. One final non-REM disorder is _____ (84), where 4–11% of individuals seeking treatment for a sleep disorder reported engaging in sexual behavior while asleep.

Disorders of REM sleep include _____ (85), in which a person enters REM sleep suddenly and directly from full consciousness. One symptom of this disorder is _____ (86), in which a person becomes suddenly paralyzed but remains conscious. Both of these conditions may stem from an abnormal form of a gene for the _____ (87) receptor. Extreme physical activity during REM sleep, such as leaping out of bed, is a symptom of REM sleep _____ _____ (88). This condition is often associated with a neurological condition, such as _____ (89) disease.

Francis Crick suggested that we are in a state of diminished consciousness during REM sleep and unconscious during non-REM sleep. However, the distinction between consciousness and unconsciousness during sleep is hardly clear. _____ (90) dreamers report awareness of their dreams as they happen and also seem to be able to control the content of their dreams. Sleepwalkers and those with REM sleep behavior disorder carry out complex behaviors while asleep (such as driving a car). Perhaps consciousness exists on a(n) _____ (91), and different states such as wakefulness, sleep, and dreaming reflect different levels of awareness.

## Short Answer and Essay Questions

Answer the following questions.

1. Why did the study of consciousness fall out of favor among psychologists in the early 20th century?

2. Describe the adaptive explanation for sleep and provide supportive evidence.

3. How may jet lag account for the fact that West Coast baseball teams playing in East Coast cities lose more often than East Coast teams playing in West Coast cities?

4. What is the difference between circadian and ultradian rhythms? Where is the clock for the sleep/wake cycle located in the brain, and how do we know this? What role does melatonin play?

5. How are blind individuals able to synchronize their circadian cycle if the zeitgeber is light?

6. What underlying brain activity do alpha and beta waves reflect? How are these brain wave patterns related to the states of arousal associated with them? How do these brain wave patterns change during sleep?

7. According to the reverse learning hypothesis, what is one function of REM sleep? What evidence supports this hypothesis? Identify other explanations for REM sleep.

8. Describe the role of the basal forebrain area, hypothalamus, and pons in sleep and arousal.

9. What are possible causes and biological explanations for the sleep disorders insomnia and narcolepsy?

## The Neural Bases of Consciousness

### Summary and Guided Review

After studying this section in the text, fill in the blanks of the following summary.

Although experts disagree as to a specific definition of consciousness, most would probably concur that being conscious includes awareness, _____ (92), and a sense of self. There is probably no single brain area responsible for consciousness, but rather it arises from the interaction of several different brain areas.

Awareness and consciousness seem to depend on a group of brain areas called the _____ _____ (93) network, including the lateral prefrontal cortex, posterior parietal cortex, and the thalamus. How the brain integrates or binds information from different areas into a unitary whole most likely involves the _____ (94) of neural activity. This type of activity occurs mostly in the _____ (95) frequency range, between 30 and 90 Hz. For example, when researchers presented a light that had been paired with a shock, activity became synchronized between the _____ (96) cortex and the _____ (97) area of the somatosensory cortex. In one study, electrodes were implanted in the brains of people who were being evaluated for surgery to treat seizures. When words were presented there was initial localized gamma activity recorded from the _____ (98) area, but if the words were recognized there was synchronized activity in occipital, parietal, and temporal areas. However, awareness is not required for all of our behavior. For example, people with _____ (99) can locate objects that they claim not to see, and considerable learning occurs without awareness.

_____ (100) is the brain's means of allocating its limited resources. Much of the stimuli around us go unnoticed, although highly relevant stimuli such as one's name may be attended to. _____ _____ (101), which occurs when the brain is presented with two different visual stimuli apparently in the same location, results in attention being alternately focused on each object, as demonstrated in the _____ _____ (102) effect. PET scans revealed that when participants were instructed to attend to an object's color, _____ (103) became more active, and when told to attend to the object's shape, the _____ _____ (104) cortex became more active, and when attention was directed toward the object's movement, the activity switched to _____ (105). The shifts were clearly due to _____ (106), because the particular area was active whether the object possessed the feature or not (colored vs. not colored, for example). The gateway for sensory information to the cortex is the _____ (107); the cortex can selectively inhibit input from this area to determine which information will reach it. Imaging suggests there are two networks involved in attention. The _____ (108) network operates under goal-directed control, whereas the ventral network responds to _____ _____ (109). In addition, the _____ _____ (110) cortex may play an executive role. This area is active during complex tasks, like the _____ (111) test in which subjects are asked to identify the color of a word that spells out a conflicting color name (for example, saying "red" when the word "green" is presented in a red color).

Our sense of self includes identity and the sense of _____ (112), in which we perceive ourselves as the source of actions or effects. Children over _____ (113) months of age appear to recognize themselves in mirrors, indicating that they have a sense of self. This is true of only a few other animal species. For example, among the primates, chimpanzees and orangutans pass the mirror test, but _____ (114) fail it. Damage to specific brain areas can result in impairment in self-awareness, including failure to recognize one's own reflection. The sense that we are causing an action or event may be due to activity in the _____ _____ (115). However, the sense of self is not represented in a single brain area, but probably results from several distributed functions.

The sense of loss in individuals who have undergone limb amputation, and people with body sensory disorders, suggests that an intact body image is a part of our sense of self. The majority of amputees experience some manifestation of the _____ _____ (116) phenomenon, such as the sense that the missing limb is stuck in a particular position or that one still has control over it. Even individuals born with missing limbs can experience this phenomenon; therefore body image does not have to be _____ (117).

_____-_____ (118) memory is also a source of our sense of identity. People with severe retrograde _____ (119), such as that resulting from Alzheimer's disease or Korsakoff's syndrome, may engage in _____ (120); this is hypothesized to result from a failure to suppress irrelevant information due to damage to the _____ (121) lobe. Sacks suggests that confabulators are constantly creating both a past and a present, interspersed with fragments of actual experiences.

The ability to empathize with others and understand others' intentions may lie in _____ (122) neurons; it has even been suggested that malfunction in this system is responsible for some of the symptoms of autism, such as the inability to develop a(n) _____ of _____ (123).

Studies of split-brain patients can tell us something about consciousness and the self. Although most of the time people whose hemispheres have been disconnected perform normally, occasionally they act as if they have two selves. In laboratory studies, when information is presented only to the nonverbal _____ (124) hemisphere, the person is unable to identify it verbally; and the left hand (controlled by the right hemisphere) must sometimes be restrained to prevent it from helping the right hand perform a(n) _____ (125) task. While some researchers speculate that each hemisphere is capable of a separate consciousness, Gazzaniga argues that the left hemisphere is the brain _____ (126), which integrates cognitive functions occurring throughout the brain. An alternative perspective is that because the right hemisphere lacks _____ (127) ability, it is simply unable to report on its own contents and therefore appears to be less conscious or aware than the left hemisphere.

Individuals with multiple personality, or _____ _____ (128) disorder, show shifts in consciousness and behavior that appear to be distinct personalities or selves. Diagnosis of this disorder is controversial, and some experts believe that patients who display it are conforming to their therapists' expectations. However, a few studies have found different physiological profiles (heart rate, immune functioning, EEG activity) when different "personalities" were present, which suggests that there may be a(n) _____ (129) basis for the disorder. For example, some studies indicate that one explanation is that this disorder represents a case of _____-_____ (130) learning. There are several indications of possible involvement of the brain structures of learning including hippocampal changes during personality switches and frequent backgrounds of childhood abuse (associated with hippocampal damage) and temporal lobe differences between personalities.

Most researchers believe consciousness requires a widely distributed neuronal network. For example, stimuli outside awareness activate only the sensory area, but when the stimulus enters consciousness, activation is more widespread. When the frontal and parietal cortices decrease activity, such as during deep sleep, general anesthesia, coma, and near death experiences, coordinated activity disappears. Many theorists believe network activity is coordinated by gamma oscillations generated by a feedback loop between the _____ (131) and cortex. Some scientists believe that while there is no brain structure that houses consciousness, there must be something that acts as a(n) _____ (132), directing activity in other structures. Candidates for this role have included the thalamus, the _____ _____ (133) cortex, and the _____ (134), but no structure has convincing support. Consciousness researchers are beginning to regard the _____ _____ (135) network (DMN) as the most important to consciousness; its activity varies with level of consciousness across many conditions. Understanding consciousness is more than academic; determining level of consciousness is crucial in making decisions about care. For example, patients with _____-_____ (136) syndrome are fully conscious, but they are so paralyzed that their communication abilities are greatly restricted.

## Short Answer and Essay Questions

Answer the following questions.

10. Describe a research study that indicates we can learn without being aware of what we have learned.

11. How is binocular rivalry, such as the Cheshire cat effect, achieved? What does this tell us about brain activity underlying attention?

12. How can we test for self-awareness in preverbal children and nonhuman animals?

13. What evidence is there that one does not need to learn body image?

14. Why does Gazzaniga argue that the left hemisphere is more highly conscious than the right hemisphere? What is the significance of the brain interpreter in his argument?

15. What is state-dependent learning? How might state-dependent learning explain the occurrence of dissociative identity disorder?

16. Most researchers believe that consciousness is distributed across much of the brain; describe their thinking about networks in relation to consciousness.

17. Why is understanding the nature of consciousness more than just an academic exercise? What practical benefits might there be for patients with severe brain damage?

## Post-test

Use these multiple-choice questions to check your understanding of the chapter.

1. In the late 19th century, consciousness was studied primarily
   a. by using introspection.
   b. with the EEG.
   c. by examining sleep and dreaming.
   d. by observing others' behavior.

2. Currently, brain researchers
   a. are interested only in studying sleep as a form of consciousness.
   b. agree on a definition of consciousness.
   c. integrate philosophical, biological, and computer science perspectives to study consciousness.
   d. agree that consciousness cannot be studied objectively.

3. Which of the following animal species sleeps the LEAST?
   a. bats
   b. humans
   c. lions
   d. kangaroos

4. Which of the following statements regarding shift work is TRUE?
   a. Night shift workers perform their jobs as well as day shift workers.
   b. Shift workers sleep less than day workers.
   c. Night shift workers generally sleep through the day on their weekends or days off.
   d. Job-related accidents are most likely to occur between 10:00 p.m. and midnight.

5. Which of the following baseball teams is LEAST likely to win a game?
   a. the Boston Red Sox playing at the Houston Astros
   b. the Houston Astros playing at the Boston Red Sox
   c. the San Francisco Giants playing at the Atlanta Braves
   d. the Atlanta Braves playing at the San Francisco Giants

6. Circadian rhythms for sleep and waking arise in the
   a. suprachiasmatic nucleus.
   b. hypothalamus
   c. pineal gland.
   d. medulla.

7. The MOST significant zeitgeber for the sleep/wake cycles appears to be
   a. moonlight.
   b. sunlight.
   c. clocks.
   d. social contact.

8. Research suggests that in order to increase worker productivity, night shift workers should
   a. sleep in complete darkness.
   b. work in bright light.
   c. take naps every 2 hours while working.
   d. a and b

9. Assuming that the day shift is from 8:00 a.m. to 4:00 p.m., the swing shift is from 4:00 p.m. to midnight, and the night shift is from midnight to 8:00 a.m., which of the following shift-rotation schedules would be MOST beneficial to workers?
   a. day shift to swing shift to night shift
   b. day shift to night shift to swing shift
   c. swing shift to day shift to night shift
   d. night shift to swing shift to day shift

10. How have researchers explained evidence that the internal clock operates on a 25-hour cycle?
   a. The effect is related to the 30-day lunar cycle.
   b. It is just an artifact of allowing people to use alarm clocks to start their day.
   c. Body temperature moves the cycle from 24 to 25 hours.
   d. none of the above

11. ___ is a hormone released by the pineal gland that induces sleepiness.
   a. Melanopsin
   b. Adenosine
   c. Melatonin
   d. Hypocretin

12. All of the following are true EXCEPT:
   a. mice lacking rods and cones are unable to show normal entrainment and cycling.
   b. light is able to activate the SCN by way of the retinohypothalamic pathway.
   c. the small percentage of ganglion cells that respond to light directly contain melanopsin.
   d. melanopsin is most sensitive to light that occurs at dusk and dawn.

13. The circadian clock for sleep and waking
   a. is found in the brain, but it may control clocks in other organs.
   b. involves a feedback loop of two groups of genes and their protein products.
   c. must be reset each day by light.
   d. all of the above

14. Which of the following cycle lengths would be considered an ultradian rhythm?
   a. 24-hour
   b. hour
   c. 48-hour
   d. 36-hour

15. The basic rest and activity cycle
   a. is a circadian rhythm.
   b. is a 60-minute cycle that occurs throughout the day.

    c. shows up in a 90-minute daydreaming cycle.

    d. is controlled by temperature.

16. Which of the following statements is NOT true about sleep?

    a. It is an active process.

    b. It is the cessation of activity due to fatigue.

    c. It involves turning some brain structures on and other structures off.

    d. It includes both active and inactive periods of brain activity.

17. An EEG pattern showing low-amplitude, high-frequency (13–30 Hz) waves characterizes

    a. alertness.

    b. relaxation.

    c. light sleep.

    d. slow-wave sleep.

18. Sleep spindles and K-complexes are MOST likely to be observed in

    a. REM sleep.

    b. Stage 4 sleep.

    c. Stage 2 sleep.

    d. Stage 1 sleep.

19. What type of EEG characterizes Stages 3 and 4 of slow-wave sleep?

    a. alpha activity

    b. beta activity

    c. delta activity

    d. theta activity

20. Which of the following is NOT a typical characteristic of REM sleep?

    a. low-amplitude, moderate-frequency EEG

    b. eye movements

    c. arm and leg movements

    d. genital erection

21. Dreams

    a. occur only during REM sleep.

    b. are more vivid in slow-wave sleep.

    c. have no personal meaning.

    d. probably occur in all people.

22. Someone who is deprived of REM sleep will

    a. spend more time in REM and slow-wave sleep when allowed to sleep without inter-
ruptions.

    b. develop temporary narcolepsy or cataplexy.

    c. come to understand the symbolic contents of her dreams.

    d. spend more time in REM sleep when allowed to sleep without interruptions.

23. The activation-synthesis hypothesis of dreaming

    a. states that dreaming is merely a by-product of spontaneous neural activity.

    b. was first proposed by Freud.

    c. involves brain stem areas that generate random activity, but not forebrain areas.

    d. suggests that dream content is not important or significant.

24. Infants spend about ___% of their total sleep time in REM sleep.

    a. 10

    b. 50

    c. 20

    d. 75

25. The developmental hypothesis of REM sleep
    a. states that REM sleep promotes neural development during childhood, especially during infancy.
    b. argues that REM sleep encourages maturation and myelination of higher brain structures.
    c. is supported by the finding that genes involved in neural plasticity are upregulated during REM sleep.
    d. all of the above

26. Slow-wave sleep
    a. promotes cerebral recovery, especially in the prefrontal cortex.
    b. occurs in response to low body temperature.
    c. occurs in response to low brain temperature.
    d. is not affected by caffeine, although REM sleep is.

27. Learning and memory
    a. decrease REM in the night following the task.
    b. involve both REM and non-REM sleep.
    c. are related to the circadian cycle of sleep, but not the type of sleep.
    d. are linked to REM sleep in animals but not humans.

28. Which of the following structures is most important in neuronal replay that occurs during sleep?
    a. the visual cortex
    b. the hippocampus
    c. the pons
    d. the basal forebrain region

29. Which of the following mammals does not experience REM sleep?
    a. elephant
    b. whale
    c. echidna
    d. feline

30. Which of the following hypotheses suggests that inappropriate neural connections are discarded during REM sleep?
    a. neural development
    b. learning
    c. reverse learning
    d. activation synthesis

31. Slow-wave sleep is LEAST likely to increase if a person
    a. swims 25 laps in a chilly pool.
    b. runs 10 miles on a hot day.
    c. has a fever.
    d. works in an overheated office.

32. Caffeine affects sleep by
    a. facilitating the effects of adenosine in the preoptic area.
    b. stimulating the adenosine receptors in the locus coeruleus.
    c. activating the cells in the basal forebrain region.
    d. inhibiting adenosine in the preoptic area.

33. Sleep involves all of the following structures EXCEPT:
    a. the preoptic area of the hypothalamus.
    b. the basal forebrain region.

c. the pons.

d. the ventrolateral thalamus.

34. Muscular paralysis accompanying REM sleep is moderated by the
    a. magnocellular nucleus of the medulla.
    b. lateral geniculate nucleus of the thalamus.
    c. occipital cortex.
    d. basal forebrain area.

35. Which of the following statements about the arousal systems of the brain is NOT true?
    a. One arousal pathway originates in the pons and produces acetylcholine.
    b. One arousal pathway activates the cortex by the release of norepinephrine from the locus coeruleus.
    c. Cells in the raphé that release dopamine are part of the arousal system.
    d. Histamine from the tuberomammillary nucleus activates the cortex.

36. Neurons in the lateral hypothalamus release ___ to stabilize the sleep and waking system.
    a. serotonin
    b. orexin
    c. histamine
    d. acetylcholine

37. PGO waves
    a. travel from the pons to the thalamus and on to the cortex.
    b. begin about 80 seconds before the start of a REM period.
    c. initiate the desynchrony of REM sleep.
    d. all of the above

38. All of the following are true about insomnia EXCEPT:
    a. it is associated with disorders such as obesity.
    b. it is usually diagnosed in a sleep laboratory.
    c. it may involve cortisol release during the night.
    d. it is common in people with depression.

39. The best treatment for delayed sleep syndrome is to
    a. take benzodiazepine sleep medications.
    b. stay up later on consecutive days.
    c. increase your body temperature at bedtime.
    d. go to bed 3 hours earlier for a few days.

40. Sleepwalking
    a. occurs during slow-wave sleep.
    b. may have a genetic basis.
    c. is most common during childhood.
    d. all of the above

41. Narcolepsy is a condition in which a person
    a. suddenly goes from being awake directly into slow-wave sleep.
    b. falls directly into REM sleep from wakefulness.
    c. has too much orexin.
    d. sleeps much more than people without narcolepsy.

42. Someone who literally acts outs dreams is probably experiencing
    a. lucid dreaming.
    b. cataplexy.
    c. REM sleep behavior disorder.
    d. insomnia.

43. All of the following are components that most researchers agree are part of consciousness EXCEPT:
    a. attention.
    b. personality.
    c. sense of self.
    d. awareness.

44. Which of the following is evidence of learning without awareness?
    a. recognizing that our unconscious mind is capable of motivating our behavior
    b. following a coach's instructions for hitting a ball with a bat
    c. using proprioceptive information to sit erect and walk
    d. reading instructions for assembling a computer prior to putting it together

45. The Cheshire cat effect is an example of
    a. binocular rivalry.
    b. lucid dreaming.
    c. binocular disparity.
    d. unconscious learning.

46. Attention
    a. is the same as awareness.
    b. is a concept rather than a physiological process.
    c. is a reflection of changes in brain activity.
    d. all of the above

47. Which of the following is LEAST likely to recognize herself in a mirror?
    a. a 16-month-old human
    b. an adult rhesus monkey
    c. an adult chimpanzee
    d. a 24-month-old human

48. All of the following contribute to the sense of self EXCEPT:
    a. arousal.
    b. body image.
    c. memory.
    d. mirror neurons.

49. Phantom limb sensations may be experienced
    a. by amputees.
    b. by people born with missing limbs.
    c. even before an individual has developed a learned body image.
    d. all of the above

50. Which of the following statements regarding confabulation is FALSE?
    a. It often includes elements of real memories.
    b. It is often consistent and meaningful.
    c. It is usually intentional.
    d. It is associated with long-term memory loss.

51. Split-brain patients
    a. are unable to perform behaviors requiring coordination from both sides of the body.
    b. are able to give verbal descriptions of objects in both visual fields.
    c. clearly demonstrate that the left hemisphere is more highly conscious than the right.
    d. usually perform spatial tasks better with the left hand than the right.

52. Which of the following statements regarding dissociative identity disorder is FALSE?
    a. It is not included in the APA's *Diagnostic and Statistical Manual.*
    b. It was formerly called multiple personality disorder.
    c. It is believed to result from childhood abuse or trauma.
    d. Individuals exhibit different physiological patterns when manifesting different identities.

53. In which of the following conditions is default mode network activity most likely to be normal?
    a. coma
    b. locked-in syndrome
    c. minimally conscious state
    d. vegetative state

54. A single center of consciousness may not exist, but the ___ has been proposed to be an "executive" area that coordinates all of the areas involved in consciousness.
    a. thalamus
    b. anterior cingulate cortex
    c. claustrum
    d. all of the above

# Answers

## Guided Review

1. introspection
2. behaviorists
3. cognitive
4. biology
5. sleep
6. restorative
7. adaptive
8. 80
9. toxins
10. shift
11. West Coast
12. jet lag
13. circadian
14. suprachiasmatic nucleus (SCN)
15. 25
16. zeitgeber
17. bright
18. later
19. delays
20. melatonin
21. insomnia
22. retinohypothalamic
23. melanopsin
24. genes
25. protein
26. light
27. SCN
28. ultradian
29. 90–100
30. beta
31. alpha
32. Theta
33. sleep spindles
34. delta
35. rapid eye movement
36. paradoxical
37. atonia
38. decreases
39. activation-synthesis
40. development
41. temperature
42. prefrontal
43. caffeine
44. learning
45. consolidation
46. nap
47. recalled
48. stored
49. hippocampus
50. reverse-learning
51. echidna
52. pruning
53. basal forebrain
54. preoptic area
55. cool
56. ventrolateral preoptic
57. magnocellular
58. adenosine
59. REM
60. acetylcholine
61. asynchronized
62. thalamus
63. norepinephrine
64. serotonin
65. histamine
66. acetylcholine

67. lateral hypothalamus
68. orexin
69. block
70. narcolepsy
71. PGO
72. Insomnia
73. little
74. high-frequency
75. cortisol
76. psychological
77. sleep
78. sleep-onset
79. chronotype
80. delayed sleep
81. slow-wave
82. immune
83. sleep-related eating
84. sexsomnia
85. narcolepsy
86. cataplexy
87. orexin
88. behavior disorder
89. Parkinson's
90. Lucid
91. continuum
92. attention
93. prefrontal parietal network
94. synchronization
95. gamma
96. visual
97. finger
98. occipital
99. blindsight
100. Attention
101. Binocular rivalry

102. Chinese Cat
103. V4
104. inferior temporal
105. V5
106. attention
107. thalamus
108. dorsal
109. stimulus demands
110. anterior cingulate
111. Stroop
112. agency
113. 15
114. monkeys
115. anterior insula
116. phantom limb
117. learned
118. Long-term
119. amnesia
120. confabulation
121. frontal
122. mirror
123. theory of mind
124. right
125. spatial
126. interpreter
127. verbal
128. dissociative identity
129. biological
130. state-dependent
131. thalamus
132. executive
133. anterior cingulate
134. claustrum
135. default mode
136. locked-in

## Short Answer and Essay Questions

1.  The behaviorists, in their attempt to make psychology a completely objective discipline, found fault with studying consciousness, because the primary method was introspection, which was inherently subjective.

2.  The adaptive explanation for sleep states that the amount of sleep is determined by safety considerations and access to food. Evidence for this hypothesis comes from studying sleep in different animals. For example, vulnerable animals like horses and cattle sleep very little, and those with low vulnerability, like lions, sleep much of the time. Bats and burrowing animals also sleep a lot, because they can find safety by hiding.

3.  One possible explanation is that when we travel from west to east, we must adopt a phase advance schedule; this results in sleep loss because we have to try to get to sleep earlier as well as get up earlier than we are used to. Traveling east to west requires a phase delay, or going to sleep and getting up later, which is much easier to accomplish. Baseball players traveling east to play may be at a disadvantage because they are less rested than those traveling west to play.

4.  The circadian has a length of a day, whereas ultradian rhythms are shorter than a day. An example of an ultradian rhythm is the basic rest and activity cycle that has a rhythm of about 90–100 minutes. The circadian clock is located in the SCN (suprachiasmatic nucleus). Evidence for this is that when the SCN is lesioned in animals, they do not stop sleeping but they sleep in naps throughout the 24-hour day. The circadian cycle is entrained by cues in the environment such as light; when not synchronized to these zeitgebers the cycle drifts. The SCN controls the pineal gland's secretion of melatonin, a sleep-inducing hormone that has been used to treat jet lag and insomnia in shift workers.

5.  Apparently some blind individuals are able to entrain to the light-dark cycle because light stimulates the photopigment melanopsin in a small percentage of retinal ganglion cells, which signal the SCN via the retinohypothalamic pathway.

6.  Alpha waves are associated with relaxation; these brain waves are of moderate amplitude and lower frequency than beta waves. Beta waves, which have low amplitude and high frequency, are associated with alertness. The beta waves indicate more asynchronous neural activity, whereas alpha waves represent more synchronous activity. In Stages 3 and 4 of slow-wave sleep the EEG is made up of high-amplitude, slow delta waves, whereas in REM sleep the EEG activity looks more like the waking but resting pattern of smaller, faster waves.

7.  According to this hypothesis, REM sleep serves to eliminate neural connections that are not useful and to conserve the connections that are useful. This hypothesis is supported by neural net simulations in which reverse learning enhances performance. Such a process may allow smaller brains to be more cognitively sophisticated. Mammals that do not undergo REM sleep have larger brains relative to their body size than mammals that do undergo REM. REM sleep may also be important for promoting neural development and for learning and memory consolidation, although non-REM sleep is also important.

8.  Areas involved in sleep include the basal forebrain and the ventrolateral preoptic area of the hypothalamus. Both regions inhibit arousal-producing neurons in the pons. Adenosine in the preoptic area and the basal forebrain area play a role in sleep; one way that caffeine keeps us awake is by blocking adenosine. There are two main arousal systems. One arises from specific nuclei in the pons that produce acetylcholine. This area shifts the synchronous EEG to a desynchronized pattern, which is observed during both waking and REM sleep. The second pathway activates the cortex by release of norepinephrine from the locus coeruleus and serotonin from

the raphé; both of these systems originate in the brain stem. Furthermore, neurons in the lateral hypothalamus send axons to the basal forebrain region and several brain stem areas. These cells release orexin, which seems to stabilize the sleep and waking system.

9. Insomnia is a disorder related to many factors, including stress, psychological disorders such as depression, disruption of the circadian and temperature cycles, and even sleep medications. There is no single biological cause of insomnia, but excess high-frequency activity in slow-wave sleep, increased release of cortisol, and genes involved in circadian rhythms have been studied. Narcolepsy is a disorder that occurs when the "stabilization switch" fails and the person falls asleep during the daytime and experiences REM sleep at inappropriate times. Low levels of orexin are found in people and animals with narcolepsy. Genetic factors affecting the immune system may play a role in the disorder, based on the study of canine narcolepsy.

10. The book describes two studies. In one, participants learned to predict where a target would appear on a screen, although they were unable to verbalize how they were predicting its location. In another study, people formed associations between facial features and personality characteristics but were unaware they had done so.

11. Binocular rivalry occurs when two images are made to appear as if they are in the same location (by presenting one image to one eye and the other to the same retinal location of the other eye). The brain attends alternately to one image and then to the other. While these attention shifts are occurring, activity also shifts between different groups of neurons in the visual cortex, suggesting that attention is "caused" by shifts in neural activation.

12. Self-awareness can be assessed by applying a colored mark to the face and then observing whether the child uses the mirror image to examine or remove the mark. Also, examining one's body using a mirror, rather than examining the mirror image or attacking it, suggests self-awareness.

13. Young children who lose a limb and people born with a missing limb experience phantom limb sensations, which suggests that body image is not necessarily learned.

14. Gazzaniga argues that because the left hemisphere has language and inferential capabilities the right lacks, the right hemisphere's consciousness is more "primitive." In addition, he explains the tendency of the left hemisphere to confabulate reasons for behaviors generated by the right hemisphere (based on stimuli presented to it and not shared with the left) as evidence of a "brain interpreter."

15. State-dependent learning is demonstrated when an individual in a particular state of consciousness (such as under the influence of alcohol, or in a particular emotional state) exhibits better recall for information learned in that state as opposed to some other state. Bower suggests that stress such as abuse (found in the history of 90 to 95% of DID patients) induces an altered state of consciousness, including thoughts and memories, which develops into a distinct personality.

16. According to Tononi, consciousness depends on the brain's ability to integrate information, and some of the results of studies of networks support this idea. For example, when a stimulus enters consciousness, activity spreads beyond the sensory area to other brain areas. Some theorists think awareness requires coordination in networks by gamma-frequency activity, which is generated in a thalamus-cortex loop; damage to the thalamocortical system produces unconsciousness. Recent attention has turned to the default mode network; coordination in this network decreases as a result of several conditions of altered consciousness, including sleep, sleep deprivation, anesthesia, unconsciousness, and brain damage that affects level of consciousness.

17. People with brain damage may be in a coma, minimally conscious, in a persistent vegetative state, or in a locked-in state. They are often unable to communicate with caregivers and family due to the nature of the damage. Hence, it is difficult to make informed decisions about appropriate care, prognosis, and whether therapeutic intervention is possible. A rare but informative example is the case of locked-in syndrome, in which a person is fully conscious but with little or no ability to communicate. The ability to assess their level of consciousness is necessary for deciding treatment strategies and goals. Low serotonin is a marker for impulsive behavior, regardless of psychiatric disorder. Studies have found lower levels of the metabolite 5-HIAA in suicide attempters and in impulsive suicide attempters compared to nonimpulsive attempters. However, in individuals with two particular gene alleles, serotonin reuptake inhibitors can increase suicide risk.

## Post-test

1. a   2. c   3. d   4. b   5. c   6. a   7. b   8. d   9. a   10. d   11. c   12. a   13. d   14. b
15. c   16. b   17. a   18. c   19. c   20. c   21. d   22. d   23. a   24. b   25. d   26. a
27. b   28. b   29. c   30. c   31. a   32. d   33. d   34. a   35. c   36. b   37. d   38. b
39. b   40. d   41. b   42. c   43. b   44. c   45. a   46. c   47. b   48. a   49. d   50. c
51. d   52. a   53. b   54. d